SEX, LITERATURE
and CENSORSHIP

SEX,
LITERATURE
and
CENSORSHIP

JONATHAN DOLLIMORE

Polity

First published in 2001 by Polity Press
in association with Blackwell Publishers Ltd

Editorial office:
Polity Press
65 Bridge Street
Cambridge CB2 1UR, UK

Marketing and production:
Blackwell Publishers Ltd
108 Cowley Road
Oxford OX4 1JF, UK

Published in the USA by
Blackwell Publishers Inc.
350 Main Street
Malden, MA 02148, USA

ISBN 0-7456-2763-3
ISBN 0-7456-2764-1 (pbk)

A catalogue record for this book is also available from the British Library and has been applied for from The Library of Congress.

Typeset in 10.5 on 12 pt Sabon
by SetSystems Ltd, Saffron Walden, Essex
Printed in Great Britain by TJ International, Padstow, Cornwall.

This book is printed on acid-free paper.

Contents

Acknowledgements

The author and publisher are grateful for permission to reproduce copyright material:

James Baldwin: extract from *Another Country* (Michael Joseph, 1963), copyright © James Baldwin 1962, 1963, reprinted by permission of Penguin Books Ltd and the Literary Administrator for the James Baldwin Estate

Elizabeth Bowen: extract from *Eva Trout* (1968), copyright © Elizabeth Bowen 1968, reprinted by permission of Curtis Brown Ltd, London, and Alfred A. Knopf, a division of Random House, Inc.

Ted Hughes: lines from 'A Motorbike' from *Moortown: New Selected Poems 1957–1994* (1995), reprinted by permission of the publishers, Faber & Faber Ltd

Philip Larkin: lines from 'An Arundel Tomb' and from 'Tops' from *Collected Poems* (1988), copyright © 1988, 1989 by the Estate of Philip Larkin, reprinted by permission of the publishers, Faber & Faber Ltd and Farrar, Straus & Giroux, LLC

W. B. Yeats: 'Leda and the Swan' and lines from 'Sailing to Byzantium', copyright © 1928 by Macmillan Publishing Company, copyright renewed 1956 by George Yeats; lines from 'The Second Coming' and 'Blood and the Moon', copyright © 1924, 1933 by Macmillan Publishing Company, copyright renewed 1952 and 1961 by Bertha Georgie Yeats; lines from 'Man and the Echo', copyright

Preface

This book is motivated by a sense that much current writing about literature and desire, be it ostensibly progressive or conservative, 'theoretical' or traditional, in the academy or the media, promotes complacent deceptions congruent with our time.

Part I takes issue with the spurious radicalism of some fashionable ideas about sexual dissidence. There is a belief that dissident desire has to be theorized; only theory can liberate this desire, and put it into a challenging political confrontation with those who would repress it. But this kind of thinking has become self-deluding, and is itself in need of being subjected to the challenge of the dissident desire it theorizes. Much of this thinking comprises 'wishful theory', by which I mean a pseudo-philosophical refashioning of the world according to a preconceived agenda; a kind of intellectualizing which is self-empowering in a politically spurious way, and which, despite its ostentatious performance of a high sophistication, tends to erase the complexity and diversity of the cultural life it addresses. Bits and pieces of different theories are stitched together in a way which is also a stitch-up, and sex is made into an elaborate, self-confirming intellectual fiction. It's a fiction which is most fully indulged in interpretations of literary texts, where, for example, the world of an oppressively dominant sexuality – usually heterosexual and masculine – is imagined to be permanently, almost automatically, destabilized by its deviant others.

Some of those I take issue with in these early chapters already have their vociferous opponents. A growing and influential reaction against late twentieth-century 'radical' ways of engaging with the humanities has been mobilized by those who favour a return to a more traditional approach, most especially to literature. If my own position is at odds with the moderns' in these culture wars, Parts II and III show why it differs much more from the traditionalists'. The reasons are several. For now it may suffice to remark that some of the most earnest of these traditional defenders of art have been its most effective censors; in celebrating art they made it respectable only by stifling it. If wishful theorists fabricate an elaborate kind of theoretical censorship, traditionalists have indulged in a less elaborate yet far more effective mode of aesthetic censorship.

Traditionalists castigate the theorists for undermining the exalted status of art. This is misleading. Arguably, traditionalists who have accorded art that status have done the greater damage by making art so respectable it remains incapable of challenging anything. Instead of challenging complacent thinking about the arts they encouraged it. This is one reason why theorists have been able to show that traditional assumptions about art are no longer tenable intellectually or aesthetically. However, those assumptions survive as the props of a cultural establishment wherein few are inclined to examine them. And with two good reasons: first because conservative aesthetics are an edifice whose foundations have eroded; second because the cultural establishment more than ever needs these traditional assumptions about art, and the respectability they confer, since it is itself increasingly propped up by commercial, business and market interests in search of cultural capital. Often radical in their own terms, these commercial interests are conservative if not reactionary in cultural terms. In fact, this is a pecuniary relationship in which a radical capitalist agenda is often facilitated by a culturally respectable one. There's a stark irony here: the traditional defence of art's exalted status is today increasingly dependent upon what, in the nineteenth century, it was a reaction to: this defence of art was once inseparable from a critique of the philistinism of commerce and the destructiveness of capitalism.

And yet, in institutional terms it's hardly surprising that traditional academic critics have domesticated literature. How else could they justify the subject pedagogically, especially its central place in a liberal, humanities education? Could we ever hope to persuade parents to allow their children to study a subject which, in today's security-obsessed society, should probably have an ethical/psychological health warning attached to it? In a culture ever more anxious to protect the young from itself, the necessity for such warnings is only avoided by methods of reading which muffle the truth, that art constantly transgresses the limits which define what it is to be decently human. And since education too has been thrown into the marketplace, the need for such readings to sustain vested interests is greater than ever.

The case for saying literature all the time violates the decently human could be made persuasively enough with disreputable kinds of writing like pornography, or the semi-respectable, like gothic fiction[1] or Jacobean tragedy ('excluding Shakespeare', as some classifications still have it). But I've endeavoured to take the argument to the heart of canonical respectability – including, albeit briefly,[2] Shakespeare and Yeats.

To take art seriously must be to recognize that its dangerous insights and painful beauty often derive from tendencies both disreputable and deeply anti-social. We know that the aesthetic vision has the power to threaten reactionary social agendas. Indeed, for most defenders of art today, though by no means all, that is welcome enough because they have a moderately liberal agenda. But art can also seduce us into attitudes which threaten progressive, and humanely responsible, social agendas as well. In fact, to take art seriously is to recognize that there are some very reasonable grounds for wanting to control it. Lovers of art have promulgated well-intentioned lies: they tell us that great art and the high culture it serves can only enhance the lives of those who truly appreciate it; that such art, unlike say, propaganda, popular culture or pornography, is incapable of damaging or 'corrupting' us. Such an attitude not only fails to take art seriously enough, but rests on a prior process of pro-art censorship more effective than anti-art state censorship. The defence *of* art is more often than not a defence *against* art, and an exaggerated respect for it becomes a way of not seeing, and nowhere more so than in mainstream theatre, where such respect leads audiences into a state of uncritical, even stupefied reverence.

To avoid misunderstanding I should declare that I share with others an implacable, libertarian hostility to state censorship. But this is not because I think the usual objects of censorship, including literature, film and pornography, are not capable of being socially harmful. Whether or not they are, or might be, depends on many factors, including the kind of society being defended or fought for. I would, incidentally, challenge many of the actual claims made about the harmful effects of, for example, pornographic art. But an effective opposition to censorship has to recognize that in principle such things *may* harm, and not just in terms of a morality which one does not accept, but in terms of one's own. A libertarian opposition to censorship is self-deluding if it refuses to recognize that the things it wants to defend from censorship may be harming someone, somewhere. And if that harm is proved to be great enough, state censorship has reason and ethics on its side. Bluntly: civilization is inseparable from censorship of all kinds, and most people, civilized or otherwise, are in favour of censoring something.

Fantasy is a recurring focus of this book. The creative imagination is inseparable from fantasy and where there is fantasy there is immorality and amorality. In fantasy the unconscious surfaces, and norms of morality, reason and humanity are violated. It has been said that cultured people are more inclined to enact in fantasy harmful desires which others might enact more directly. If so, that is one virtue of culture. But we shouldn't then be surprised to find the art of the educated full of such fantasies.

The renewed realism I advocate recognizes art as frequently – not invariably – a medium of dangerous knowledge. It's ill-advised, I know, to deploy such a slippery and contested term as 'realism'. What I mean by it, is anything but the view that we should accede to what is straightforward or self-evident; rather, I mean a willingness to engage with what is refractory and intractable in human history and human desire, and to undertake a more searching intellectual engagement with past thought. In particular we need to recover, via intellectual history, aspects of our cultural past which currently are all too often ignored or disavowed – be it by fashionable postmodernists on the one side, or by the respectable spokespersons for traditional high culture on the other.

The separate chapters of this book address different topics but follow sequentially in a developing argument. My general concern is sexual desire, and my specific examples include homosexuality, bisexuality, sexual disgust, and the disturbing connections between desire and death, and art and inhumanity. Most persistently this book is about how the experience of desire in life and art compromises our most cherished ethical beliefs; how it sets dissident desire against not just oppressive social life, but also what are widely agreed to be the necessary limits of civilization itself.

Many have helped me write this book, some of whom are unaware of having done so. Rachel Bowlby and Sally Munt read the manuscript with more patience and insight than I deserved.

PART I

Desire and Theory

In his first letter he wrote of this restless longing which would connect with something about his lover so slight it only added to the confusion, like the way he glanced across a street, offered a cigarette or took one. Fleeting moments having nothing in common except that they were fleeting. Later he wrote: 'everything I desire about him reminds me of something that hurts in my desire for him, a hurt so removed from present consciousness I can't reach it. So I linger at the edge of that past loss which has become the urgency of now – him and me inseparable only in this moment. Am I wrong to sense something like this in him too? Sometimes, when he comes, he sighs in a way I'll never forget; it's like a sigh from the past – his, mine, others, all separate and unreachable.'

Anon., 1953–87

[T]he character of the ego is a precipitate of abandoned object-cathexes and . . . contains the history of those object choices.

Sigmund Freud, The Ego and the Id

1

Too Hot for Yale?
The Challenge of
Queer Theory

It was a scary class. I knew that if I couldn't control this escalating argument between two students, then not just that one seminar, but the entire course might be wrecked for the rest of the term.

Class warfare

The course in question was part of the Sexual Dissidence programme at the University of Sussex. It attracted some notoriety for being the first of its kind in the country. You can imagine the scene: right-wing Members of Parliament proclaiming loudly that the university should at least be shut down, and preferably bombed as well. The tabloid press agreed, conjuring up lurid fantasies of what exactly we did on such a course.

It's characteristic of academics to get highly indignant about this kind of publicity – and not a little self-righteous as well. In truth it did us little harm, being so obviously ludicrous that informed opinion had to mobilize in our support. But it did lead some students to assume that an in-your-face radical stance on homosexuality was a guarantee that one would complete the course successfully. The argument that blew up in the class that day involved one such student, a young gay man who was insisting that homosexuality was a revolutionary force in western culture, with the power to subvert its heterosexist underpinning entirely. And a good thing too: he disliked that culture, and wanted sexual dissidence to be the spearhead of all the forces that would overthrow it. The other student, also gay, insisted that this was wishful thinking: homosexuality could exist comfortably alongside heterosexuality and it was only a residual outmoded prejudice that led some people to think otherwise. Education could and would change all this. And part of this process of education involved gay people showing straight people that we really were not that different – that we can be parents, teachers, politicians; as socially responsible as anyone else. He insisted too that the course that had brought us together in that class should be a part of this rational, reformist programme and *not* the platform for the self-deluding revolutionary rhetoric being advanced by the radical student.

The battle lines were drawn up. Silence fell and each deferred to me – or rather, looked menacingly my way, implicitly demanding support. I needed to buy time. I could try 'Goodness, look at the time' and break for a coffee, or resort to the no less diversionary tactic of asking the views of some other, hitherto silent, student. I opted for the latter, choosing someone who looked cooperative: 'Jeremy, what do you think?' Jeremy's looks belied his thoughts: 'I feel excluded and oppressed by this discussion. It completely ignores bisexuality, and I'm bisexual.' Suddenly a new battle line was drawn onto the existing map, and for a moment the revolutionary and the reformist students suspended combat. As out gay men, each distrusted the bisexual, not least because they regarded him as sitting on the fence, unable to make up his mind; avoiding commitment because lacking the courage. 'Goodness,' I exclaimed, 'look at the time . . .' Angry silence on all sides; nobody moves. The day was only saved by a mobile telephone going off in the radical student's satchel. He hastily left the room to take the call while the rest of us broke for coffee.

I helped devise that course on sexual dissidence, and at times like that I half wished I hadn't. It could be impossible to teach, and not just because of clashing personalities: something much more significant was implicated in that three-way seminar stand-off that day, something which made the presence of such a course as worthwhile as it was difficult to teach. Unbeknown to them (at the time), those two gay students were re-enacting one of the most fundamental antagonisms within the politics of sexual dissidence over the past century. As for Jeremy, little did he realize that in just a couple of years bisexuality would cease to be regarded as the dishonest third option. Marjorie Garber's 1995 book, *Vice Versa: Bisexuality and the Eroticism of Everyday Life* consolidated bisexuality's return as a viable and progressive sexuality. Meanwhile in the academy, a new bisexual politics, increasingly influential in Britain and the USA, would be claiming this to be the quintessentially postmodern sexuality – mobile, unfixed and subversive of all existing sexual identities, including the gay one. I return to this in the next chapter.

If one central objective of that course was to get students to engage with the longer history of such contemporary arguments, one central difficulty it encountered was that they were already so embroiled in the current arguments that the effort of historical understanding seemed, to them, to be beside the point. We encountered that strange but familiar position in debates about modern sexuality: if recent history has profoundly changed the ways the young think about sexuality, it has also led them to experience *their* sexuality in ways which make history itself seem obsolete.

Too hot for Yale?

Let's for a moment stay with that stand-off between the radical and the reformist gay students. Their argument not only remains with us, but has if anything become more conflicted now that the so-called sex wars and the culture wars have been mapped onto each other. Consider the front cover of the American paper *The Village Voice* for 29 July 1997. It proclaims: 'It's Here, It's Queer, [and] It's Too Hot for Yale.' The sub-heading reads: 'Gay Studies spawns a radical theory of Desire.' The story, by Richard Goldstein, was about how Yale was allegedly trying to play down its earlier reputation as a centre for gay studies, declining an offer of several million dollars from Larry Kramer to fund a professorship of gay studies, on the grounds that this was not yet a proven academic discipline. This was met with loud charges of homophobia. Without taking up a brief for Yale University, scepticism is justified here. Not of course because homophobia doesn't exist, but on the contrary because it does, and to an extent which gives plausibility even to false claims that it's operating. Moreover, as gay and queer studies have become increasingly fashionable in the American academic marketplace, spurious claims are made on their behalf. This *Village Voice* article is a prime case in point. I don't want to dwell on yet another squabble in the American academy, but this one does focus a problem fundamental to education, and in particular the project of an engaged cultural critique. Bluntly, much sexual radicalism today is not radical at all, but tendentious posturing symptomatic of the way that much critique has become relatively ineffectual because academic, metropolitan and professionalized. It's in the American academy that the problem is most obvious, and in ways not unrelated to the more general cultural imperialism of this country.

Leo Bersani among others has remarked the lack of self-criticism in the lesbian and gay community. The reason is partly a fear of the gay/academic thought police, who brand as homophobic any criticism of gay culture (this being a prime instance of the point just made about the spurious deployment of the charge of homophobia); more understandably, it is because such criticism is felt to betray the gay cause and give ammunition to the enemy. But, says Bersani,

> we have enough freedom, even enough power, to stop feeling like traitors if we cease to betray our intelligence for the sake of the cause, and if . . . we admit to having told a few lies about ourselves (and others). (*Homos*, p. 53)

Bersani is to be admired for the way he's prepared to take on the gay thought police, and also some no less censorious feminists, lesbian and otherwise. His writing is important for the way it takes issue with the comfortable and sometimes spurious radicalism that some gay academics currently propagate. He mentions in passing speaking at a lesbian and gay conference about gay men's love of the cock, only to be reproached by a lesbian colleague for having given a talk which 'marginalised women'. I've no idea which conference this was, but I can guess at its kind. It aspires to be the most radical of occasions while being at heart deeply conformist. Tyrannized by the punitiveness of a certain kind of academic sexual politics which listens only for the opportunity to castigate the speaker for exclusions which fatally discredit the significance of anything they have actually said, some speakers spend so long covering their arses against any suggestion of racism, phobia, imperialism, class bias etc., etc., that they have little of significance to say anyway. Instead they tell the audience what it wants to hear in the desperate hope of becoming its favourites, or at least of avoiding the dreaded reproach of discrimination-by-omission. The complainant at this conference recalls those who have been so resentful that Eve Kosofsky Sedgwick hasn't spent as much time talking about lesbians as about gay men, sometimes with the implication that this is a deeply damaging, even conspiratorial, exclusion. In practice, the reverse is the case: the very success of Sedgwick's project actually helps create a space for someone else to do what she hasn't: her omissions became others' opportunities. Such complainants should heed Oscar Wilde's celebrated maxim: 'we girls make history, but not in conditions of our own choosing.'

Returning to that *Village Voice* article, we learn that the radical theory of desire too hot for Yale has been spawned not by gay studies but by the more recent queer theory. Major strands of queer theory took off in part as a reaction to lesbian and gay studies because the latter were deemed not radical enough. In fact, for some, 'gay' came to seem as boring and (almost) as repressive as 'straight'. In 1996 Mark Simpson edited a collection of essays called *Anti-Gay*. Unashamedly controversial, it argued, among other things, that gay culture is boringly mediocre, intolerant of criticism, and bigoted when it comes to the sexuality of people who do not define themselves as gay. Unsurprisingly, it generated a heated debate. By 1998 Simpson is even more angry with 'gay'. In a review in the *Independent on Sunday* (25 January) he lambasts the contributors to *Lesbian and Gay Studies: a Critical Introduction* (eds Medhurst and Munt) as (again, among other things) boring, irrelevant, middle-aged, bitter, suffering from intellectual incontinence, and hilariously paranoid. It would be easy to take one side or the other in this debate, and send even more bitchy rhetoric up to the fan. Instead, I try to take a longer view of some of the important cultural issues this debate at once raises and obscures.

Although queer theory has been very influential in academic and metropolitan circles in the last few years, it's difficult to define exactly. Certainly the author of the *Village Voice* article had great difficulty in doing so. After heroically struggling through the language of the major queer texts, the most famous of which, Judith Butler's *Gender Trouble*, he finds 'as dense as a black hole', the only radical agenda he can derive from them is that – wait for it – nothing is really fixed and we are or should be free to be and do what we want. And Goldstein is, remember, a sympathetic commentator.

To be fair, queer theory also celebrates sexual perversions, although it's hardly original in doing so. Fetishism is quite high on its agenda, and also what is sometimes called part-object sexuality. If a lesbian, or gay man is foolish enough to be overheard saying something incredibly old-fashioned like 'I am attracted by the person rather than their superficial attributes' they are likely to be met with howls of derision by queer theorists. For them, such sentimentality is a huge sexual turn-off. They have great sympathy with the size queen who famously declared that he was in love with the cock but had to settle for the whole person. This is of course a quintessentially postmodern anecdote[1] because, depending on who you tell it to, you can substitute bits of anatomy as you wish. Erring here on the side of caution, I settle for the penis. In truth, my sympathies, ironic if not erotic, tend in the direction of this anecdote. To the extent that the English can be said to be European (and some of us are trying), we are learning from the decadent traditions of the old world. But that's hardly the point – or if it is, only to the extent that queer theorists are often oblivious to the history which has anticipated them.

There's an important sense in which queer theorists are right about a certain kind of gay/lesbian activist of the 1980s whose radicalism was steeped in petty-bourgeois anxieties: for all their apparent radicalism, he or she could only accept their own homosexuality, and especially other people's, if it was at heart respectable and self-policing, and was represented to self and others via positive images. Their indignation at homophobia was genuine and justified, but was also intensified by – and helped to conceal – anxieties about aspects of homosexual behaviour, including perhaps their own, by which they felt threatened and/or disgusted. Their counterparts today are those gays who are trying to square the circle with a homosexuality which is hugely subversive but at the same time politically correct.

Something comparable to the queer challenge to gay happened within feminism at least a decade ago. Some feminists imagined a unified movement around the so-called homosexual continuum – roughly, the idea of being women-identified without the lesbian sex. This was wickedly caricatured by the Lesbian activist Pat Califia:

> After the wimmin's revolution, sex will consist of wimmin holding hands, taking their shirts off and dancing in a circle. Then we will all fall asleep at exactly the same moment. If we didn't all fall asleep something else might happen – something male-identified, objectifying, pornographic, noisy, undignified. Something like an orgasm.[2]

More recently Julie Burchill, in her *Absolute Filth: an A to Z of Sex* tells us that orgasm is 'The point, the whole point and nothing but the point of having sex in the first place. If what you want is cuddling, buy a puppy' (entry for 'Orgasm'). Califia has been leading a campaign to put sex back into lesbianism, whereas here Burchill is apparently speaking for everyone.

So the challenge of queer theory, rather like this earlier challenge, was something of an internal, family affair – queers arguing with gays rather than with the world at large; engaging in the pleasurable strategy of upsetting the prescriptive agenda of one's own radical (or not so radical) movements by promoting the sexual practices it ignored or excluded. Califia has especially recommended sado-masochism. And in the name of sexual libertarianism this strategy of upsetting the new normative agendas seems to me to be not only pleasurable but productive. But as the grounds for claiming a radical new theory of desire? I think not. More often than not what we're given is little more than a libertarianism which dovetails fairly conveniently with a lifestyle politics of the well-heeled and well-insulated metropolitan.[3]

On a more intellectual level, queer rehearses a familiar postmodern move whereby it rejects not just the old religious idea of the soul (barely remembered anyway), but also the modernist secular soul-surrogates. So, for instance, even the idea of having a comparatively fixed sexual identity is rejected as too soul-like. Some queer writers will even say it is a form of self-oppression for gay people to claim or assume such an identity. This is particularly exasperating for those who came to gay consciousness believing it was a form of self-oppression *not* to make such a claim. But times change and today the radical agenda is less a question of what one is, more of what one does; as an early queer manifesto urged:

> Queers, start speaking for yourself! . . . Call yourself what you want. Reject all labels. Be all labels. Liberate yourself from the lie that we're all lesbians and gay men. . . . Queer is not about gay or lesbian – it's about sex![4]

The following anecdote, apochryphal or not, nicely queers the relation between sexual identity and sexual behaviour. An American student eventually gets to meet a cult writer in the lesbian S/M scene whom she admires greatly. The writer asks the student what kind of person she sleeps with. The student, grateful for the opportunity to do so, eagerly announces that she too is lesbian.

> WRITER (surprised): Are you telling me that you never fuck men?
> STUDENT: Definitely not. Like I said, I'm lesbian. Like you.
> WRITER (after reflective pause): You mean you don't even fuck gay men?
> STUDENT: Well no – I mean they're still men, aren't they? And anyway gay men don't sleep with women.
> WRITER (after further pause): Well, you sound like a pretty straight dyke to me.

The beauty of insisting on sexual practices rather than identity is that anyone can now be queer. It's a very democratic form of radicalism. Carol Queen writes:

> Heterosexual behaviour does not always equal straight. When I strap on a dildo and fuck my male partner, we are engaging in 'heterosexual' behaviour but I can tell you it feels altogether *queer*, and I'm sure my grandmother and Jesse Helms would say the same.[5]

Actually I doubt if 'queer' would be the first word which sprang to the lips of granny and Jesse, and certainly not 'queer' as it has been refashioned by postmodernism. But you never know, and I certainly don't want to be patronizing, at least, not to Granny. But the real issue here is whether such sexual practices are ever *inherently* radical. To imagine that they are is to be closer in thought to granny and Jesse than Queen realizes: after all, to regard a sexual practice as inherently radical is really just the obverse of regarding it as inherently evil or, indeed, as inherently normal.

One thing we learn from the history of dissidence is that the subversiveness of a dissident culture derives in part from the force which resists it. That means there is a severe and violent dialectic between the two. In a rather trivial sense this is apparent from Queen's claim: somehow the 'queering' of that particular sexual practice required, if not the actual presence of granny and Jesse, then certainly their imagined disapproval. The transgression has to be regarded, discussed, known about in order to be transgressive. Which is one reason why today sexual transgression is talked about so much. But as we talk up our transgressions, let's never forget that historically the working out of this dialectic has involved the murder, mutilation, incarceration and censorship of sexual dissidents. I repeat: the subversiveness of a dissident culture derives in part from the force which resists it. Hence that violent dialectic and all the broken people left in its wake.

But maybe I'm becoming too serious and missing the new queer insistence on the importance of pleasure for the dissident agenda. I would indeed hate to be associated with the puritanical attitude which used to say that nothing pleasurable could be radical, and that politically effective action had to painful. If it wasn't hurting either the activists or those they were trying to change, it wasn't working. Depending on its size, maybe that couple with their dildo were upholding the puritan political tradition after all. Of course there's nothing wrong in principle with the new insistence on mixing politics and pleasure. The error is to pretend that because it's pleasurable, sexy and shocking, it's almost certain to be subverting patriarchy, heterosexuality, masculinity and whatever else we don't like. It's obvious of course that pleasure, sex and shock are neither necessary nor sufficient conditions for radical political effect. To want them to be so, corresponds to a more general move today whereby the truth that sexuality is political through and through, has allowed some to delude themselves into believing that sexuality is the only political focus worthy of attention. This is a development which goes hand in hand with an increasingly naive notion of the political, and very probably an abdication of the political.

Radical versus reformist sexual politics

This in turn has left contemporary sexual politics caught in a real contradiction between what I earlier described as the radical and the reformist agendas, as epitomized in the stand-off between the two students. The radical position represents gay people – or rather queers and dykes – as disturbing, disruptive, anarchic, ludic and more. They express the militant, radical, subversive difference of queer desire, especially when seeking deliberately to pervert hetero-sexuality, *à la* Queen, the dildo and her partner. Queer radicals welcome the idea that there remains something ineradicably opposi-tional about homosexual desire; it is why they think, or hope, it can never be accommodated within an existing respectable sexual order, and why gay people themselves should not tame it through respect-able self-representations and positive images.

But of course queer radicals, far from liberating the full and dangerous potential of homosexuality, also tame and rework it in various ways, one of which is especially relevant here: they tend to represent themselves as personally immune to the subversiveness of desire. It's an immunity which comes with being radical, since to be radical is not to be repressed and, via a simplification of Freud, it is only the repressed who can be wrecked by desire. In other words, sexual radicals are the agents of the disruptiveness of desire but rarely, if ever, its victims. If they are the victim of anything it is social discrimination against their desire – embodied in Jesse and granny – rather than the desire itself. Yet the tone of much radicalism suggests otherwise: often supercilious, it is also anxious, defended and sometimes paranoid. Eve Kosofsky Sedgwick has written a perceptive and, I hope, influential piece on paranoia in the American academy and beyond. One hesitates, however, to agree with Sedg-wick's claim – she is writing in 1997 – that 'to theorize out of anything *but* a paranoid critical stance has come to seem naive, pious, or complaisant' (*Novel Gazing*, p. 5). Sedgwick is speaking specifically of gay and queer theory, although she gives the paranoia in question a certain intellectual pedigree by tracing its origins, via Paul Ricoeur, to the so-called 'hermeneutic of suspicion' in philoso-phers and analysts like Marx, Freud and Nietzsche. In fact, queer theorists might be less paranoid if they paid more attention to such writers. Maybe this paranoia has more to do with the professional

in-fighting in the American academy, in which, it seems, the higher
you go and the more powerful you become, the greater the paranoia.
That Sedgwick is herself assuming this frame of reference is suggested
not only by her actual examples of paranoid writing, but by her need
to state the obvious rather defensively: 'To be other than paranoid
... does *not*, in itself, entail a denial of the reality or gravity of
enmity or oppression' (p. 7). Obviously not, and in the context of
the writing of gay, lesbian and bisexual historians and theorists one
could cite the distinctly non-paranoid writings of, among others,
Dennis Altman, Marjorie Garber, Mary McIntosh, Alan Sinfield and
Jeffrey Weeks. Such writing also indicates that, contrary to what
Sedgwick implies, the critical strategy of seeking to expose a concealed truth is not an intrinsically paranoid activity. Nor should it be
assumed to be definitively modern, given its origins in the fundamental distinction between appearance and reality as it evolved in diverse
areas of human thought including philosophy, theology, and astron-
omy, to mention only some of the oldest, and on the way inspired
fatalism, religion and revolution.

In complete contrast to the radicals, the reformists emphasize the
sanity of homosexual identity and they tend to do so in non-paranoid
ways. They deem negative attitudes to homosexuality to be irrational:
in a more enlightened, non-homophobic culture homosexuality
would be accepted. What is required is not full-scale radical social
change so much as the elimination of outmoded prejudice. This
reformist position is by no means necessarily a conservative one, but
its conservative wing is conveniently reflected in the title of recent
books: Bruce Bawer's *A Place at the Table* and Andrew Sullivan's
Virtually Normal.

If the radical and the reformist positions were represented as a
clear stand-off between those two students in my seminar, most
queer theorists, especially those in the American academy, seemingly
want it both ways. This compromised position is starkly apparent in
the way we have witnessed such academics keen to out-queer each
other on the conference circuit with ever more provocative papers,
only to then become self-righteously indignant when the right-wing
press responds exactly as anyone could have predicted. The radical
agenda is in the deliberate provocation; the reformist agenda in the
indignation at the response provoked. To some of these academics it
seems unthinkable that sexual dissidence may have a price in terms
of professional standing. But why not if it really is deeply challenging
politically? Where else would such dissidence be free of risk? Some
of the anger of sexual radicals against contemporary society is
justified. But in the academy, and in the disputes which spill over

from the academy into the public domain, anger is also manufactured: the academically ambitious, especially sexual politicians within the academy, empower themselves through indignation.

Moreover, they have been known to keep themselves empowered by controlling rather carefully who is allowed to be dissident. We sometimes speak of pushing back 'the frontiers of knowledge'. Of course, it's misleading to speak of knowledge as if it's a geographical, territorial strategy of expansion. And yet the professionalization of the US academy keeps this way of speaking half-applicable because its knowledge frontier moves all the time, but in predictable, limited and market-controlled directions. Those actually on the frontier – i.e., in the prestigious university departments – are rather few and highly influential in deciding who else might come up alongside. One consequence of the professionalization and commodification of knowledge is that its frontiers are policed even as they are unfolded. And again, this is nowhere more apparent than in the patronage system of the academy. In certain respects nothing has been more conformist in recent years than the 'radical' output of a younger generation of US scholars whose careers are dependent upon the approval of the 'stars' who control the field. Simon Jarvis observes the double bind on queer-theory students: their need to be transgressive is acted out within an academic regime which encourages 'cowed tutelage' ('Reflections in the Golden Bowl', p. 25).

The problem has become serious enough for some to question whether the academy is any longer the right place for dissident social critique. The scholar and Palestinian activist Edward Said has more than once criticized a professionalizing attitude to ideas in our universities which leads to theory being taught 'so as to make the student believe he or she can become a Marxist, a feminist, an Afrocentrist, or a deconstructionist with about the same effort and commitment required in choosing items from a menu' (*Culture and Imperialism*, p. 389). It's a menu offering even more choice now queer is on it. The consumerist dimension to this raises a related problem going well beyond the universities. More than ever before, movements like postmodernism and queer theory thrive in a larger metropolitan culture. This was forcefully brought home to me in a very different context, at a conference on post-colonialism in South Africa in 1996. African delegates spoke critically of what they called metropolitan theory – that is, theories of post-colonialism originating not just within the major western cities, but within centres of western capital. It was felt not just that these theories were inapplicable to the African context, but that they misrepresented it in ways which seemed almost like a new colonization or at least a form of intellectual imperialism. Some of the US speakers at this conference were especially resented because they seemed to regard the South African context as like any other: just somewhere else to take the same old roadshow with its American-centred focus. What made the resentment of those South Africans so acute was that they had to work through a double bind: the theory which misrepresented the African reality was also the theory which had helped make the conference possible and given some visibility to the issues.

It was there in South Africa that I came to realize that, for all its cosmopolitan affect, much metropolitan thought thrives on a new parochialism – that self-absorbed, inward-looking and relatively insulated existence which has always, to a greater or lesser degree, characterized academic life and which now, albeit very differently, is also a feature of intellectual, urban avant-garde culture. Which means that, even as this theory gestures towards cultural difference, it remains insulated from it. The geographies of some modern cities graphically epitomize this of course, with the privileged and the deprived tightly juxtaposed yet still effectively segregated. Increasingly, cultural and intellectual life in the metropolis partakes of this situation of segregated proximities. Diverse cultural networks crisscross with each other yet avoid each other in their very proximity, and avoid too the greater complexity to which they belong. Of course interaction does occur, but it is often regulated by the sophisticated communications characteristic of advanced capitalism – communications which, in many ways, have only refined the more traditional kinds of segregation based on class and race.

Queer theory is quintessentially metropolitan and, at its worst, little more than intellectual style-politics (for which, nevertheless, there should be a place in every fallen world). Its claim to a poised and perfect radicalism reflects the influence of a facile postmodernism, the kind which competes to be always on the forward edge of our own contemporary moment, and from there clamours to announce a profound new insight into the here and now, telling us that today radical change is in the air while knowing that tomorrow it will all change again, and is anxious to be in on the diagnosis when it does – hence the prevalence in academic titles of 'post', 'after', 'beyond' and the like. Postmodernism of this kind partakes of wishful theory: a preconceived view of the world is elaborated by mixing and matching bits and pieces of diverse theories until the wished-for result is achieved (see chapter 3). If anything in 'reality' offers resistance, splice in or jump-cut to another theory better suited to erasing the difficulty. But the most interesting aspect of queer theory is hardly theoretical at all, namely its affirmation of perversity, for which the better name might be 'queer erotics'.

Interlude: differences in a small space

At this point I risk the first of a few remnants of personal history. I had my first gay affair at 28; he was a bit older. It was supposed to be casual. In fact he had made a bet with a third party that he could get me into bed. He could: he did, and he won his bet. But what neither he nor I reckoned on was that we would fall for each other. I left an existing relationship to live with him in a very small single-room flat. I had arrived in gay culture from a hitherto exclusively straight life; he had made an even more radical move: a Guyanese immigrant, he had only recently arrived in England. It was spring and there were differences in the air, or rather there were differences in a very confined space; differences which, by summer, were in conflict. The affair ended – though we remain close friends to this day – but not before changing my life, and affecting everything I subsequently thought and wrote. But, contrary to the experience of many gay people, I didn't feel I had discovered my true self. There was a great deal of pressure from gay culture for me to feel and acknowledge that I did; but I didn't – not quite.

In other words, I didn't fit a classic coming-out narrative: I had not at last become the person I had always really been. On the contrary, almost overnight, so to speak, I had become a different person. This wasn't so much a self-discovery as a bewilderingly radical transformation of the self. I was going to say 'self-transformation'. But that wouldn't be right either, because it felt like a transformation of the self by everything but the self. From that experience, that first homosexual affair, came the profound realization, the conviction, that not only could I change, but everything had the potential to be radically different. I felt on the pulses what hitherto I had only known intellectually, namely that much of what we experience in the world as inevitable, natural, and unalterable, is only contingently in place and could be different – and better.

To that extent my experience put me closer to the radical agenda than the reformist one. But something else had already happened which meant I couldn't accept the radical agenda either, at least not in its liberationist form. As someone who had left a secondary modern school at fifteen and started his working life barely literate and unqualified and in a car factory, I already knew how difficult it was to escape from one's social circumstances, let alone change them.

To realize that a particular social arrangement is a reflection *not* of the natural order but of history and of existing, contingent social relations, may lead us to think that it is therefore easily changed: after all we can't change nature but we *can* change our social relations. But it isn't. And if the potential to be otherwise seems to derive from the same contingencies of history which makes things almost unalterably as they are, that tension is nowhere more apparent than in human desire. Put differently, there will always be something deeply mysterious about desire. From that first relationship I intuited how our desires – his and mine – were at once an effect of our different histories, and a refusal of them. Desire can be so amazingly compliant with the history of our culture and, more immediately, with our own socialization, that it comes to seem nothing but. To borrow a metaphor from the seventeenth-century philosopher John Locke, it's as if desire begins as a tabula rasa which then has the social script written upon it. But then, in another context, desire is so intransigently, perversely resistant to history and socialization, that the opposite seems equally plausible, namely that the real force of desire is pre-social libido. And then again, it can seem that the most recalcitrant kind of desire is not pre-social at all, but that which we know to be the effect of prolonged socialization.

For such reasons one becomes preoccupied as much with the past as the present, including the remote and not just the immediate past. Reasons why things are so hard to change then are partly to be found there. By the same token, the knowledge of what has to be overcome for change to now occur is also partly there. Just now we are increasingly allowed to disregard the past, be it by postmodern history that claims we can't really know it anyway, or by facile millennial speculations about a radically different future in prospect, or just by an education system that fails to give an adequate historical sense. In the situation described by Said earlier, students embrace contemporary kinds of cultural critique in ignorance of the past – especially the intellectual past in which the pioneers of such critique were themselves steeped. Over the two decades that I've been teaching courses on homosexuality, I've noticed an increasing tolerance of all kinds of dissidence, but it is a tolerance ungrounded in historical awareness. At its best this tolerance is a precious thing. But it remains vulnerable to the extent that it is ahistorical. The late Angus Wilson once told a story about how he gave a coming-out lecture to some young gay people. He spoke of his long-term relationship with another man. The audience's response was cool, if not hostile: why, asked one young man, did he feel this need to ape heterosexual monogamy? A little while later he gave the same lecture to a group of even younger gay people (all were teenagers) from whom he anticipated even less sympathy. In fact, their response was very different: they seemed to empathize with, and even to revere him. The reason became clear when one youngster, prefacing his question with a sincere concern for the difficulties of being gay in earlier times, asked: 'Mr Wilson, were you a close friend of Oscar Wilde's?'

In the arena of human sexuality it may be that the pull of the past exerts a far greater influence on the twenty-first century than we can possibly imagine. But let's for a moment assume not, and imagine that the reformist position wins through. Its advocates will success-fully persuade the majority that hitherto demonized practices like homosexuality are more or less compatible with society as it is: they present no threat, for example, to the family, which anyway will evolve into new and diverse forms. Homosexuality is at last inte-grated as an option, no more remarkable than say, those married heterosexuals who choose to have no children, or four. Some reform-ists go further, seeking even wider reforms, yet with the same insistence that sexual behaviour in itself is not the ethical, legal or political issue – what precisely one does, and the gender of the person with whom one does it, is irrelevant – what matters are the relation-ships, and most especially the power relationships, that obtain within human sexuality. Absence of exploitation, consent, agreement, responsibility, and above all, equality before the law, will be the deciding factors.

Suppose then that the reformist has this completely free run across the new century and manages finally and fully to demystify human sexuality. Looking back, people then will marvel at the obsessive significance of sexuality through the nineteenth and twentieth centur-ies: the way it became a surrogate religion, even, or rather, especially, in the most apparently secular and progressive areas of life. Current queer theory, if remembered at all, will seem equally bizarre – though probably not as ridiculous as the current obsession by some in the Church of England to prevent the practice of homosexuality (as distinct from *being* homosexual, which is regretted but tolerated). In its own way this will be regarded as no less absurd than the fear of masturbation a century ago. The norm will surely be bisexuality. Not in the sense that most people will be having partners of both sexes. Rather, bisexuality will be the unremarkable, unprescriptive norm, and those people who happen to cohabit predominantly or exclusively with a person or persons of one sex will stand out no more nor less than those who do otherwise.

What will seem strangest of all is our current obsessive binary division between heterosexual and homosexual: the classification of people according to the sex/gender of their partners, or desired partners. There will doubtless be other kinds of dominant classification. In the context of AIDS, penetrative sex has taken on new significance. If sexually transmitted disease cannot be controlled it may even be that a 'straight' and 'gay' pair doing penetrative sex might be classified as more alike than (for example) two gay pairs in which one is doing penetrative sex and the other not. Likewise with gay and straight people practising auto-eroticism rather than inter-personal eroticism.

The challenge of the past

Enough speculation: no matter how successful it might be, the enlightened, reformist agenda for sexuality could never have a completely free run across the next century. Culture evolves through conflict, resistance and contradiction. But where might the challenge come from? Not, I think, from the radical view of sexual dissidence, so influential in the last half-century, nor from the conservative view it was in reaction against. But it may come from a mutation of a conception of sexual desire which preceded both the conservative and the radical political agendas and from which both borrowed, often unawares. This is the idea of sexual desire – especially deviant desire – as ineradicably dangerous and disruptive in its very nature.

The reformist position tends to deny this view: there is nothing inherently anti-social about human sexuality – it only becomes so, if at all, when thwarted and distorted by repressive social arrangements. In taking this line the reformist inherits the great rationalist legacy of the Enlightenment, for which the problem is indeed not sexual desire so much as the society which distorts and persecutes it: if only desire could be freed from superstition, discrimination and other irrational constraints, we would be happier as individuals and society would be the better for it. By contrast, the reformist's radical counterpart inherits a much older idea of desire as inherently dangerous and always potentially disruptive. This has been the prevailing view the last two millennia in western culture. We associate it mainly with Christianity, but it goes back further – the Greeks were clear about the dangers of unrestrained desire – and it continues right up to Freud's claim that there will forever remain a fundamental struggle between the demands of instinct and those of civilization. The conservative response to this struggle is to side with civilization against desire: social cohesion requires that desire be controlled, harnessed, restrained and, in so far as is possible, educated. The radical response is to side with desire against civilization, seeking to liberate repressed desire and use its energies to revolutionize the way we live.

And yet the radical view remains indebted to the conservative view it breaks away from. We seem unable to conceptualize momentous cultural development except in terms of such breaks. Postmodernism especially has been obsessed with going beyond, with rapid transition, the moment of complete change. But we should recognize too what I can only call, with deliberate awkwardness, 'radical continuity'. By this I don't mean tradition – that slow, more or less conscious process of selective development. Rather, this refers to the way something can seemingly disappear, yet actually be mutating in the form of its (apparent) opposite or successor. In other words, the two things are strangely complicit, the radical break both disguising and facilitating the radical continuity. So it is that the sexual radicals connect with the sexual conservatives. They – the radicals – reject the idea of original sin, and even the modern (diluted) Christian distrust of sexual desire. They break too with the secular philosophies which succeed Christianity, for instance psychoanalysis, to the extent that such philosophies regard the repression of desire as inevitable and necessary. But the indebtedness of sexual radicalism to these older views remains apparent in the way it still imagines sexuality as a potent force. Only now it is the source not of evil but freedom, not of social disintegration but of revolution, not of misery but, potentially, of happiness. This is accompanied by a secularization of the soul whereby freedom comes to be identified with our capacities as unique individuals and, increasingly, our capacities as rational, civilized beings, while unfreedom is associated more with social existence: man is born free but is everywhere in chains. Above all, freedom is sexual: sex is both the inner dynamic of the individual and the means of his or her liberation. Desire freed has the potential to overthrow the unjust society which represses the individual and everything else truly human. Religious antecedents are yet further apparent in the sexual radical's idea of sexual desire as an identity: the source of an essential, authentic selfhood for which we must be prepared to fight and suffer. In short, a spiritual conception of the self has been appropriated for a sexual politics and Saint Augustine doubtless turns in his grave. And let him: he of all people should know that culture evolves through such audacious appropriations.

The reformist view, in that it believes homosexuality, viewed rationally, will be accepted and seen as not fundamentally different from heterosexuality, is obviously less extreme than the radical view which invests sexuality with this power to transform and even overthrow. And yet, in so far as the reformist position seeks to break entirely with an older conception of desire to which both conservative and radical remain indebted, it can be said to be the more radical.

Queer sexual radicals are half-aware of the problem: as we've seen, they are embarrassed by the religious implications of the idea of desire as the basis of authentic identity. Not for them any suggestion of inward essence. But they are suspicious too of the idea of desire as an energy or force because that smacks of another kind of essentialism almost as bad as religion: 'biologism'. So what exactly is left of the radical agenda for queer theory? It's a good question: the very things which once made desire disruptive have been systematically (or not) deconstructed, while the wish to keep it disruptive has, if anything, increased. One move is to mask the problem with ever more sophisticated theoretical analysis: hence the difficulties of our *Village Voice* journalist and many others struggling to get to grips with what queer theorists really mean.

Take the notion of desire as dangerous, but loosen its connections with both the conservative and the radical agendas: from, that is, the one which says it must be rigorously controlled by religion and morality, and the other which says that it has the potential to liberate us from a society being stifled by a repressive religion and an oppressive morality. That gives us our contemporary moment within which echoes of an older conception of desire can be heard again. (I shall return to this, but briefly anticipate it here.) In the very same month that the *Village Voice* article appeared, Michelangelo Signorile wrote a rather more disturbing and controversial piece for the magazine *Out*.[6] He drew attention to the growing numbers of people having unsafe sex in contexts in which the risk of HIV infection is high. According to Signorile, these people are not being merely careless; on the contrary, they are deliberately eroticizing the risk factor. High-risk unprotected sex is called 'barebacking'. He further identifies a trend towards eroticizing the HIV virus itself, in fantasy and in actual practice. Signorile writes this article because he fears this tendency may be widespread, and growing. It connects with the culture of drug use. The explanation that drugs make us sexually careless is not the complete story. The encounter with risk and danger is sometimes more deliberate, and initially at any rate, more calculated than any rational approach to either sexuality or drugs, wants or can afford to allow. 'Barebacking' is not obviously widespread, but it has attracted much attention since Signorile's article, and also for a while had its own website ('xtremesex') where, among other things, people wrote about the incomparable sexual thrill of being, or imagining they were being, infected with the virus. In one of the many recent articles devoted to it, Celia Farber concludes that barebacking is a powerful reminder that sex is never safe ('Unprotected', p. 63). At the very least it confirms what we always knew: an experience of desire as daemonic continues to circulate in fantasy, and in ways which are making even the queerest of postmodern radicals pause for thought as they encounter the past they thought they had escaped.

2

The New Bisexuality

In the previous chapter I was largely critical of queer theory. I begin this chapter by acknowledging a debt to it.

Across the last two decades of the twentieth century everyone was 'theorizing' identity and the mobility of desire. Influences were diverse: I remember especially the impact, for gay writing, of Barthes' dream, or plea, in 1975, for a radical sexual diversity. There would no longer be *homosexuality* (singular) but *homosexualities* (plural), a plural so radical it would 'baffle all centred discourse to the *point* where it seems . . . pointless to talk about it'. Or Derrida's even earlier call for an affirmation which would determine the non-centre otherwise than as a loss of centre. But whatever the influences – and there were many more – we converged with this one conviction: desire and identity are not – must not be; can never be – fixed or essentialized. Identity is contingent and mobile, desire is fluid and even more mobile. To try to fix or naturalize things like femininity, masculinity or heterosexuality; to see them as stable, natural categories was reactionary crap – at best, the last throes of an obsolete humanism. For those of us thinking lesbian and gay theory, 'nature' and 'essence' were the metaphysics of the heteronormative.

Was 'homosexual' equally 'non-natural'? There we were less sure. On the one hand we quite liked the idea of being non-natural, even unnatural, but only on our own terms – which meant under strictly theorized limits – and if anyone else found us unnatural: well, that was rampant homophobia.

During all this, somewhat unexpectedly, I found myself in a relationship with a woman. Experientially it was somewhat bewildering, but I took consolation from the fact that I was at least on theoretically safe ground – after all, hadn't we just proved beyond doubt, the radical mobility of desire/identity; and wasn't this being surprised by desire exactly what the theory predicted? Actually I really should have asked for theoretical clarification before embarking on this relationship, since for some sexual politicians it marked me out as a traitor: one lesbian was heard to snarl that I'd gone straight, gone 'nuclear', and, worst of all, become a 'breeder'. But the charge that most intrigued me was the one which said that I'd only ever been gay for my career. Initially, I was tempted to say, Well, you should have been at Sussex when Alan Sinfield and I launched the country's first gay MA programme, meeting with hostility not just from politicians and the press, but also from the powerful at the centre of our own university. But then I thought, hang on: actually, any guy who could spend his life being fucked from pillow to bedpost by other guys, presumably faking perfect orgasms on the way, deserved to have a fabulous career. I for one can't think of anyone more employable. Anyway, I decided to lay low for a while. In truth it was something of a relief. Now that I no longer needed to be a good gay object I found myself writing and exploring ideas which had hitherto been off-limits. But eventually the phone started to ring again and I was asked if I'd write or speak on the subject of bisexuality. But, I said, hadn't we theorized the bisexual as the biggest hypocrite of all in the sex arena, a bullshitter, a hedge-sitter, someone who wanted the best of all worlds without committing to any? Yes, yes, came the impatient reply, but that was before. Before what? Before bisexuality was re-theorized by queer theory. And you know he was right – books on the subject were appearing from the publisher, Routledge, and the culture journalists were chattering it up with all the glibness that meant it had arrived.

What little credibility I managed to regain is owed entirely to the way queer theory sidelined some of the moralists in sexual politics, celebrating a sexual practice somewhat closer to the theory. It recognized – or I should say rediscovered – the complexity and diversity of human sexual practice; and yes: the mobility of human desire, the unpredictability of human fantasy and, above all, our capacity to make profoundly perverse identifications in the sexual imaginary. None of this was new, but it was useful to have it restated and to see the judgemental sexual politicians either silenced or having to retool. (That's an unfortunate metaphor, but one which, on quick reflection, I think I'll keep.)

Defended desires

What then, of the new bisexuality which queer theory has made possible? Bisexuals had hitherto been variously vilified as promiscuous, immature, undecided, treacherous, cowardly, and carriers of AIDS into the straight community. Now though, they were being hailed not only as one of the most politically radical of all sexual minorities, but provocatively and sexually postmodern as well. Was this the ultimate liberation – or just another version of wishful theory?

Some of bisexuality's most perceptive and incisive recent defenders include Sue George, Elisabeth Däumer, Clare Hemmings, Jo Eadie and Nicola Field.[1] They show that some of the strongest hostility to bisexuals comes not from bigoted straights but out and proud gays, some of whom have promoted kinds of discrimination which they themselves experienced and loudly protested against. Eadie suggests that the lesbian and gay wish to exclude bisexuals is based on the fear of contamination and miscegenation; he says, contentiously, 'bisexuality is a miscegenate location' ('Activating Bisexuality', p. 158). Clare Hemmings makes a similar point, in this paraphrase of gay hostility to bisexuals:

> I'd never sleep with a bisexual because they bring men into the lesbian community / are responsible for the spread of HIV / always leave you for someone of the opposite / same sex / can't be trusted etc. ('Resituating the Bisexual Body', p. 130)

For both Eadie and Hemmings, the main problem is the current dominance in lesbian and gay culture of so-called identity politics, the objections to which have been tabled many times but rarely as succinctly as by Susie Bright: 'It's preposterous to ask sexual beings to stuff ourselves into the rapidly imploding social categories of straight or gay or bi, as if we could plot our sexual behaviour on a conscientious, predictable, curve' (cited in Garber, *Vice Versa*, p. 83). Identity politics is suddenly out of fashion – which means that increasingly, queer and other theories dismiss it without even trying to understand it. The fact is, we all aspire to a sexual identity of some kind. But it is wrong to suggest that we do this as a relatively straightforward expression of our orientation or desires. Identity (as single orientation) can be as much a defence against, as an expression of, desire.

Notoriously in human history, those who have made progress have then wanted to deny the same rights to others. To the extent that it sometimes entails this, identity politics becomes the ground of a turf war in which the rhetoric of liberation is a cover for self-empowerment of a politically conservative kind. An apparent case in point, cited by Eadie and others, concerns the announcement by Brett Anderson, the lead singer with the group Suede, that he was a bisexual who had not so far had any homosexual experience. A writer in the gay *Pink Paper* snarls in response: 'a "bisexual who's never had sex with a man" . . . stinks as bad as a white boy blacking up.'[2] Would a gay man who came out without as yet having had any homosexual experience be equally derided? Presumably not. Perhaps the difference is the (questionable) assumption that bisexuality has more kudos than homosexuality? In which case we glimpse the increasingly hypocritical policing of the coming-out process in contemporary sexual politics: if you don't come out it's because you're afraid of the stigma; if you do it's only because you want the (putative) kudos. It should be said that most gays' response to bisexuality is rarely as crass as in this instance, and for the very good reason that it is other lesbian and gay writers who have helped develop the libertarian, anti-discriminatory perspective which makes it seem so crass in the first place, and who would be the first to reject its exploitation of anti-racism for new discriminatory purposes of its own.

Another scenario is both more representative and more significant of identity politics: such politics are often most invested when the fortunes of a minority have improved, but not securely; in some cases the identity remains precariously dependent upon that improvement, and in a context where hostility not only remains, but has actually intensified, in part as a response to the increased social visibility which the emerging identity entails. A vivid case in point is the eruption of hostility in Scotland during 1999–2000 over the proposed repeal of Section 28 (legislation passed in 1988, forbidding municipalities to spend public money in ways that might 'promote homosexuality', especially in schools). Identity politics are inseparable from a consolidation of this ground recently gained and precariously held. Such consolidation is inevitably also a struggle for survival, which includes a struggle for the means of continuing visibility.

In the field of sexuality this overlaps with another, and to me equally significant aspect of this consolidation and brings us back to the point made just now: such politics are a defensive formation not only against discrimination, but against desire itself. We protect ourselves against those instabilities intrinsic to desire and which threaten to dislocate us psychically and socially; and which do so even, or especially, when our sexuality or object choices are relatively settled. An endearing instance of this is given by Sukie de la Croix, a gay man, who meets a straight African-American woman called Troy:

> She was hot, she was raunchy and she scared the shit out of me. Why? Because she raised some heterosexual feelings in me that I thought had disappeared years ago . . . It took me years to sort out my true sexual identity, and the last thing I need at this point in my life is to do a turnabout.

Four days later he is still sufficiently worried to confide in a friend. The friend laughs and reveals the 'truth': 'Troy is no woman. Troy is a man. And honey . . . I don't mean part-man, I mean all-man!' Sukie exclaims: 'Oh god, the relief, the blessed relief!'³ At one level this story illustrates two momentously ironic situations around which so much modern thought revolves. First, we are defined as much, if not more, by what our identity excludes as what it includes. Second, our desire, in all its perversity, is drawn to the very exclusions which constitute it; no sooner have we 'made' ourselves than we desire what threatens to 'unmake' us. But we shouldn't conclude too quickly that Sukie is just being haunted by his excluded other. Can we confidently say whom or what Sukie really desired in this scenario *prior to* the point of his friend's disclosure about Troy? I can't, and I'm not sure he can either. Was he responding to the 'woman' on the surface, or the 'all-man' underneath? If the first, would that really have made his desire clearly heterosexual any more than, if it were the second, it would have made it clearly homosexual? And if he was responding to both, would that have made it clearly bisexual? And isn't it just possible that he was being other than consciously disturbed by his own homosexuality? And even assuming we could decide, what difference does his friend's disclosure actually make? One thing is for sure: gay identity, as distinct from homoerotic fantasies of identification, far from being the direct social counterpart of our desires, may in part be a protection against their complexity, including the complexity of those desires sanctioned by the identity. This is one of the less obvious reasons why sexual politics can be so censorious and punitive; so quick to repudiate and blame; so committed to clear identities and so intolerant of complex ones.

In this respect then, a confident gay identity may be closer to straight identity than some like to imagine. Isn't Sukie saying as much when he implies that the years-long struggle to achieve what he calls a 'true sexual identity' entailed an organization of desire which was also a policing of it (or, less contentiously, an imposition of restrictions upon it)? If so, then at the heart of a new-found and hard-won gay identity there re-emerges not raw heterosexuality or bisexuality, so much as an old-fashioned notion of restraint – something to which, at other levels, the discourses of sexual liberation have been vociferously opposed.

The problem with identity politics isn't so much its need for restraint, exclusion and boundaries, but its refusal to develop an adequate political understanding of that need, preferring instead a self-righteous language of self-evident authenticity and orientation. And this is one reason why gay identity, and the hostility to heterosexuality and bisexuality which it entails, may end up, as Jo Eadie puts it, sustaining a ghetto gay mentality, impeding political alliances. This, he rightly adds, is 'a luxury of those whose oppression is apparently so restricted to sexuality that alliances are not an issue'. Even more to the point is his further observation that the demonizing of heterosexuality polices those within gay spaces as effectively as it keeps the straight-identified out of them (p. 155).

As I remarked earlier, most of us, even the queerest of all, aspire at some level to a sexual identity. Even queers, keen to be seen as disturbing, subversive and deviant on the one hand, are also anxious to be seen as essentially healthy, 'together', hip and free on the other. Surprising as it may seem, even most queer radicals want to be normal in this sense. And it's obvious why, given how powerfully sexual deviance has been pathologized by medical and psychiatric discourses. But by the very same token, this need to be regarded as healthy, hip and free is itself a need for an identity, and one with an embarrassingly 'straight' (i.e. normal) history at that.

One reason why a political identity is threatened by the desire it wants to sanction is because of the process of identification which inflects desire. We need a double distinction here: between identity and identification, and between desire and identification. Do we ever simply desire the person we love, or is our desire not also partly an *identification with* him or her? Simply put, the 'I want you' of desire is complicated by the 'I want to be you' of identification. This seems especially plausible when we realize that the process of identification we are talking of is not necessarily, nor only, with the lover, but the 'other' which he or she stands for. Who might this other be? Someone completely different from us, or someone obscurely familiar to us: an actual parent or sibling perhaps, or maybe the parent or sibling we wanted but didn't have? And if this sounds too incestuous for those of us with, say, gay identifications well outside of the conventional 'family romance', we might still wonder whether (for example) the person desired might resemble the person we once were; or the person we always wanted to be; or the person others wanted us to be; or the person we would still like to be? It's sometimes assumed that identification is especially strong in same-sex relationships; I suspect that it may be particularly complex in some expressions of bisexuality, conscious or otherwise. But if Freud is right in thinking not just that we are all inherently bisexual, but that *all sexual acts* are so as well, then the potential for complex identification is there for all of us.[4]

Desire and identification: two scenarios

Consider two sexual scenarios, the first resonant of a partial meaning of what it might mean to be gay, the second with an equally partial meaning of what it might mean to be bisexual. Far from being the proving ground of identity, these scenarios are places where it's compromised so immediately as to suggest that this is the rule of desire rather than its exception, and it is so because of a dialectic between identity and desire whereby we embrace an identity only to have it compromised by the very desire it was supposed to stabilize.

The gay scenario: the adoration which a self-identified gay man feels for another male as he goes down on him may or may not be implicated in the politically offensive constructions of phallic masculinity in our culture (it depends on the moment, the man, the scenario). But this gay man discovers that gay pride includes not feeling guilty about the fact that it might be; and not really wanting to apologize for it, if it is. But, being a thoughtful man (he is a student) he is also pro-feminist and actually was one of the first in his seminar last week to repudiate 'phallocentrism'. But here, in the cruising ground, a political identity conflicts with the very desire it sanctions. And since our student also happens to be into rough trade, there's another identification here which further compromises the political. And I wonder – only in passing – if this kind of conflict isn't the source of relatively new kinds of anxiety inside identity politics: anxieties which are only half-allayed by being punitively projected as 'sexual politics'? (Our student is the first to trash 'real men' and to castigate any trace of misogyny in gay culture.)

The other scenario: a bisexual male partakes of a threesome in which he watches a man fucking with a woman. His identifications here are multiple: he identifies with the man (he wants to be in his position, having sex with her) but he also wants to be her. And I mean *be* her: he doesn't just want to be in her position and have the man fuck him as himself (though he wants that too); no, he wants to be fucked by the man with himself in the position of, which is to say, as, the woman. He knows of no pleasure greater than to be fucked by a man, but in this scenario he also wants to be the woman: he wants to be fucked by him in a way he imagines – fantasizes – only a woman can be. Maybe he desires the man through her. And in this same scenario there may be a further kind of pleasure where desire and identification are inflected by voyeurism: for our bisexual male the sexual attractiveness of the male is heightened by the fact that the latter is apparently desired by the woman – he excites the more because he's desired by her.

This bisexual is also a thoughtful type (he is a trainee therapist), and he (briefly) pauses to wonder about the relative degree of sexual objectification in this encounter: is the woman more objectified than the man, and should the fact that objectification of women is greater than of men give him pause for thought – or can he reassure himself with the queer celebration of *all* desire as objectification? And anyway, maybe such considerations are displaced by another, more urgent one: in this scenario, desire circulates between sexual subject positions but not necessarily as a free flow: there may be a tension, a resistance, even an impossibility here. Put simply, this bisexual male may desire to be where he can't be, and desire to become what he cannot become (at least if he desires to remain what he is). Here his identity as a coherent sexual (never mind political) subject is very much in question, and in ways which suggest that the problems for identity politics are problems for us all, even bisexuals.

It might be said that these scenarios, especially the last, represent the homosexual and the bisexual as damaged subjects. To which it could be replied that we are all damaged, and life itself, one source of the damage, is also an exercise in damage limitation – whence identity politics. Alternatively we might reflect that although we are all damaged, we aren't all damaged in equally interesting ways. Bisexuals, like homosexuals, are definitely interesting, which is why I want to save them from, rather than for, postmodern theorizing.

Being sexually postmodern

Both Jo Eadie and Clare Hemmings write persuasively about bisexuality. From their respective articles one can draw three implications. The first, and most obvious, is that the problems bisexuals experience are mainly a consequence of discrimination by society – straight society still, but also, and increasingly, the lesbian and gay community. Second, that bisexuality as a form of desire is relatively problem-free. And third, that a sexual orientation free of aversion, restraint, and the need to exclude, is the ideal, and bisexuality is the closest there is to it. If all three implications have a prima facie plausibility, then this is especially so with the last, and for the following reason.

It's an orthodoxy in cultural theory to reject difference in its negative, binary and usually antagonistic sense (white as opposed to black, heterosexual as opposed to homosexual, man as opposed to woman, and so on), but celebrate difference in a multiple and egalitarian sense, and to argue that when we recognize cultural diversity and plurality as a good thing, we will coexist without conflict. Ideally, difference in the positive sense doesn't just replace its negative form but actually subverts it; the hope is that the binary opposition which maintains the status quo will become so overloaded with cultural diversity that it will short-circuit and eventually self-destruct. In this context then, bisexuality becomes a sexuality which is more inclusive of difference: it is obviously less restricted in object choice, but also, and more excitingly, it crosses and confuses the most fundamental binary organizing desire in terms of exclusion (homosexual versus heterosexual). Hey presto, bisexuality is suddenly in the vanguard of postmodern sexual politics and cultural theory.

Even so, I would question all three implications, and especially the last. To begin with, all kinds of desire potentially eroticize difference in both its positive and negative senses. And where there is preference of any kind there is exclusion. Leo Bersani remarks: 'I have always been fascinated – at times terrified – by the ruthlessly exclusionary nature of sexual desire' (*Homos*, p. 107; cf. p. 59). Bisexuality is no exception. But perhaps I've oversimplified the arguments of Hemmings and Eadie. It's true after all that both acknowledge the bisexual as a figure of instability. This is Hemmings (p. 129):

> The 'I' in 'I am bisexual' is not simply an insubstantial assumption of fixed identity, as in 'I am lesbian' – rather, it signifies transition and movement in itself. To say 'I am bisexual' is to say 'I am not I'. . . . The process of being/becoming bisexual [is] one that is ever re-centring, re-emerging and re-creating the 'I'.

Unstable, yes, but not in a self-challenging way: this is a liberating, dynamic state of unfixity, apparently secure in its very instability. This is mainly because the instability is represented as simultaneously a state of freedom for the bisexual, and a subversion of the more rigid identities of others. Instability is not what any of us *might* experience, but the effect of 'my' desire upon 'your' desire: that which empowers me, destabilizes you. So, for example, Hemmings' need to prove that bisexuality is 'both politically and theoretically viable' is inseparable from her insistence that 'the bisexual body' is 'a figure of subversion and disruption'. Actual bisexuals are theorized as ' "revolutionary double agents" ' who can not only *dis*assemble fixed gender relations, but may also have new insights into the tenuous nature of the oppositions which sustain them (pp. 118, 131). To me this sounds like bisexuality passing, if not closeted, as postmodern theory, safely fashioning itself as a suave *doxa*. The main problem isn't the writer's overt political intent; what gives most pause for thought is the assumption that bisexuality – a form of human sexuality with histories and contemporary cross-cultural expressions so extensive as seemingly to implicate us all, even to the point of making the idea that it needs defending at all seem half-absurd – must be theoretically 'reconfigured' to become, as Hemmings puts it, 'politically and theoretically viable'.

Eadie too sees bisexual politics as about 'dismantling the entire apparatus which maintains the heterosexual/homosexual dyad'. Now this was of course a classic ambition of lesbian and gay theory, and remains so for some in that tradition. But not, according to Eadie, for its most influential current advocates: they, on the contrary, are promoting a 'dominant lesbian and gay sexual epistemology' which now wants to 'cement' rather than dismantle the straight/gay binary (pp. 142, 144). Eadie endorses Donna Haraway's repudiation of an oppressive homogeneity in favour of difference, or what Haraway calls 'infidel heteroglossia', and the imperfect, always partial and perhaps incoherent identity which that seductive phrase implies (p. 157). If this sounds risky, Eadie exhorts us not to lose our nerve: we can 'profit from that incoherence'; this very uncertainty will enable new communities of difference. Hemmings, likewise, affirms a bisexual erotics of difference which actively dismantles binary thinking and challenges a Freudian structure of desire, without being left with 'a mass of tangled signifiers' (pp. 135, 136). But what, I wonder in passing, about being left with a mass of tangled desires and identifications? I can't help but feel that the more theoretically sophisticated this celebration of difference becomes, the more experientially unconvincing it also becomes. In that sense it is wishful theory.

Reflect on some of the metaphors for the alleged subversiveness of the bisexual: the revolutionary double agent (Hemmings); the infidel (Eadie, via Haraway); hybridity (Eadie); miscegenation (Eadie). Taking the last first, there may be some who are understandably anxious at such a casual appropriation of racial history for sexual subversiveness. For my part, I only want to register that what is excluded in this appropriation is any sense of the psychic difficulty of being in a 'miscegenate location', to use Eadie's phrase. As for the double agent, we might recall that he or she is someone whose political fate has included torture, incarceration and murder (a fate, incidentally, more applicable to the history of the homosexual than that of the bisexual). But again my point would be that there is no sense of the manifest psychic dangers inherent in being the double agent, even assuming those real physical dangers have been metaphorically evaded. The physical dangers facing the infidel have if anything been worse, although her chances of maintaining psychic integration somewhat better, assuming she can adhere to a dissident identity which has marked her out as infidel in the first place (unlikely if she's a postmodern infidel since she will already have repudiated identity as an oppressive fiction).

Earlier I suggested that identity politics might be in part a defence against the instabilities and difficulties of desire itself. I'm now suggesting that the new theoretical version of bisexuality presented by Hemmings and Eadie might be a similar kind of defence. But again perhaps I'm misrepresenting the theory. After all, and commendably enough, both Hemmings and Eadie ground their theories in a celebration of difference. But the sexual embrace of difference is rarely without its own problems. For sure, there are no more-intense kinds of desire than those which transgress the borders separating 'us' from those who are 'other'. But at a cost: difference is fraught with difficulties for desire which already has difficulties of its own. It's here for example that we discover that our fantasy lives rarely live up to our political ideals. This is not necessarily a cause for guilt or even apology. Arguably, any sexual politics that can't embrace the inevitable political incorrectness of at least some of our desires is useless.[5] And as Marjorie Garber suggests, it may above all be bisexuality that compels us to confront the fact that 'eroticism and desire are always to some degree transgressive, politically *in*correct'. Garber here describes a conference at which a lesbian 'observed matter-of-factly that one of her most erotic turn-ons was male–male pornography. Many women at the conference, (myself included) nodded agreement; more than a few men, older and younger, looked stunned.' Garber plausibly argues that fantasy, in virtue of its psychic mobility, may also be inescapably bisexual (*Vice Versa*, pp. 31–3). Over and again Garber's remarkable and extensive documentation of bisexual eroticism in 'Everyday Life' confronts us with the challenges and difficulties of the actual desiring encounter with difference, as distinct from the comfortable postmodern invocation of it.

Leo Bersani goes further, repudiating the postmodern obsession with difference. In the past lesbians and gays have fiercely resisted the idea that homosexuality involves a turning away from the embrace of difference (by which was meant sexual difference) in favour of a narcissistic love of someone of the same sex; they pointed out that homosexuality was full of other kinds of difference beyond sexual difference, for example differences of race, age or class. They retained the positive evaluation of difference, giving it a different content. Bersani does not follow this route. He argues firstly that, behind the respectable wish to embrace difference, we are likely to find a deeper wish to actually annihilate the other and maybe even 'a hopeless dream of eliminating difference entirely' (*Homos*, pp. 39–40, 146). Secondly he advances the provocative claim that the homosexual preference for the same is not the cowardly dis-avowal of difference it is often said to be, so much as a necessary and positive transcending of difference altogether: 'same-sex desire, while it excludes the other sex as its object, presupposes a desiring subject for whom the antagonism between the different and the same no longer exists' (p. 59). Homosexual desire is the desire to repeat, to expand, to intensify the same. And, speculates Bersani,

> The desire in others of what we already are is . . . a self-effacing narcissism, a narcissism constitutive of community in that it tolerates psychological difference because of its very indifference to psychological difference. *This* narcissistic subject seeks a self-replicating reflection in which s/he is is neither known nor not known; here individual selves are points along a transversal network of being in which otherness is tolerated as the non-threatening margin of, or supplement to, a seductive sameness. (*Homos*, p. 150)

Radical and safe

Nothing I've read in the postmodern defences of bisexuality even hints at the fact that bisexuality may on occasions (contingently, not necessarily) resonate even more acutely than homosexuality or het-erosexuality with the difficult, fascinating complexities which inerad-icably mark any human desire which is vulnerably alive. At several points in the following chapters I shall have occasion to remark such complexities. The dominant narrative of this postmodern version of bisexuality is over-dependent upon the belief that freedom, stability and completeness lie somewhere beyond this fallen world of social discrimination.[6]

But wait: Eadie tells us that he *does* encounter bisexuals who are anxious about their identity as bisexuals, and moreover, does so 'with alarming regularity':

> Monogamous [bisexuals] feel they should be having more relationships, and [bisexuals] in multiple relationships feel they are perpetuating a stereotype. [Bisexuals] who have had primarily same-sex relationships feel they are expected to have opposite-sex relationships, and [those] in opposite-sex relationships feel they have not proved themselves until they have had a same-sex relationship. (p. 144)

But for Eadie this it isn't a problem intrinsic to bisexuals or even to sexuality; its cause is, once again, entirely socio-political: all these people have been made to feel, socially and politically, that they should be doing something different. And they have been made to feel this by the implicit demands of identity politics, and the straight/gay dyad, both of which lesbians and gays are oppressively endorsing. Eadie is undoubtedly right, to some extent: identity politics can be normative and coercive and certainly can make people feel anxious about their sexual practices or lack thereof. But it isn't as simple as that. As so often, a plausible but partial social truth obscures a psychic reality which is inseparable from immediate social pressures but not reducible to them.[7]

Identity, we know, is formed socially, not just in the here and now but also, and much more so, by the past. So too is desire. To a degree that we can never exactly know, our conscious desires of the here and now are constituted by the history of what we have desired and perhaps lost in the past. Freud once speculated that something similar was true of the ego generally: 'the character of the ego is a precipitate of abandoned object-cathexes and . . . contains the history of those object choices'; that is to say, we identify with, or introject, those we have desired and had to give up, and this makes the ego inevitably melancholic (*The Ego and the Id*, pp. 367–9). History is the 'outside' of desire, but is also inside it. That is one reason why desire tends to be politically awkward, as our fantasy life testifies. I do not mean this in an essentialist, transhistorical way. On the contrary, desire is unpredictable because so affected by history in all its ineluctable contingency: its seemingly arbitrary mix of the social and the personal. I could elaborate this in the abstract for some time, but anyone who has been wrecked by sexual infatuation or unrequited desire knows it. Likewise with anyone who remotely identifies with Tristan or Isolde, Romeo or Juliet, Catherine or Heathcliff. And if that list sounds too straight – and it needn't, depending on whom you are and who you're identifying with – then there are homoerotic texts which convey even more acutely what it is to have one's identity wrecked by desire: the Greek lyric poets, including Sappho's famous fragment,[8] James Baldwin's *Giovanni's Room*, Thomas Mann's *Death in Venice* and more.

For all its radical affect, there's something predictably safe about the new bisexual politics, not least its apparent reluctance to concede that desire always retains the potential to disturbingly unfix *my* identity, and not only that of my oppressive other. Hemmings speaks of bisexuality in terms of 'the variety of personal and political positions that a person may *choose* to occupy' (p. 25, my emphasis). But surely desire can also wreck the rational subject presupposed by such choices? Desire can unfix identity in ways which are liberating; it may compel a gay person to come out, and to experience that incomparable elation which derives from swopping an inauthentic straight identity for an authentic gay one. Desire can also unfix identity in ways which liberate by destroying an existing identity without replacing it with another. It can wreck us and bring us back to life and maybe both at once. Don't imagine that this is a didactic warning against desire; I'm only remarking some of its seductive and dangerous aspects disavowed by much sexual politics. But when identity *is* destabilized by desire we shouldn't underestimate the potential cost. It's then that we can become flooded by apprehensions of loss endemic to our history and our culture more generally, and which it's partly the purpose of identity to protect us against. In this sense too identity can be as much about surviving, even evading desire, as about expressing it.

To be wrecked by desire is one thing; to be permanently if elusively dislocated by it, is another. We do not have to accept Freud's theories of melancholy and ego formation to know that we are vulnerable to desire pressured and haunted by loss. To grow up, to become individuated, is obviously about growth and becoming, but it is also, and traumatically, about restriction and loss. Psychoanalysis offers various explanations as to why a sense of loss pervades socialized desire so acutely, including weaning from the breast, the enforced abandonment of an original 'polymorphous perversity' and being pressured into the restricted and repressive world of gender difference and normalized sexuality; the loss of parents as the first incestuous love objects, the loss of oneself as a narcissistic ideal, and so on.[9] But are these really explanations, or mythic intellectual elaborations of the experience? Again, we don't have to commit to the psychoanalytic mythology to know this loss, both in the sense of having had to relinquish and abandon earlier love objects, or more directly in the sense of simply losing them through, for example, death, betrayal, or being abandoned, or just being left behind at a railway station. The experience of loss pressures the process of identification, making it the more urgent. At the opening of 'The Waste Land', T. S. Eliot says that April is the cruellest month, 'mixing memory and desire'. Desire is always desire for something which is not yet; in that sense it is forward-looking, addressed to the future. But desire is also about the past and memory, and in that sense it is about going back. Ecstasy pressured by loss.

In some elusive and incomplete way we are the embodiments of something called sex. 'Desire' is the correct word, but let's for once use 'sex' if only because it has a density, directness and yet a degree of indeterminacy which makes it occasionally right. We cannot step outside the force-field of sex any more than we can step outside the language we speak. Sex is profoundly cultural and not simply a natural given. And yet any attempt to explain it exclusively in terms of culture will always fail. And when it does, we relive the experiential complexity of sex, and realize the futility of trying to evade it via the spurious complexities of theory. To be alive is to desire; to desire is to be deeply and maybe destructively confused, sooner or later.

3

Wishful Theory

What is wishful theory? So-called 'critical theory' originally sought to integrate theory with praxis. But what did that mean, exactly? For some of the Frankfurt School it entailed a commitment to emancipation inseparable from rigorous historical analysis – praxis as the pursuit of philosophy by other means. Marx had said, famously, that hitherto philosophers had sought only to understand the world; now they were to change it too. But of course the effort to change the world itself required an ever greater effort to understand it. To change in the direction of emancipation required above all an understanding of the ideological conditions which prevented change. Whatever we may now think of the Frankfurt School, its sustained analysis of the historical conditions which prevented change has to be respected. Arguably, those who now completely reject Marxism have abandoned not only any serious intention of *changing*, but also the serious commitment to *understanding*. Certainly an aspect of the tradition of cultural critique has been lost: the effort to understand the historical real as we inherit and live it. Marx said, famously, that we can make history, but not in historical conditions of our own choosing. And the conditions about which we have no choice profoundly affect the choices we do make. Wishful theory is akin to trying to make history in conditions of our own choosing. Too often the observation that 'we need to retheorize the problem of x or y' means: 'let's use theory to redescribe, analyse and describe the problem so that it goes away (for us)'.

Let me be more specific. There is a particular model of social struggle which has been influential in recent theory. Very briefly, it concentrates on the instabilities within the dominant culture and/or identity, identifying, for instance, ways in which the marginal is subversive of the dominant, especially at those points where the latter is rendered unstable by contradictions intrinsic to it. Other conditions which make the dominant vulnerable include the fact that it is dependently connected to the subordinate, and that while these connections are disavowed by the dominant, they become known, to a degree, by the subordinate. If this model originates with Hegel its modern form has been deeply influenced by, among other movements, Marxism, psychoanalysis and deconstruction. It's because I've been influenced by this account of social struggle,[1] and remain persuaded by it, that I can't subscribe to what I regard as a wishful theoretical use of it most pronounced in some strands of postmodernism. Bits and pieces from diverse theoretical sources are expertly spliced together, often with the aim of demonstrating a repressive dominant always allegedly on the brink of its own ruin and about to be precipitated over the edge by one or another marginal challenge to it. For example, some queer theorists regard male heterosexuality (it's rarely, if ever, female heterosexuality) as so intrinsically insecure as to be always about to self-destruct under the pressure of the homosexuality it is repressing. Dream on.

And then there is the way that certain marginal sexual cultures and practices – cross-dressing and sado-masochism have been especially fashionable in this regard – are theoretically worked over so as to become the last word in avant-garde subversion. Scepticism about this claim in no way implies a scorn for such practices; on the contrary, such scepticism may now be the precondition for a more thoughtful encounter with them. The result of such theoretical workovers is not so much a demonstration of the intrinsic instability of the social order, or its effective subversion by marginal forces within or adjacent to it, but an abstract, highly wrought re-presentation of it – a theoretical narrative whose plausibility is often in inverse proportion to the degree to which it makes its proponents feel better. To that extent wishful theory is also feel-good theory. And if, as Rudiger Safranski has argued (*Schopenhauer and the Wild Years of Philosophy*, p. 309), modernity remains inside the old problematic of freedom and unfreedom, this is nowhere more so than in wishful theory: on the one hand such theory emphatically repudiates old ideals of individual freedom by dissolving the 'subject' back into the structures, discourses, and ideologies which he was once thought to be master of; on the other hand these same theorists replay this 'lost' freedom in their own fantasies of subversion and disruption. And this same sublimation of freedom might be discernible in the fact that so much theoretical denial of freedom is written in the tones of the masterful and the omniscient, not to mention the supercilious.

The contrived narratives of wishful theory insulate their adherents from social reality by screening it, and this in the very act of fantasizing its subversion. So much so that in some contemporary theory, the very concept of subversion has become a kind of disavowal. Theory is deployed in a way which is usually self-exonerating, hardly at all in a way which is self-questioning. This kind of theory can be so quickly updated because it is so tenuously connected with the real. Drop this bit of theory, splice in that and the whole thing can be updated to correspond to intellectual fashion. Want some political street cred? – then mix and match a bit of post-colonialism with a bit of queer theory. But hang on: isn't there a suspicion on the conference circuit that queer theory is already passé? And don't forget, it could be up to two years before publication. Far better to frame the whole thing with reference to an as yet obscure intellectual from some war-torn part of the world. It's difficult to be against fashion; as someone once said, it has to be forgiven because it dies so young. None of the advocates of the new postmodern queer and/or bisexual politics produce wishful theory in this worst sense, but they borrow from it, especially when they 'retheorize' sex into an agreeable intellectual fiction.

What does heterosexuality want?

> INTERVIEWERS: This leads us to the question of heterosexuality –
> JUDITH BUTLER: I don't know much about heterosexuality!
> INTERVIEWERS: Don't worry, it's a theoretical question.
> 'Gender as Performance: an interview with Judith Butler', p. 32.

Previously I've looked at how some advocates of the new bisexual politics use theory to refashion bisexuality as a radically destabilizing force. I turn now to how theory has been used, equally implausibly, to represent heterosexuality as the epitome of a wretchedly destabilized sexual identity. The writer in question, Judith Butler, is someone who earns respect as the most brilliantly eclectic and influential theorist of sexuality in recent years. Yet her account of heterosexuality as elaborated in *Gender Trouble* also borrows from wishful theory. This is how she summarized her argument in an article published a year after that book:

> heterosexuality is always in the process of imitating . . . its own phantasmatic idealization of itself – *and failing*. Precisely because it is

bound to fail, and yet endeavors to succeed, the project of heterosexual identity is propelled into an endless repetition of itself.[2]

A couple of pages later she reiterates the same claim, equally emphatically: 'heterosexuality is an impossible imitation of itself', only now adding the crucial additional factor that it is *homosexuality* which precipitates heterosexuality into this state of high ontological insecurity, not to say contradiction:

> the parodic or imitative effect of gay identities works neither to copy nor to emulate heterosexuality, but rather, to expose heterosexuality as an incessant and *panicked* imitation of its own naturalized idealization. That heterosexuality is always in the act of elaborating itself is evidence that it is perpetually at risk, that is, that it 'knows' its own possibility of becoming undone: hence, its compulsion to repeat which is at once a foreclosure of that which threatens its coherence. That it can never eradicate that risk attests to its profound dependency upon the homosexuality that it seeks fully to eradicate. (pp. 22–3)

Here is a version of that relationship between the dominant and the subordinate described earlier, now being played out between heterosexuality and homosexuality: the latter subverts the former by exposing its inherent contradictions and insecurities.

Let's assume, just for the sake of argument, that heterosexuality is a monolithic evil and that the most urgent task is to secure its overthrow. Even with these assumptions, indeed *especially* with them, Butler's description of it seems to me hopelessly wrong.

First, because she gives us a representation of heterosexuality which is at once universalized, essentialized and reductive, far removed from the diversity of what most straight people are, and what they might do. This could be regarded as legitimate given that Butler is talking not about individuals as such, but about concepts or discursive constructions. But that would accentuate the problem, not solve it, since she crudely 'psychologizes' these constructions in terms that could only be applicable precisely to such individuals: thus heterosexuality is said to be paranoid; impossibly imitating itself; knowing it can only ever fail; panicked by its own impossibility; etc.

Second, because this 'psychology' does not correspond to any plausible discursive or materialist history of heterosexuality. On the contrary, the crude psychology at the heart of this theoretical sophistication, erases that history in all its stubborn contingency and surprising complexity. It is a psychoanalytically-inspired fantasy. Further, this claim about heterosexuality's endemic contradictions, paranoia, impossibility etc., hardly squares with its obvious resilience.

Institutions like marriage and the nuclear family may be collapsing or at least undergoing extensive change, but heterosexuality per se is proving adaptable to say the least. As for individual heterosexuals, even some of them seem surprisingly resilient. If it's replied that the contradictions, paranoia and impossibility are not manifestly structural, but unconscious, that just begs a whole lot of new questions, not least the question of symptoms. In effect, the evidence for Butler's diagnosis of the permanent instability, panic and crisis of heterosexuality is the very fact of its survival and persistence. But when demonstrable historical 'success' becomes the main evidence of radical failure, and actual real-world perpetuation the sure sign of an innate impossibility, things are getting wishful in the extreme.

There's a touching irony in the fact that those most insecure about their heterosexuality are not 'real men' but people politically sympathetic to the lesbian and gay cause; they include straight feminists, bisexuals, the men of men's studies. Certainly, some of the most anxious straights are those men trying not to be heterosexist; men who have internalized feminists, gays and lesbians as their significant others – only to then get trashed by these others for trying to be 'new men'.

This connects with two further aspects of the potential of desire to disturb. Firstly, such disturbance is indeed a potential and not a structural condition or foregone conclusion. And when we ask *who* is most susceptible in this respect we find that it is often those marginal to the dominant formations, be they heterosexual or otherwise. Conversely, it is often the case that those most central to the dominant formations are also most protected by them: what has always been true of, say, social class, is also true of sexual identity.

Secondly – and this is something generally missed by those who have mis/appropriated her work for a facile politics of subversion – in Butler's account gay desire usually figures *in an intense relationship to* heterosexuality; so much so that it might be said to have an antagonistic desire *for* it. Reading Butler one occasionally gets the impression that gay desire isn't fully itself unless somehow installed subversively inside heterosexuality. Again, my point isn't so much that Butler's argument may be offensive to gays or straights or both. I willingly disregard such considerations because I'm bored by the tendency in gender politics to accumulate cultural capital by occupying the high ground of the offended, and then launching into the punitive critique which it's supposed to licence. Too often that strategy is prompted more by professional paranoia and *ressentiment* than by political critique. My point is that, as a generalized description of how homosexuality and heterosexuality relate, Butler's account strikes me as just wrong. And heterosexism is just as likely to be aided as undermined by an argument that deploys totalizing reductions to erase the complexity and diversity of heterosexual identifications and desires.

On this last point – the specific relationship of heterosexuality to homosexuality – it isn't just the advocates of bisexuality (including those whom, for other reasons, I was critical of earlier), who write more perceptively about it. Lynne Segal, recalling Marjorie Garber's anecdote about the lesbians who get off on gay male pornography (which I mentioned in chapter 2), writes engagingly of how she 'became "straight"' through identifications made available by the novels of James Baldwin:

> Situating myself in the place of the desiring male longing for the body of another male, homosexual imagery provided the perfect – seemingly the only possible – route into sexual pleasure, into having it both ways, as every straight woman, at least in masturbatory repose, must want and need.[3]

She remarks too that the attraction of the male homosexual as an identificatory figure for the heterosexual female can hardly have been unusual, and finds confirmation of this in Cora Kaplan's observation that women readers, whatever their sexual bias,

> could take up shifting and multiple fantasy positions within [Baldwin's] fictional narratives: that possibility, itself wonderfully, if terrifyingly, liberating, allowed an identification not just with specific characters but with the scenarios of desire themselves.[4]

By the time of her later book, *Bodies that Matter* (1993) Butler has in part changed her arguments but also claims, plausibly enough, that *Gender Trouble* was misunderstood and misappropriated. But on this question of the fundamental relationship of straight and gay there seems to be no major change; the same argument is confirmed in the interview with which this section began:

> One of the reasons that heterosexuality has to re-elaborate itself, to ritualistically reproduce itself all over the place, is that it has to overcome some constitutive sense of its own tenuousness. (p. 34)[5]

She adds that, to take up a particular 'sexual position *always* involves becoming haunted by what's excluded. And the more rigid the position, the greater the ghost, and the more threatening it is in some way. . . . one is defined as much by what one is not as by the position that one explicitly inhabits.' So here is an insistence that *all* sexual subject positions are equally tenuous, equally open to being thus haunted by what they exclude. I share Butler's scepticism about the person who claims that their own exclusions are only a matter of indifference; for instance, the straight person who claims that they have an attitude of indifference to homosexuality – 'I haven't thought about it much, it neither turns me on nor turns me off. I'm just sexually neutral in that regard' (pp. 34–5). We are indeed often haunted by what we exclude, and the person who claims not to be may well be performing a disavowal. But, as the remarks of Segal and Kaplan indicate, these aren't the only options: fantasy correlates even less to sexual subject positions than does sexual behaviour[6] but is at the same time inseparable from, and constitutive of them. What that means for the thoughtful is that their sexual subject positions are not necessarily petrified identities forever haunted by what they ruthlessly exclude: they may actually facilitate access to scenes of sexuality which already, *and pleasurably*, include what in other respects are excluded. Or to put it another way, for fantasy, exclusion/inclusion is one of the most unstable of all binaries. Further, by way of trying to avoid speaking of desire in a totalizing way – another tendency now endemic to theory and epitomized by the fact that we (I include myself) hardly ever speak about desire in the plural – we should recall that desire is not only haunted, but radically enabled, by its exclusions. When Bersani ponders the ruthlessly exclusionary nature of sexual desire (see above, chapter 2) he is remarking the way it confidently proceeds, not the way it falls into paranoid failure.

In *Bodies that Matter* Butler now writes compellingly about melancholia and the inherent difficulties of desire. But, if anything the inscription of homosexuality inside heterosexuality becomes more insistent. We are now told that drag does not oppose heterosexuality, and nor will the proliferation of drag 'bring down' heterosexuality; rather drag 'allegorizes *heterosexual melancholy*', a melancholy which is 'constitutive' of it – of heterosexuality that is, not drag (pp. 235, 237). Heterosexual identity is now construed in terms of the homosexuality it excludes, only to then experience this as absence and loss; this produces:

> a culture of heterosexual melancholy, one that can be read in the hyperbolic identifications by which mundane heterosexual masculinity and femininity confirm themselves. The straight man *becomes* (mimes, cites, appropriates, assumes the status of) the man he 'never' loved and 'never' grieved; the straight woman *becomes* the woman she 'never'

loved and 'never' grieved. It is in this sense, then, that what is most apparently performed as gender is the sign and symptom of a pervasive disavowal. (*Bodies that Matter*, p. 236)

Or, as she had put it just before: 'In this sense the "truest" lesbian melancholic is the strictly straight woman, and the "truest" gay male melancholic is the strictly straight man' (p. 235).[7] This is of course such a theoretically exquisite irony that it seems churlish to wonder whether it's true, or whether Butler is not herself partaking of the hyperbole she has just exposed as the definitive strategy of 'mundane heterosexual masculinity and femininity'.

Sexual/intellectual failure

Butler writes confidently about the failures of heterosexuality. I am more concerned with the failures of theory, and, beyond that, of all of us who write as intellectuals. It seems more than ever right to reflect on the way that intellectuals necessarily live inside, not outside, the failures of their predecessors. By briefly addressing this in a different but related context, I can, I hope, indicate how my own scepticism about wishful theory differs from the recent, emphatic and growing reaction against all theory per se. My argument with wishful theory is in defence of intellectual engagement; that the reaction just referred to is anti-intellectual is apparent from a book which has become a rallying point for it, Brian Vickers' *Appropriating Shakespeare*.[8]

But perhaps the most damaging thing about this book is not the credence it gives to undiscriminating reaction, but the way intellectual history, an important antecedent of contemporary theory, and one it still has a great deal to learn from, gets silently censored and reduced in the process. In fact, if there is one thing that some anti-theorists share with some postmodernist theorists, it is this ignoring of intellectual history, and with it, the complexities of intellectual inheritance.

Resisting the temptation to illustrate this by challenging Vickers on what I regard as his weakest ground – his dismissal of political criticism – I propose instead to confront him on his strongest ground, namely his critique of Freudian-inspired criticism. 'Strongest' in the sense that Vickers is at least right in this: some highly implausible criticism of Shakespeare has proceeded in the name of Freud, criticism which might well be regarded as a precursor of contemporary wishful theory. But in his critique of Freud, Vickers seems to me to betray the very scholarship he invokes to discredit theory. He demands careful attention to literary texts which he then denies to other kinds of writing, most spectacularly Freud's. In an unremitting rejection of everything Freud argued for, Vickers relies entirely on selective quotation from secondary sources. No work of Freud appears in his bibliography. Vickers criticizes Freudian critics for being ahistorical and unscholarly. Nothing is more ahistorical and unscholarly than Vickers' second-hand take on Freud. *Appropriating Shakespeare* suffers from intellectual reductiveness and a sensibility apparently blunted by *ressentiment*. Each of these limitations discredits his own claim to a superior scholarship, since the best scholarship (of which I for one know I am not capable) requires both intellect and sensibility.

Most of Vickers' attack is designed to show that psychoanalysis is a failed science. He assumes that this totally discredits Freud,[9] himself failing to realize that intellectual interest in Freud today virtually begins with the understanding that psychoanalysis is a failed science: the seduction, the danger, and the necessity of concepts like repression, displacement and fantasy to name but three, begin here. Like so many anti-theorists, Vickers can't comprehend that most-crucial yet difficult of intellectual activities: being historically and imaginatively inside a perspective which one is also critically resisting; struggling to escape its failures while seeing that one has already been changed by it. Such is the history of much dynamic thought, and the best intellectual history recognizes this. Vickers might learn from what Leo Bersani has written of his own long encounter with Freud: 'If Freud has determined more than anyone else the ways in which I read art, his theories have been less important to me than the experience of having followed the modes of theoretical failure and even collapse in his work.' Although I am not persuaded by Bersani's claim that these moments of collapse in Freud provide us with 'the *most* authentically psychoanalytic events in his writing' (*The Culture of Redemption*, pp. 3, 44; my emphasis), my own reading of the importance of the theoretical failure of psychoanalysis with regard to sexual disgust – the subject of the next chapter – is indebted to Bersani.

4

Sexual Disgust

Why is it that we read so much about desire but very little about how it is haunted – created, even – by its opposite, disgust? If this is one of the more significant of the many repressions within academic sexual politics it's hardly surprising, since disgust, one of the least explored human emotions, has even been described as the forgotten emotion. As we'll see, one good reason for exploring the strange and elusive dialectic between desire and disgust is the way it resists the simplistic judgements of the moralist, the X-ray vision of the analyst, and the reductive perspective of wishful theory.

'Disgust' is the strong word, 'aversion' the weaker. And then there is the evasive alternative to both of these: 'indifference'. If I use the strong word it's because disgust is often in fact what is being felt, even though what is admitted is usually something else: sometimes aversion, but more usually a claimed indifference – 'not my scene'. The relationship between desire and disgust is especially significant in the arena of sexuality where, as we've already seen, complex responses are at once registered, concealed and indeed repressed in that misleadingly simple designation, 'sexual preference'.

Some would say that even to talk about sexual disgust is to be gripped by a residual puritanism. But if anyone remains in the grip of such a thing it's those who would pretend that sexual or bodily disgust is only for Victorians and prudes. In fact, some of the most uninterestingly neurotic people one can meet are those who want everyone to know that they are really at ease with their own sexuality, and as the politically correct counterpart of this personal bill of health, at ease with everyone else's too.

Disgust, both in its subjective experience and its social expression, is dense with cultural significance, a dynamic component of the most exalted philosophies and the most murderous political ideologies. It can work to protect cultural and bodily boundaries; but often does so in ways which indicate their vulnerability to disruption, and the psychological and social cost paid for securing them. It can be a reaction which consolidates individual identity, or a disavowal of what threatens it; it can be a symptom of repressed or ambivalent desire for something with the potential to liberate or threaten the self, or it can liberate *and* threaten it almost indistinguishably.[1]

Disgust is typically experienced at the boundaries of a culture, and of the individual identities of those who belong to it, and its focus is typically what is excluded by those boundaries and especially what is just the other side of them. Social cohesion requires that the securing of the boundaries of the larger culture and the individual identities within it, should coincide, whereas in practice of course they often do not. To be sure, they *do* coincide, more or less, and this greatly contributes to social cohesion. From one angle it is the coincidence which seems conclusive; from another, the mismatch; from yet another it is the seemingly unbridgeable gulf between those differently positioned in relation to the boundaries: what to one person is the most ecstatically beautiful experience in the world, to another might be so repulsive it deserves reprobation, punishment, mutilation and death, and never more so than where sexuality is concerned.

Because of all this, the active incitement of disgust can be an effective strategy of satirical critique and political opposition: a confronting of culture with its constitutive repressions, a provocative violation of cultural boundaries and bodily proprieties. And if, as Laura Kipnis has shown in her account of *Hustler* magazine, the counter-reaction provoked by such a strategy is typically relentless and no less aggressive, then that is some measure of what is at stake (*Bound and Gagged*, esp. pp. 122–60).

Sexual disgust is also a prime motor of censorship, and in a way which reveals its relationship to social control. Later I shall be looking at the banning of Radclyffe Hall's *The Well of Loneliness*, a now legendary novel about lesbian love. The book was banned on several grounds. Those against the book said that it was disgusting because lesbianism was morally dangerous, obscene; a threat to children, nation, Christianity, etc. In fact, as we can see from the private views of those who mounted the campaign against the book, the disgust at lesbianism was less a reaction to its putative dangers, than a motive for imagining or inventing them.

For sure then, disgust is where the struggle between dissidence and domination can become especially violent, and just because it reveals so much about ourselves and our culture. At the same time it suggests how little we really know about either. There is something mysterious or at least elusive about the dialectic between desire and disgust, within both the individual psyche and the larger culture, and I want to hold this in mind throughout as central to the larger project of this book.

The way people go at it

In his frank and controversial 1920 autobiography, *Si le grain ne meurt* (*If it Die*), André Gide recalls witnessing a sexual encounter which took place in Algiers in 1897. Gide's friend, Daniel, fucks an Arab youth called Mohammed. Gide recalls that Daniel 'looked gigantic leaning over this little body which he hid from view – he might have been a huge vampire feeding upon a corpse. I could have screamed in horror.' Although undoubtedly occurring within an exploitative context, this sexual act was not obviously rape: Gide confesses that he was horrified, equally, by 'Daniel's way of going at it and by the willing cooperation of Mohammed'. Gide does not judge; on the contrary he uses the occasion to reflect not just on the diversity of human sexual practice, but on the irrational revulsion we experience, and the difficulty we have in understanding the way, in Gide's words, that other people 'go at it'. Nothing, he adds, 'is so disconcerting'. If we were able to see the way our neighbours make love it would seem as 'strange, ridiculous and, let us admit it, as revolting' as the sexual coupling of animals and insects. And, crucially, 'no doubt this is why misunderstandings in this matter are so great and intolerance so ferocious' (pp. 286–7). Undoubtedly this thoughtful take on his own personal revulsion was a crucial strand in Gide's rationalist defence of his own and others' sexual non-conformity, a defence whose historical importance needs to be remembered. Gide's response to Daniel and Mohammed is especially commendable in that Gide's own preference was for what today might be called 'vanilla' sex; in his own words here, he 'can only conceive pleasure face to face, reciprocal and gentle and . . . find satisfaction in the most furtive contact' (p. 287). Vanilla or not, as Bersani shows in *Homos*, Gide's sexuality, or at least his representation of it in *The Immoralist*, intimates a kind of intimacy devoid of intimacy, an eroticism with the potential to challenge nothing less than the western conception of desire as 'a drama of personal anguish and unfulfilled demands' (*Homos*, pp. 125, 128).

How striking then to find Gide, in one of his journal entries, displacing his own disgust into exactly the intolerance he here avoids, and doing so at around the same time as he wrote up his recollection of the earlier traumatic episode.[2] It is a brisk early instance of a certain kind of identity politics – that self-exoneration inseparable from a repudiation of others. Gide classifies homosexuals into three groups: the pederast, the sodomite and the invert, and declares that it is only the inverts – men who like to be anally fucked – who deserve the reproach of 'moral and intellectual deformation' which is commonly addressed to all homosexuals. He adds: 'most often the differences among [homosexuals] is such that they experience a profound disgust for one another, a disgust . . . that in no way yields to that which . . . (heterosexuals) fiercely show toward all three' (*Journals*, vol. 2, pp. 246–7).

Despite their alleged disgust for one another, homosexuals (collectively?) resist the homophobic disgust of straight culture. This ambivalent solidarity – one which incorporates, reproduces and displaces what it also resists – persists today, albeit in different terms, and not only within gay identities.

Since Gide we have benefited from the sexual liberation to which he contributed in no small part. And liberation has greatly changed not just the objects of disgust, but the ways in which its expression is interpreted. For example, one kind of conservative attitude has always regarded aggressive disgust as a proper response to any sexual deviation. In our more liberal climate that response survives but on a much reduced scale. In fact today we are more likely to turn the tables, and pathologize not the deviant practice, but any extreme attitude of disgust towards it. Like Shakespeare's player, the disgusted are thought to protest too much. This change derives in part from the liberation movements of the post-war period which tended to either demystify and/or pathologize disgust. To demystify disgust entailed seeing it as symptomatic of a repressive sexual ideology; to pathologize it, as symptomatic of a 'screwed-up' individual. And in practice of course the latter usually, and conveniently, presupposed the former. One of the more successful examples of this was the way the gay liberation movement was able, with considerable success, to argue that it was not the homosexual who was neurotic but the disgusted homophobes; and the reason they were so disturbed was because they were concealing their own repressed and possibly unconscious homosexuality behind cultural bigotry. Additionally – and this is a nicely ironic instance of how disgust doesn't so much disappear as find new objects – the disgusted individual becomes vaguely disgusting. This very example tells us that the influential origins of this change whereby disgust is pathologized are in Freud. Yet my mention of Shakespeare might suggest that the psychological insight which enables this reversal is much older (Freud would have agreed).

Closeted disgust

And yet it seems to me that liberation, far from eradicating the kind of sexual disgust felt by Gide may have intensified it; certainly it has helped produce new ways of concealing or repressing it, and of encouraging people to displace and project their experience of it into politically acceptable forms of bigotry. We are still invited to express disgust publicly in relation to many things, most of all perhaps, to paedophilia. The virulence of such expressions is partly a consequence of the suppression of others. Misogynistic and racist disgust have been freely expressed for centuries.[3] Today, in certain important public contexts at least, the overt expression of such disgust has diminished, but not gone away. It remains the case that the sexuality of some straight men is organized around not just a barely-concealed contempt for, but also a fundamental disgust with, women. Crudely, they fuck them despite, or because of, not much liking them.[4] Ostensibly that has changed. Yet I would guess that for some men it hasn't changed very much, while for others, while much has changed, anxious aversions remain. Another instance: one of the most embarrassing aspects of gay history has been the overt misogyny of some gay men. Commendably, some other gay men tend to be among our most vigilant critics of misogyny. But does this necessarily mean they themselves are free of anxieties about the female body? Might not this political vigilance in some cases also be symptomatic of the continuing shadowy presence of such anxieties rather than their complete absence? It is one of the many deceptions of contemporary sexual politics that the adoption of a progressive political attitude is naively taken to guarantee the presence of a 'together' – i.e., untroubled – psyche. One suspects that some people have only adopted the first by way of laying claim to the second. Does it work? Amusingly, Camille Paglia suggests not, at least not in relation to those American men who tried to make themselves more attractive by adopting the persona of 'new men', only to find that the very feminists who demanded this of them are attracted even less to new men than old men. Paglia is given to the odd overstatement, but the disjunction between attraction and approval she here identifies is familiar enough.

And then there is the new 'body theory'. The body has become a fashionable topic: athletes work out; cultural theorists 'work on' the body, and with a tenacious abstraction which to me suggests evasion if not aversion.[5] Here's an exchange between an older and a younger academic, overheard at a cocktail party (you'll know which is which):

'So what do you work on?'
'The Body.'
'The body – how interesting; [longish pause in which both sip drinks] in what sense exactly?'
'I see the body as an effect of repressive discursive constructions and in particular the site of the inscription of power.'
'Right. So this is a body in chains, as it were?'
'Well, yes and no: I also theorize the body as the site of subversion and subjugated knowledges.'
'Interesting.'

Explicit attention to the question of aversion puts back into the picture what the abstractions of postmodern body theory usually evade, namely the body. I'm not foregrounding disgust and aversion as the key terms in a new theory of desire. It's probably apparent by now that the last thing I want is yet another theory of desire. I'm much more interested in using disgust to interrogate the limits of the theories we have. Bored by body studies, I yearn for a body that is material in the sense that it is recalcitrant, not malleable to theory; and in particular a body which impedes rather than surrenders to wishful theory – not with the intention of repudiating theory, but getting it to be more 'worked-out', that's to say, more truthful, not more elaborate. If William Miller's recent book, *Anatomy of Disgust*, is more enlightening about the body than any body theory could ever be, it's partly because his common-sense approach confronts the empirical realities of disgust which theoretical abstraction precisely avoids. Similarly with Mary Douglas's pioneering work in *Purity and Danger*, in which she shows how relatively small changes in the object or its location can precipitate us from one attitude into its opposite, from desire to loathing: hence the famous formulation that dirt is [nothing more than] matter out of place.[6] The same food which was enticing on the plate becomes repulsive in the dustbin. This is a spatial difference which has a temporal counterpart: the food which is desirable on the plate *now* may be perceived as disgusting in exactly that same place several hours later. Small differences of space and time affect the desire/disgust dialectic to a remarkable degree and in a way which suggests how the vicissitudes of human desire more generally are likewise affected by equally small differences.

Vile bodies

Aversion to the body is hardly surprising since for many human beings nothing has greater potential to disgust. And if writers as diverse as Augustine and Freud are right in thinking that we are repulsed by the realization of having being born between faeces and urine, it's even more pertinent that the very same bodily orifices which disgust us because of their excretions – vomit, urine, shit and blood, to name but four – also excite sexually. Which is, perhaps, why disgust in its 'purest' form can *only* be experienced in relation to the human body – the selfsame body which, for those in love, can also be the most beautiful, the *least* disgusting, thing in the world. But, if the truth were told, for most of our lives we are not in love in quite that sense and the mundane fact remains: where the bodies of others are concerned, anxious aversion rather than spontaneous attraction is the norm.

I've already mentioned three types of the disgusted: the racist, the misogynist and the homophobe. Now in each case we can, if we like, pathologize the disgust – or at least regard it as only or mainly a problem of individuals not like us. But expressions of disgust can sometimes be politically respectable even, or dare I say especially, for people like us. Not so long ago a feminist writer spent some time demolishing the myth that older men make better lovers. In the process she spoke of ailments of the ageing male body with contempt and distaste (a more intimate rendering of the familiar 'dirty old man', a figure who probably collects more displaced/frustrated disgust today than any other). It was another woman writer who pointed out that, had a man spoken of women in such terms it would have been construed as virulent misogyny. Another example: lesbian and gay people sometimes parody, and sometimes earnestly reciprocate homophobia by expressing contempt for straight sex,[7] and both gays and straights have been known to express aversion to bisexuality; so much so that a new word has recently entered the arena of sexual politics: biphobia.

In current debates, bisexuals are sometimes categorized as pathologically greedy because they are imagined to be out to fuck everyone in sight. Some bisexuals turn the tables by celebrating this sexual openness as a measure of how pathology-free they are: at least they aren't afflicted with the constitutive aversions of the rigidly straight or the rigidly gay. But, as we've already seen, it isn't that simple. I once heard of a (self-identified) bisexual male who had been interrogated by a psychiatrist intent on finding out whether he was really straight or gay. This bisexual confessed to finding some men's bodies repulsive in a way that he rarely found women's bodies repulsive. Relieved, the psychiatrist concluded that this proved his 'patient' to be more straight than gay, and only in need of a little aversion therapy. Unfortunately he didn't wait to hear that this bisexual also found his aversion to some men matched by an intensity of desire for others which he never quite felt for women.

Of course, this man does not have to be classified sexually. The utopian potential of refusing sexual classification is only now being imagined, with the advent of queer erotics. But there is some way to go, since at the moment many gays, as well as straights, share the psychiatrist's desire to pin down our bisexual on one side or the other: they all find the apparent sexual indeterminacy of the bisexual troubling to their own identity. So, if we can't resist the temptation to classify him, then I'd bet he was more gay than straight. So yes: I'm suggesting that to experience an aversion to some men matched by an intensity of desire for others may make him more gay than straight. If so, then something like body aversion is integral to the make-up of our sexual being and not just to specific sexual choices. And that has the interesting consequence that strong aversion to some people of the *opposite* sex may be a constituent part of heterosexuality rather than, or as well as, homosexuality, while feelings of aversion to some members of the *same* sex may actually be prima facie evidence of homoerotic inclination. One thing is for sure: sexual aversion isn't just a hostile dynamic between groups characterized by *different* sexual orientations or identites – straight, gay, bisexual. As the earlier example of Gide made clear, there's a long tradition of people of the same – the very same – sexual orientation being disgusted with each other. Proust of course made the same point; and there is a particularly challenging section in *Homos* where Bersani says that Proust deserves our attention for suggesting that 'the aversion of inverts to the society of inverts may be the necessary basis for a new community of inversion' (p. 131).

But to return to the question of orientation: what about a feeling of aversion to the *whole* of the opposite sex – surely that would be conclusive evidence of homosexuality? Presumably so; yet how many people ever really experience sexual desire in terms of such a blanket, almost a priori form of aversion and exclusion, any more than we desire *all* members of the same sex if we're gay, or the opposite sex if we're straight? And if, say, a gay man does experience total aversion to the opposite sex, isn't he being over-determined by an identity formation which is historically very recent, and not unconnected to the 'straight' person's total aversion to the idea of any kind of erotic contact with people of the same sex? These are questions, the point of which is to suggest that the experience of aversion is all the while telling us more than we want to hear or to know.

'Disgust always bears the imprint of desire'

One idea that became popular with sexual liberation was that disgust is always a masking symptom of repressed or unconscious desire: 'disgust always bears the imprint of desire.'[8] It derived vaguely from the Freudian idea that disgust was a reaction formation to a desire which was threatening the coherence of the civilized ego. Attractive as this idea may be, it is just wrong to believe that disgust is always an expression of a repressed desire whose return promises mayhem. That it may be is an indispensable insight which also contributes to the almost inevitable misapplication and discrediting of psychoanalysis. Approaching the subject from an anthropological perspective, a very different picture emerges: aversion is not necessarily about a repressed desire for its object, but about protecting boundaries and maintaining the inner coherence of an existing formation of desire. This makes a real difference. In a strong Freudian model there is a desire 'inside' the disgust which is a force for instability: identity is constantly, and constitutively, being threatened or destabilized by its own repressed desires. On the anthropological account, aversion is not so much about the surfacing of repressed desire, but the policing and containing of a socially acceptable desire. Boundaries and identities are not being threatened but, on the contrary, secured through learned and imitated behaviours.

Another problem with the repression model is that it can't quite comprehend why we may construe something as disgusting just because we *consciously* desire it. Perhaps because we're infatuated with someone we deem unworthy of us; perhaps because we know we desire what threatens our survival, even our very life. And then there is the related scenario where the desire comes first and then transmutes into disgust in the context of surfeit.[9] Further, there are the mournful effects of time and change, the stuff of literature and philosophy. For an instance of this I glance back a couple of millennia to indicate the cultural continuity, but also the cultural relativity, of what I'm describing. Plutarch (*c*.46 to *c*.126) describes how in Ancient Greece the love which a man felt for a boy would disappear abruptly when body hair appeared; a single hair, he says, would cancel the obsessive love just like that, turning desire to aversion.[10] (A nice irony here of course: in Greece they were disgusted by men loving boys who were too old, while today most people are disgusted by men who love them too young; thus Camille Paglia: 'Greek pederasty honored the erotic magnetism of male adolescents in a way that today brings the police to the door' (*Sexual Personae*, p. 115)).

Consider another, much more recent instance. In James Baldwin's *Giovanni's Room*, the narrator, David, describes how he comes to be disgusted by the body of his female partner:

> I trace it to something as fleeting as the tip of her breast lightly touching my forearm as she leaned over me to serve my supper. I felt my flesh recoil. Her underclothes, drying in the bathroom, which I had often thought of as smelling even rather improbably sweet and as being washed much too often, now begin to seem unaesthetic and unclean ... I sometimes watched her naked body move and wished it were harder and firmer, I was fantastically intimidated by her breasts, and when I entered her I began to feel that I would never get out alive. All that once delighted me seemed to have turned sour in my stomach. (pp. 118–19)[11]

Anyone who has read this novel would probably agree that it would be somewhat evasive to describe David as bisexual. But if we're to describe him as homosexual that raises the uncomfortable prospect that his is a homosexuality somehow inseparable from a disgust with, and in flight from, the female body. We could of course avoid such uncomfortable issues by simply dismissing David as a misogynist. But that too would be an evasion since, as Marjorie Garber, who cites the above passage in *Vice Versa*, points out, for the body of a loved one to become the focus for such disgust is a familiar if unwelcome recognition for many people – straights, gays and bisexuals alike (p. 129). Surely it is rather that in this novel disgust finds expression in terms of a misogyny it is not, and cannot be, reduced to. To engage in such a reduction is convenient. Likewise with the charges of homophobia and racism: to see aversion only in these terms allows us to avoid confronting the uncomfortable complexities of desire itself, and a crucial but partial truth becomes an evasion. To think harder about aversion might get us back to that complexity and makes us confront the evasion.

Note for example how in this passage from Baldwin the disgust emerges not from some new aspect of the other (as in the instance from Plutarch), nor even from some hitherto unseen or ignored aspect of them, but from the selfsame details which hitherto were erotic: the 'fleeting' contact of the breast on the forearm, the smell of the underclothes. What once was desirable has become disgusting. David feels this to be the physical manifestation of something much greater – the process 'of love turning to hatred'; not indifference, note, but hatred. And this change is, says David, 'far more terrible than anything I have ever read about it, more terrible than anything I will ever be able to say' (p. 118).

Here disgust is, among other things, the compelling expression of the terrifying *mutability* of desire. So why then has the simplistic interpretation of disgust as always being the symptom of *repressed* desire gained such currency – doubly erroneous here since repression is usually regarded as a constant rather than mutable factor in desire? (Which is not to suggest that the mutability of desire never involves repression.) One obvious reason is that it is an interpretation which empowers those who invoke it. The person experiencing the disgust (read as symptom) is 'known' from a superior position: we diagnose his or her inner 'truth' to be one of conflict, repression, insecurity, bad faith, inauthenticity; he or she is, in short, 'fucked up'. Disgust in its expression can obviously be violent. But so too can disgust as an analytic concept. That is one good reason for being suspicious of this particular concept of disgust as the expression of desire. Another is that it works with a crude version of the Freudian theory of repression. A third is that it is in danger of becoming an uncritical orthodoxy in theory, or rather, wishful theory.

Aversion and exclusion can be 'positive' components of desire. This is nicely treated in the German gay film *Taxi Zum Clo*. A gay teacher, on his way home, cruises some toilets. As I recall – and I fear I may be wishfully idealizing the scene – he's sitting in a cubicle waiting for action. Being a conscientious teacher he's filling in time marking student scripts. Suddenly there's interest from the next cubicle. Through the glory-hole the teacher posts a note: 'What are you in to?' The message comes back: 'Everything. Anything.' Now who, I find myself wondering, could have been on the other side? Perhaps a postmodernist. Or maybe it was only the kind of person I mentioned earlier, at ease with their own sexuality and everyone else's. Whoever – our teacher does the only decent thing: he gathers together his scripts, and leaves. He, at least, knows that discrimination is the essence of culture.

To repeat, disgust may mark the inherent instability of identity in relation to desire. But, as we shall see, the desire which is imprinting disgust rarely ever returns in a condition newly freed of socialization, but in a condition ineradicably altered by it.

Freud: overriding disgust

I mentioned earlier that liberation discourse tended to demystify and to pathologize disgust, seeing it as symptomatic both of a repressive sexual ideology, and of the 'screwed-up' individuals produced within that ideology. We might expect Freud to be the crucial precursor in the second respect (disgust as symptomatic of individual neurosis), but actually he's also a significant precursor in the first (symptomatic of repressive ideology). Since most of what follows will be critical, I want to say again that I believe there are ways in which Freud was quite right, and on both counts.

In brief, his theory is this: disgust, along with morality and shame, are civilization's defensive strategies against unbridled instinct. Disgust keeps instinct in check; it is part of the process of repression which keeps illicit desire unconscious. For Freud of course, there is an unending conflict between the demands of instinct and those of civilization. The evolution, not to say the very survival, of civilization depends especially upon the repression and sublimation of sexual desire. Anal eroticism becomes a striking paradigm of all this; according to Freud, once upon a time, when we went around on all fours, we were all into anal sex. But as we get up on two legs, the evolution of civilization requires the repression of anality. It becomes, says Freud, with a nice choice of word, 'unserviceable' for civilization. Hence the disgust with which it is now regarded.

But there is an inherent, momentous instability in this process: '*the sexual instinct in its strength enjoys overriding . . . disgust*'; it 'has to struggle against' disgust (and shame) which in turn are struggling to keep the instinct within the bounds of the normal (*Three Essays*, pp. 64, 72, 76, my emphasis). A major challenge to civilization's defensive strategies comes from the sexual perversions; they above all transgress the cultural boundaries between desire and disgust. Actually it might be more accurate to speak here not of transgressing boundaries but of shifting them: perverse desire pushes back the boundaries, claiming ground from disgust but only under a state of tension with it. An example of this is provided by Rupert Haselden describing his feelings on visiting for the first time in the late 1970s the gay New York club, The Mineshaft, legendary for its sexual extremism:

> I had never seen anything like it: fist fucking, racks, and the stench of piss and poppers and everything else and the heat and the men and the light was all red and I remember thinking standing there, adrenalin

thundering round me and thinking, 'This is evil, this is wrong'. I
remember being very frightened; it seemed so extreme. But later I was
thinking about it a lot, and wanking when thinking about it, and the
next thing I knew I was back there and within weeks it felt like home.[12]

Desire more or less permanently overrides aversion. Or does it?
Sometimes the boundaries close back in.[13] Whatever, Freud suggests
that in the individual there is a continuing struggle between desire
and disgust which replicates the struggle between instinct and civilization. In a sense the human subject is just the walking casualty of
that struggle.[14] And when we recognize that this struggle between
desire and disgust can be intensified by sublimation – intensified
rather than escaped – 'casualty' does indeed seem the appropriate
word.[15] Our psyche is the battleground for the opposition between
these terms, even while our libido is energized by their violent,
dialectical intimacy with each other. Desire now finds, in what was
once disgusting, a pleasure whose intensity it could never have
known without that history of disgust; *now* desire gives way to a
revulsion the more intense because its history is grounded in the very
desire it displaces.

So far this theory raises questions, but it's reasonably consistent. It
soon ceases to be so, as one would expect of something so central to
what Freud wryly calls 'the human privilege of becoming neurotic'
(*The Question of Lay Analysis*, p. 311). Like others of Freud's
concepts, disgust becomes inconsistent as he elaborates it and extends
its explanatory power to new instances. To explore this inconsistency
reveals more than the confusions of psychoanalysis. The most striking inconsistency in Freud is apparent in those places where he
briskly announces that disgust is 'purely conventional' – that is,
something easily dismissed as a local, ignorant and irrational prejudice. In the *Three Essays* he is even prepared to regard the most
obdurate form of sexual disgust, namely the revulsion felt at the
thought of anal intercourse, as also purely conventional. Indeed,
Freud insists on this, even to the point of being concerned that he
might be construed as a propagandist for the practice:

I hope . . . I shall not be accused of partisanship when I assert that
people who try to account for this disgust by saying that the organ in
question serves the function of excretion and comes in contact with
excrement . . . are not much more to the point than hysterical girls who
account for their disgust at the male genital by saying that it serves to
void urine. (*Three Essays*, p. 64)

How does this square with his other argument, just alluded to, that anal eroticism has become 'unserviceable' for civilization yet remains the site of the eternal struggle between instinct and civilization? On the one hand disgust – here, specifically anal disgust – is an expression of a repression which itself is the necessary condition for the evolution of civilization; on the other, disgust is no more rational than hysterical girls who don't like the idea of sucking cock (it is fellatio which Freud has in mind). Is the man who, for the same reason, also finds disgusting the thought of performing fellatio on another man, equally, irrationally, hysterical? I'd like to think so if only because the implication would be that a bit of brisk cognitive therapy would have all the straight boys going down on each other all the time. A sexual revolution just a lifted T-shirt away.

But never mind the boys; what about those hysterical girls? This is such a revealing moment in Freud: psychoanalysis bravely confonts an inveterate cultural prejudice, but does so only by invoking another. These girls recall Dora, Freud's most famous hysterical girl. She too experiences disgust at the penis and is reprimanded by Freud for doing so. Rereading the extensive secondary literature on this case history, I was struck by how rarely this issue of disgust was addressed directly. When Dora is fourteen years old, Herr K., a friend of her parents, tries to seduce her; he clasps her to him and kisses her. Freud writes: 'This was surely just the situation to call up a distinct feeling of sexual excitement in a girl of fourteen who had never before been approached. But Dora had at that moment a violent feeling of disgust', and broke free. Freud is unequivocal: for her to feel disgust rather than pleasure in this encounter was, he continues, 'entirely and completely hysterical. I should without question consider a person hysterical in whom an occasion for sexual excitement elicited feelings that were preponderantly or exclusively unpleasurable' ('Dora', p. 59).

Dora is suffering from what Freud calls reversal of affect, a situation in which – in this context – because of repression, desire is transformed into disgust. I remarked earlier that to interpret disgust as a symptom of desire is full of potential error not because it is simply wrong, but precisely because it is sometimes right. The same is true with reversal of affect. It happens. But that has led some to construe all manner of people as saying the opposite of what they mean, and desiring the opposite of what they say or think they desire; of telling them, in effect, that their 'no' really means 'yes'.[16] To his credit Freud says that reversal of affect is 'one of the most important and at the same time one of the most difficult problems in the psychology of neuroses', and admits that he hasn't yet cracked it (p. 59).

Freud further interprets Dora's disgust as involving displacement. She remarked in analysis that she could still feel on the upper part of her body the pressure of Herr K.'s embrace. Freud concludes that during the embrace she in fact felt the pressure of his erect penis. But because this perception was disgusting to her she repressed it and replaced it with this more respectable sensation. There occurs a displacement from the lower part of the body to the upper – from the disgusting to the respectable – a displacement which, he adds, psychoanalysis often encounters. But still Freud isn't finished: he interprets other aspects of Dora's behaviour as involving a repressed desire to perform fellatio, and in the process feels it necessary to defend himself against the charge of obscenity. In doing so he again – just as in the *Three Essays* – deviates into a defence of homosexuality. He says that the perversion 'most repellent to us', namely male homosexuality, was accepted by the Greeks, 'so far our superiors in cultivation'; and that 'this excessively repulsive and perverted phantasy of sucking at a penis has the most innocent origin' (p. 86).

What's obvious, even if you dismiss all the psychoanalytic interpretation as pernicious nonsense, is that Freud does not find these activities – male homosexuality and fellatio – disgusting. What is less clear, but to me still very plausible, and still not much dependent on accepting the psychoanalytic mode, is that it is Freud who is excited by the idea of the erect penis felt beneath the clothes. As is well known, late in the analysis – on his own admission, too late – Freud 'discovers' what is really causing the problem, and what was obvious all along: Dora's homosexual desire for Herr K.'s wife. What this means then is that Freud briskly demystifies disgust vis-à-vis fellatio and male homosexuality, while spectacularly failing to recognize it as a symptom of Dora's own homosexuality. On the contrary, he disastrously construes it as a symptom of her repressed heterosexuality (disgust bearing the imprint of desire). One way of looking at this would be to say that Freud's own homosexuality is allowed to surface while Dora's is repressed. His emerges at the expense of hers. Or is it homosexuality exactly? Does Freud fantasize about feeling Herr K.'s erect cock beneath the clothes, even perhaps of going down on him, or is it rather that he is excited by the scopophilic, bisexual fantasy of imagining Dora doing it? At the very least Freud is excited by the thought of the man sexually aroused by the young woman.

A few years earlier Freud encountered another young woman, eighteen-year-old Katharina, suffering from neurotic symptoms in which disgust, displacement and the erect penis again figure prominently, at least for Freud. Actually, he encountered this 'well-built girl with her unhappy look' at the top of a high mountain in the eastern Alps which he had just climbed, and where she approached him, asking if he were a doctor and adding: 'my nerves are bad.' Freud conducts a makeshift analysis right there, on top of the mountain. It transpires that Katharina's problems stem from a time when, aged 16, she witnessed her uncle having sex with her cousin. She was too young to realize what was happening but (on Freud's prompting) recalls that she must have felt disgust nevertheless. Initially neither she nor Freud can work out what was the object of this disgust. Then she recalls earlier occasions, when she was 14, and the same uncle made sexual advances to her. On one occasion she remembered waking up and ' "feeling his body" in the bed'. Freud concludes – and she agrees – that the disgust she felt at seeing the uncle and her cousin together was caused by a realization that what he was doing with the cousin he had also wanted to do with her. Freud makes much of the fact that she had 'felt his body'. Her symptoms – something is crushing her chest and she can't breath – might suggest it was his whole body. Freud, following again the idea of displacement from disgusting lower to respectable upper, has other ideas:

> – Tell me just one thing more. You're a grown-up girl now and know all sorts of things . . .
> – Yes, now I am.
> – Tell me just one thing. What part of his body was it that you felt that night?
> But she gave no definite answer. She smiled in an embarrassed way, as though she had been found out . . .

Freud does not leave it there; he tells his readers:

> I could imagine what the tactile sensation was that she learnt to interpret. Her facial expression seemed to me to be saying that I was right in my conjecture. But I could not penetrate further, and in any case I owed her a debt of gratitude for having made it so much easier for me to talk to her than to the prudish ladies [hysterical girls? Dora?] of my city practice, who regard whatever is natural as shameful. (*Studies on Hysteria*, pp. 190–8)

That 'whatever is natural' hardly seems appropriate, especially in the light of the chilling revelation made by Freud in a footnote added in 1924. For reasons of discretion he had distorted the original story: in reality the man who had tried to have sex with Katharina was not her uncle but her father (p. 201).

In this case, as with Dora's, Freud's concern to overcome a young woman's apparent disgust at the imagined touch of an erect penis has much to do with his own voyeuristic fantasy investment in the same. It is a voyeurism which emerges so 'professionally', yet seemingly involves a blindness, or at least an indifference, to the respective experiences of vicious betrayal which must have been central to both these young women's distress. Not only is Dora the subject of sexual advances by the husband of the woman she is in love with (Frau K.), but (we learn, from Freud) her own father is conspiring with Herr K. in allowing those advances because he himself is having an affair with Frau K. – crudely, the daughter is being exchanged for the wife. Hardly surprising then that Dora tries to kill herself. The betrayal of the 14-year-old Katharina is less intricate but just as vicious and possibly even more traumatic in that she is the subject of sexual advances by her own father.

Freud's interpretations of sexual disgust are occasions for great insights into the deep conflicts between human desire and human culture, and of courageous challenges to some of that culture's inveterate prejudices. They are also the occasion for an interpretative blindness which must throw doubt on the trustworthiness of the entire analytic procedure. The two case histories suggest first, that this interpretative blindness derives in part from that familiar blindness intrinsic to voyeurism wherein desire only sees because it does not see; second, that voyeurism is probably an inescapable part of most analytic encounters. More generally, some of the concepts central to and indispensable for the psychoanalytic encounter seem nowhere more unreliable than in these histories, including reversal of affect, displacement, hysteria, maybe even the later concept of counter-transference. It has been argued that the understanding of homosexuality was indispensable for the evolution of psychoanalysis (Freud himself admitted as much) but, by the same token, proved its stumbling block. Something similar is true of disgust and not only for psychoanalysis; as I suggested earlier, not the least of its interest resides in the way it seemingly resists the very explanations it invites.

In a sense, disgust defeats Freud; it not only resists his theory but provokes it into disarray. It's customary today to explain the failures of psychoanalysis by saying that it is more 'literary' than scientific. I believe this to be an evasion, akin to the compromised liberal Christianity that keeps trying to lose its embarrassing doctrinal history in favour of something not just less literal but vaguer to the point of evasion. The truth is rather more difficult: the errors and abuses of psychoanalysis derive in part from the fact that Freud was specifically and insightfully right. And his was the problem for theory more generally. Throughout I've tried to say that a particular theory is true of some people or in some instances. In one respect this is only being empirically cautious by trying to avoid overgeneralization. This point could be rephrased to alert theoretical-political sensibilities in the way that mention of empiricism will not, by invoking the idea of respect for, and the avoidance of repression of, cultural difference. That's to say, it is cultural and other kinds of imperialism which have led to repression and exclusion through the universalizing of the culturally specific by those with the power to do so. This has been most apparent in supposedly universal, but in fact exclusionary, notions of what it is to be human.[17] Certain strains of psychoanalysis have been repressive in exactly this way, and especially in relation to unconventional sexualities. But I'm also making a further point: it is just because a particular theory or explanation is appropriate in the one context that it can have such catastrophic consequences in another. Bluntly, the damage it causes is the worse when the theory is not wrong, and not even half right, but precisely right in certain circumstances. Put theoretically, the specific, insightful truth creates, by its very success, the inevitability of its own misapplication.

So how does this leave me feeling about psychoanalysis as theory? Only that I am more than ever convinced of Freud's brilliance, and that the intellectual encounter with him is, like analysis itself, prolonged and difficult. But I'm also more distrustful than ever of having that encounter via the couch.

Bataille: death as the return to 'seething life'

There is another interpretation of disgust which coincides with but also differs from Freud's. It too figures disgust as a defence in the struggle between civilization and something else, but now the antagonist includes, but also exceeds instinct, sexual or otherwise: it is nothing less than nature itself. In this interpretation nature is not evil or fallen, as in Christianity, but nor is it the benign nature of a sentimental romanticism or politically naive ecology. Rather, nature refers to the life force in its most elemental indifference to the human, and especially the human principle of individuation – consciousness as individuation being the bed-rock of human alienation from nature. To speak of the life force suggests, of course, something distinct from and even opposed to death; but this 'force' is not: it wreaks death and generates life indiscriminately, and inextricably. Death, decay, and annihilation are inextricable aspects of the life force.

The writing of Georges Bataille (1897–1962) is speculative, controversial and to be assented to critically, if at all. But it is important for trying to articulate a material reality which contemporary intellectual thought has increasingly tried to forget or repress. For Bataille, even more than for Freud, disgust registers something profoundly significant about the formation of civilization and the identity of the individual, and the conflicts integral to, and which threaten, both.[18] He too recognizes that we exist unstably and painfully inside the dialectic between civilization and what it excludes. In a sense, civilization necessarily disavows the true nature of life itself. For Bataille life is an energy which is never conserved but perpetually squandered and wasted. Just as the sun expends its energy without any return, so all life is rooted in the destruction of life – of itself: 'the ground we live on is little other than a field of multiple destructions.' The squandering of life is inseparable from a ceaseless destruction of property and bodies; it is this fact which ultimately makes life and death inseparable (*Accursed Share*, vol. 1, pp. 10–11, 23, 28, 34–5). In fact, death and ruin – 'This colossal waste, this squandering annihilation' – are not only necessary for life, they are also its most complete expression. Death is the condition of birth, and life is a product of putrefaction. Decomposition and death become 'the source of an abundant surge of life' (*Erotism*, p. 56; cf. *Accursed Share*, vol. 2, pp. 80–4).

Bataille plausibly insists that the prevailing attitude of humankind to this fundamental truth about life is to disavow it. He goes further: the whole of civilization is built upon that disavowal, symptomatic of which is the way that, within culture, we labour to acquire, save, accumulate, store, preserve and so on. Cultural accumulation, in particular the accumulation of capital, is a reaction formation to the squandering reality of nature. Yet the underlying reality of life as reckless waste is still inside us; somewhere deep down we desire to get back to it, to shatter cultural acquisition in favour of a reckless spending and wasting: there comes upon us the irresistible desire to 'squander the accumulated riches . . . waste and lose as much as we can' (2.107). Here is that underlying longing to reject prudential living, the safe identity, the insured future, the acquisition of capital, cultural and material, in favour of its opposite: risk, and an ecstasy inseparable from destruction including self-destruction.

The insight into the scandalous truth of life as expenditure (spending and wasting) can now only be had from *inside* culture; that is, from inside the set of disavowals which constitute culture. This means that we are unavoidably divided beings. We can never simply 'get back to nature' because now we are constituted, culturally and psychically, by the very prohibitions which separate us from nature. And those prohibitions mean that '[An] abhorrence of nature [is] built into our essence' (2.23, 70). But that does not mean we can now simply comply with the prohibitions of culture since the excess of nature is still within us. Man initially reacts against nature (life as excessive, non-productive expenditure), but now revolts against the very prohibitions he established to protect himself from nature. If there is no getting back to nature, neither is there any chance of becoming completely reconciled to cultural prohibition:

> Since man has uprooted himself from nature, that being who returns to it is still uprooted, he is an uprooted being who suddenly goes back toward that from which he is uprooted, from which he has not ceased to uproot himself. (2.77, 90)

Hence our deep ambivalence toward nature; our alternation between disgust and revulsion on one side, and transgressive fascination on the other (2.48; cf. 23, 28, 50, 70). What most repels us in nature is the very putrefaction from which we emerged:

> That nauseous, rank and heaving matter, frightful to look upon, a ferment of life, teeming with worms, grubs and eggs, is at the bottom of the decisive reactions we call nausea, disgust and repugnance.

But this very revulsion 'keeps alive in some indirect fashion at least the consciousness that the terrifying face of death, its stinking putrefaction, are to be identified with the sickening primary condition of life.' Paradoxically it is death which restores us to life in the sense of dissolving us back into this 'seething life' (*Erotism*, pp. 56–7). Life understood fully, as a primal force, is a state of differentiation so extensive that it merges indistinguishably with the undifferentiation of death. This is why Bataille can speak of 'death gorging life with decomposed substance' (*Accursed Share*, vol. 2, p. 95).

Now we flee nature, taking refuge in the disavowals of culture; now we feel an irresistible urge to submit to the dissolution of nature and the eventual oblivion it guarantees to any individuated consciousness. Yes, we have a 'tormenting desire' to live, but we also yearn for that 'primal continuity linking us with everything that [is]'. Only this can restore to us 'our lost continuity' and deliver us from the pain of our 'individual isolated discontinuity' (*Erotism*, p. 15). And, I'd add, because the human remains fascinated by what it necessarily excludes in order to be what it is, the inhumane always returns most potently via – in the form of – the human.

Especially relevant are three respects in which Bataille significantly reworks older ideas. First, the fantasy of losing oneself in a larger totality is familiar enough; its sources include the religious, the mystical and the romantic. But this kind of totality is usually the ethereal transcendent of western metaphysics (the One), or the equally ethereal unity of a romantically tamed 'nature'. In western metaphysics such 'clean' self-loss via assimilation has always been an aspect of transcendence. For Bataille, by contrast, the self-obliteration we ambivalently contemplate is not this annihilating transcendent, but an immolation in natural process – 'and of the putrefaction that follows it' (*Accursed Share*, vol. 2, p. 119). In other words, we remain ambivalently attracted to the reality – death and putrefaction – which the metaphysical was supposed to transcend.

Second, the idea that Man lives in divided worlds, and is therefore constituted by division and incompletion, is long-standing. But Bataille, like other modern thinkers, gives it an obsessively erotic charge. Religious poetry could often be intensely erotic (and, for a modern reader, encountering say John Donne's *Holy Sonnets* for the first time, surprisingly, and even shockingly so), but the eroticism was arguably subordinated to the spiritual. In Bataille the spiritual origins of his eroticism are clear and acknowledged, and without which it could never be the obsession it is,[19] but now the eroticism aspires to dominate and supercede the spirituality.

Third, Bataille, like others before and after him, including Freud and Denis de Rougemont, realized that the dialectic between desire and aversion escalated with prohibition: that which was designed to contain desire might instead intensify it. We desire what is forbidden to us more, because it is forbidden; indeed we may only desire it because it is forbidden. But for Bataille what this means is that to seek security in a social order which one *also* desires to transgress and violate, is not just bourgeois hypocrisy or existential bad faith, but the inescapable condition of being human. Likewise, to be riven with ambivalence and conflicted by attraction and repulsion is no mere individual pathology but, again, a defining aspect of the human psyche: we most truly *are* that shudder of revulsion *against* which is also an intense, ambivalent desire *for*.

In *Powers of Horror*, Julia Kristeva, obviously influenced by Bataille, presents disgust as an inextricable part of the experience of abjection – for her, the most extreme threat to the self imaginable. And death, experienced through disgust, discloses the repressions of social life: 'refuse and corpses *show me* what I permanently thrust aside in order to live.' She too thinks that to recognize this cannot lead to a straightforward lifting of repression. Abjection becomes, rather, an agonising insight, momentarily, intensely, but unsustainably co-extensive with the dialectic of life and death:

> Apprehensive, desire turns aside; sickened, it rejects. A certainty protects it from the shameful – a certainty of which it is proud holds on to it. But simultaneously, just the same, that impetus, that spasm, that leap is drawn toward an elsewhere as tempting as it is condemned. Unflaggingly . . . a vortex of summons and repulsion places the one haunted by it literally beside himself. (pp. 1–3)

Bataille has also been appropriated for postmodernism. And yet his writing sits uncomfortably in that context and it does so in a way which compels us to ask: What kind of writing is it? Certainly it isn't historical in any recognized sense, and as anthropology it is suspect and erroneous.[20] And by any account Bataille sometimes seems just obviously wrong, or at least embarrassingly parochial in his views, as when he gets upset about the idea that Nietzsche might have experienced homoerotic desire, or when he tells us that 'by living in idleness, the prostitute preserves the completely feminine qualities that work diminishes' and that, in contrast, 'women subjected to a factory job have a roughness that disappoints desire, and it's often the same with the crispness of business women, or even with all those women whose dryness and sharpness of traits conflict with the profound indolence without which a beauty is not entirely feminine' (*Accursed Share*, vol. 2, p. 147).

This notwithstanding, Bataille is a writer with the ability to throw into question the ethical foundation of civilized thought. What postmodernists mostly leave out of their encounter with Bataille is his fascination with pain as the intermediary between life and death, and the dialectic whereby 'the ecstasy of the torture victim lent weight to the ecstasy of the great sadists' (J. M. LoDuca, in the foreword to Bataille's *The Tears of Eros*, p. 5). One of these sadists, Gilles de Rais, about whom Bataille wrote at length, murdered and mutilated children. This is from Bataille's commentary on the trials of Gilles de Rais:

> Ostensibly he would sit on the belly of his victim, and in this fashion, masturbating, come on the dying body; what mattered to him was less the sexual enjoyment than to see death at work. He liked to watch. He had the body cut open, the throat cut, the members carved to pieces; he relished seeing the blood. (*The Trials of Gilles de Rais*, p. 10)

Bataille also liked to watch, or at least look at pictures of, and read about, real life 'sacrifice'. The question hardly ever asked by admirers of Bataille, or more pressingly still of the writings of the Marquis de Sade, is a necessary one for any serious political and ethical perspective: How far do we follow before turning back?[21] But that is also the point of Bataille's own writing, of which it could be said that to read it and not turn back, is to have not read it properly. In the case of Sade there is a notorious tendency to evade this problem by aestheticizing his writing. The most influential advocate for this view is probably Roland Barthes, who claimed that Sade's work should be considered as writing rather than reality because 'the pleasure of a reading guarantees its truth'. By reading Sade in this way rather than for his contents or his philosophy, Barthes claims to be able to rescue him from bourgeois morality (*Sade, Fourier, Loyola*, p. 9). Without wishing to discredit this kind of reading, it's worth observing that later, in *Camera Lucida*, Barthes has a very different aesthetic relation to the real. Mourning the death of someone dear to him, Barthes 'reads' photographs of people long dead, finding in these images the mortal realities which have wounded him; a sophisticated theory of reading no longer keeps reality – what he calls the indifference of nature – at bay. Whether or not its subject is already dead, every photograph tells of death in the future. And beyond this death is that indifferent nature whose contemplation involves a 'laceration so intense, so intolerable . . .' (*Camera Lucida*, pp. 94, 96).

In the case of the careful attention Bataille gave to Gilles de Rais, this can by no stretch of the imagination be described as 'writing' in Barthes' sense; Bataille aspires to present a carefully documented history and we are more than justified in questioning his interpretation – when, for example he declares that 'Gilles de Rais is preeminently a tragic hero, the Shakespearean hero' whose crimes 'are those of the world in which he committed them. The convulsive tremblings of this world are what these slit throats expose' (*The Trials of Gilles de Rais*, pp. 11, 43). It seems to me that Bataille was fascinated by ritualized sexual violence, and he could never really acknowledge the conflict between such violence and ethical existence, or the extent to which such ritualized violence is a human practice deriving from cultural repression. In the name of profundity he prevaricated, sometimes naively. His significant essay, 'The Psychological Structure of Fascism', reveals an attraction to what he saw as the transgressive impulse in that movement.[22] But what is most disturbing at this distance from his work, and most relevant for my thoughts here, is how prevarication leads Bataille into understanding things which others carefully disavow in and through a principled moral stance. Perhaps what Conor Cruise O'Brien said in another context is also true of Bataille: 'the insights of the right are far too important, and too dangerous, to be left to the right' (*The Suspecting Glance*, p. 90). And maybe Bataille's interest in this subject was, after all, historical in that it derived from his work as a student of the medieval and early modern periods, and of western religion. The latter gave him an insight into the psychic and social dynamic of transgression largely absent today: 'to shrink from fundamental stability isn't less cowardly than to hesitate about shattering it. Perpetual *instability* is *more* boring than adhering strictly to a rule' (*Guilty*, pp. 28–9). In the culture of the medieval and early modern he encountered above all a passionate fascination with death and dissolution; a sense of mutability not as the delicate poignancy felt in the perception of the fall of a leaf, but a potent force of dissolution and decay.

It is fashionable today to regard philosophies as intellectual stories that we tell ourselves in order to make sense of the world, to make it negotiable, less threatening, more controllable and so on. One version of this is what I've called wishful theory, although it may hardly deserve to be called a philosophy. But some kinds of intellectual engagement do more, even when they are more mythological than philosophical, or obviously wrong in certain respects; or even when they fail on their own terms: they engage with realities which have been repressed but not excluded, which remain active as frustrated intensities deeply felt but hardly recognized for what they are. It's as if these kinds of intellectual engagement have to fail. However flawed they remain as theory or philosophy or science, Freud's and Bataille's explorations of the dialectic between desire and disgust are cases in point.

Most significant for my reflections here is Bataille's insistence on the opposition between human culture and nature, where the latter is understood as a life force indifferent to life itself.[23] To be human is to be profoundly not natural. A child dies: we never forget, and if we loved that child we maybe never recover. And yet nothing is more natural than for an organism to die in infancy. It is not that human culture has transcended nature or even that, in any fundamental sense, it has controlled it. Rather, human culture involves an attitude to nature which mixes repression, defiance and forgetting – a repression which can never simply be lifted, a defiance which is ethical, a forgetting which is inevitable, and all of which are the condition of love.

PART II

Dangerous Knowledge

All art is at once surface and symbol.
Those who go beneath the surface do so at their peril.
Those who read the symbol do so at their peril.

Oscar Wilde, Preface, *The Picture of Dorian Gray*

5

Daemonic Desires

Just when you thought you'd worked out a sexual identity, and built a lifestyle around it, your desire disrupts both the identity and the lifestyle. Magnified and intensified this is of course a familiar theme in literature: human desire will not be contained by safe and reassuring narratives about who and what we are, and the institutions they sustain. In literature desire is perversely dangerous and often the more seductive for being so.

To think of desire as daemonic[1] is to think of it as being to some defining extent not just incapable of socialization, but deeply antagonistic to the social – perhaps even to civilization. The daemonic in this sense is powerfully expressed in some of the great mythic oppositions of western culture including the Greek one between Apollo and Dionysus, the Renaissance ones between reason and passion, culture and nature, and most recently, Freud's account of human history as the unending antagonism between civilization and instinct. Each of these far-reaching mythic oppositions embrace a double, conflictual truth which is at once social, political and psychological. On the one hand civilization requires the education, control and supression of certain desires, especially sexual ones. On the other, the more we try to contain and control sexuality the more likely some part of it will escape or resist control, and probably return in some direct or distorted form to disrupt, and maybe subvert whatever or whoever is trying to control it.

In each case too the desire in question is obviously a life force: it is, variously, the Dionysiac, passion, nature, instinct, or drive. But this life force is untamed, unsocialized and at heart non-human. Its amoral core becomes the more potentially destructive of the human as a result of human attempts to tame it. The extreme romantic version of this was voiced by Bataille: 'eroticism is an insane world whose depths, far beyond its ethereal forms, are infernal' (*The Tears of Eros*, p. 69). And, as we saw in the last chapter, this is a life force indifferent to life itself: the life force is inseparably a force of death, dissolution and destruction. Eros and Thanatos are not enemies like God and Satan; they cleave together, but it is an embrace in which each is indifferent to the other. This is the heart of the pre- or non-Christian idea of the daemonic. Consider, briefly, how Euripides (*c*.480–406 BC) dramatized it.

Even when read in a translation with modern idiom, there is something alien and perplexing about Greek tragedy: we recognize it as the antecedent of modern tragedy, yet at the same time it seems irreducibly different. One reason for this is that what links us to it – what we comfortably call 'tradition' – is not simply a disinterested selection of the best that has been, but a constant process of interpreting and transforming the past into something which serves the present. If one of the functions of traditional critics is to ration-alize and censor what is strange and disturbing about the past, it's the job of their radical counterparts to read past literature against rather than for tradition. They rarely do so. A case in point concerns the appropriation of the Greek god Dionysus. Across the last century Dionysus has been invoked by various radicals in support of a freer sexual life. In the process 'he' has been so tamed and rationalized that those who return to Euripides' representation of Dionysus in *The Bacchae* (407 BC) in the hope of securing classical support for a modern libertarian agenda, are shocked by what they encounter. The play tells of how the shallowly sensible Pentheus, King of Thebes, tries to repress the Dionysiac cult. Dionysus' revenge includes having Pentheus' mother, in Dionysiac ecstasy, literally ripping him limb from limb: 'His mother first, / As priestess, led the rite of death, and fell upon him.' Pentheus pleads for mercy: ' "Mother", he cried, / Touching her cheek, "It is I, your own son Pentheus".' Instead,

> She grasped
> His right arm between wrist and elbow, set her foot
> Against his ribs, and tore his arm off by the shoulder.

The other women join her:

> Howling in triumph. One of them carried off an arm,
> Another a foot, the boot still laced on it. The ribs
> Were stripped, clawed clean; and women's hands, thick red with blood,

Were tossing, catching, like a plaything, Pentheus' flesh.
                                    (*Bacchae*, p. 232, 1113–33)

It is a play about the terrifying and irreducible conflict between civilization and the daemonic energies it represses and outlaws.

Bacchae was Euripides' last play; *Medea* (431 BC), one of his earliest, dramatizes a similar conflict. It tells the story of how Jason abandons his 'barbarian' wife Medea, and their two children, in order to marry Glauce, the daughter of Creon, King of Corinth. Justifying his actions, Jason reminds Medea that he brought her from 'a barbarous land' to a civilized one, 'a society where force yields place to law' and where she has known justice for the first time. Medea, 'this savage beast' (p. 61, 1406), belongs to the civilized world while still embodying the barbaric world which the civilized one defines itself against. Fearing the havoc she might wreak, Creon banishes her. She leaves but not before exacting a terrible and calculated revenge (p. 50, 1074–6):

> I understand
> The horror of what I am going to do; but anger,
> The spring of all life's horror, masters my resolve.

First she kills Glauce and Creon. Their deaths are agonizing and horrific: through a mixture of poison and fire they are melted into the unrecognizable:

> Her eyes, her face, were one grotesque disfigurement;
> Down from her head dripped blood mingled with flame; her flesh,
> Attacked by the invisible fangs of poison, melted
> From the bare bone.

Her father embraces her in grief and sticks to her, suffering the same fate. Trying to escape 'he tore the old flesh off his bones' (p. 54, 1196–8; 1217). Then, solely in order to further revenge herself upon Jason she kills her – their – children.

As in *The Bacchae*, the horror of the violence is heightened by a deliberate contrast with the human tenderness it violates. Just as Pentheus touches his mother's cheek before she tears him to bits, so here we see a father embracing the dead mutilated corpse of his daughter and literally disintegrating in agony as a result. We witness too Medea deliberately brutalizing herself in order that she be able to kill her children. In both plays the most powerful representatives of civilization become antagonistic to the alien and the foreign – those who embody energies which the civilization has excluded in order to be what it is. Equally important for a modern audience is the way that Pentheus is destroyed from within by those same forces – is seduced by them – before they literally tear him apart. Correspondingly, the violence in these plays does not arbitrarily descend upon society from outside; it is a violence which partly derives from the social order it destroys. At the same time these plays suggest that we can never reduce that violence to its social causes. The hope that if violence were shown to be entirely socially caused it might be eliminated, is a belief which tragedy rejects. This is not to say that the basic reality which confronts us is an unchanging nature red in tooth and claw. In Greek tragedy we glimpse something which will become more apparent later, namely that the virulence and intensity of the daemonic which returns to destroy the civilized derives partly from its repression.

Christian theology disavows an earlier realization of 'nature's' indifferent binding of death into life, projecting onto it some myths of momentous significance: the enmity of God and Satan (the translation of the daemonic into the demonic), and man's fundamental responsibility for bringing death into the world. The most remarkable aspect of Christianity is not that it invented God and eternal life to lessen the trauma of death, but that it intensified the trauma by making Man/Woman responsible for death. Unforgettably, original sin epitomizes that inextricable blend of abjection and hubris which is the essence of Christianity. As Elaine Pagels remarks, the power of the idea of original sin lies partly in the fact that there are times when we would rather feel guilty than helpless (*Adam, Eve and the Serpent*, p. 146). It is a sublime example of the human mind hubristically seeking to identify with, and even internalize, what threatens it.

Of course earlier realizations still influence Christian theology; one only has to recall the widely held belief from ancient times through to the Renaissance and beyond that ejaculation literally shortens the life of the male. This is what the Renaissance poet John Donne meant when he wrote: 'profusely blind / We kill ourselves, to propagate our kind' (*An Anatomy of the World*, l. 110). Donne, half inside the theological disavowal of nature's indifferent binding of death and life, translates the daemonic into the satanic, and blames Eve for bringing death into desire. This is from the same poem: 'that first marriage was our funeral: / One woman at one blow, then killed us all, / And singly, one by one, they kill us now.' Undoubtedly misogyny has a lot to do with such views – let us call them, for convenience if inaccurately, 'patriarchal' – but it is one of the delusions of a progressive sexual politics to believe this is the beginning and end of the matter. Misogyny interweaves with civilization's most fundamental disavowals, but not in a way which adequately explains them. To consider misogyny in this connection requires us to question some of the more convenient explanations of it, that is, to take it more, not less seriously.

In the myth of Eden it was Eve's transgressive desire which brought death into the world. The Christian body is imprisoned between desire and death not least because sexual desire ruins, torments and destroys us with the experience of lack. To be in its grip is to be radically unfree. To desire is to begin to die. How heroic then of later radicals to make sexuality the source of human liberation, thereby doing with sex what Christian theologians had done with death. What magnificent hubris. How the old gods must laugh! But if we hear in that cruel laughter just a hint of envy, we will not be mistaken: if it was our hubris which made the gods punish us humans, it was also what made them fall in love with us. I wrote just now that to desire is to begin to die. The Christian god, unlike his predecessors, does not desire. He is complete, wanting and lacking nothing. He absolutely does not desire because to desire is an imperfection and a limitation inseparable from mortality. Being perfect, the Christian god doesn't desire, but then he doesn't laugh, *in PL* either. At least, not since Satan left Heaven. *he does*

The pioneer Christian theologians – the Church Fathers – believed that the creation of true civilization in a fallen world requires the repression of a large measure of human instinct. But they also half knew what Freud would later formulate in psychoanalytic terms, namely that the more developed the civilization, the more it becomes vulnerable to the return of what it necessarily has to exclude and repress. And via both Freud and another of those ironic twists which mark the tortuous history of thought, this realization facilitates the appropriation of sex for agendas of radical liberation in the writings of those like Norman O. Brown, Wilhelm Reich and Herbert Marcuse (these, incidentally, are the influential though often ignored antecedents of the sexual radicalism which culminates in queer theory).

If, for these writers, the idea of the return of the repressed is crucial, so too is Freud's belief that what is repressed is never eliminated: it can never simply be expelled either from the individual psyche or the social order. Rather, it remains inside both, always threatening to destabilize them. Every individual experiences the struggle to a greater or lesser degree: instinct, the id and the unconscious are always there to wreck whatever precarious equilibrium is achieved by the ego. But the sexual radicals argued that this force, instead of wrecking the individual through repression, might be liberated and turned against the society doing the repression. It's a momentous turn-about: now sexuality is not the reason we are radically unfree, but the impetus for a radical vision of freedom. Instead of being the source of torment, guilt and death, sex now offers liberation and happiness. It is hardly surprising that this reversal involved a taming of desire which amounted to a new kind of repression. Sexual radicalism wanted desire to subvert some things but definitely not others; it had to destroy the old order but serve the new. The hope was that liberated desire would, as it were, civilize itself. But it is unwise to rely upon desire to discriminate between good and bad social orders, and the very radicalism which made so much of the idea of the return of the repressed would repeatedly encounter the return of its own repressed.

Progressive and secularist theories of desire have struggled to displace the Christian view, forgetting the daemonic which had preceded it, which in turn the Christian had sought to disavow. From the daemonic perspective desire cannot be regarded as delinquent only when denied an outlet. Such a 'wild oats' account fails to recognize that this is a force at best indifferent to civilization and probably inimical to it. On this view, the return of the repressed has the potential to disintegrate any individual and any society.

Whenever radical vision of desire (or indeed its reformist counter-part) becomes disorganized by its own repressions, the daemonic becomes half-visible again and constitutes an obscure challenge to both. In art it has never *not* been visible. Artists have always been fascinated by the daemonic, especially in terms of erotic risk, and the erotic encounter with death. A recent collection of short fiction is called *High Risk 2: Writings on Sex, Death and Subversion* (eds Scholder and Silverberg). It claims its contributors to be on 'the cutting edge of literature'. It is more likely that most of them are catching up. Some eighty-five years ago Thomas Mann was writing more insightfully about sex, death and subversion in *Death in Venice*. Thirty-five years after that he gave epic expression to the same themes in his important but now neglected novel, *Dr Faustus*. Mann made a daemonic, erotic encounter with disease and death the focus of a history of Europe in the first half of the twentieth century. It seemed, say twenty years ago, unthinkable that anyone might do the same for the first half of the twenty-first century. Now, again, it has become thinkable. But it's important to remember that in Mann, as in the literature of the Renaissance, or indeed Greek tragedy, desire is inseparable from the sexual but not limited to it.

The daemonic is being hesitantly revived by some queer theorists, most of whom are vague about its history. One queer slogan a couple of years back was 'put the homo back into homicide.' But its most controversial recent intellectual advocate has to be Camille Paglia, and she is fully aware of its cultural history. Although in her influential book *Sexual Personae*, first published in 1990, she hardly mentions him, her views were significantly anticipated by Bataille (see chapter 4 above). Paglia resurrects the idea of human history as a struggle between the Apollonian and the Dionysiac. For her the truth of the Dionysiac is not to be found in the earth's surface but in its bowels, and if we have a deep revulsion for slime, it's because that's what we came from; to be civilized is to be rightly alienated from our real origins. The essence of nature is what Paglia calls the 'chthonian', that is, 'the blind, grinding of subterranean force, the long slow suck, the murk and ooze'. All culture, including aesthetics and science, is built on the repression or evasion of the fact that we begin in a primal melting pot where the life force is also a force of dissolution and death:

> Everything is melting in nature. . . . An apple tree laden with fruit: how peaceful, how picturesque. But remove the rosy filter of humanism from our gaze and look again. See nature spurning and frothing, its mad spermatic bubbles endlessly spilling out and smashing in that inhuman round of waste, rot, and carnage. . . . Nature is the seething excess of being. (*Sexual Personae*, pp. 1–6, 41–2)

Human culture is a massive and necessary defence against this nature. But our sexuality still partakes of it. Which is why sex is unfree, inhumane, compulsive and aggressive, characterized by a 'daemonic instability' (p. 13). In sex we are caught up in a 'backward movement towards primeval dissolution'; sex threatens annihilation. This is why, says Paglia, so many men turn away or flee after sex: 'they have sensed the annihilation of the daemonic' (pp. 4–5).[2] She believes a perfectly humane, guilt-free eroticism to be impossible.

To hear academics and others dismissing Paglia as a fascist or merely a spokeswoman of the New Right, is to know they are on the defensive.[3] Paglia is given to the odd overstatement and may be said to be an embarrassing victim of her own success. She is certainly an American celebrity, which is almost the same thing. But one good reason for her success is that Paglia polemically revives, often crudely, sometimes compellingly, some of the most powerful myths of western culture, myths which both the reformist and the radical attitudes to sexual dissidence have tried to forget. Of course it remains open to question whether those myths articulate profound truths or pernicious mystifications. But they persist in the cultural memory, and they return because the realities they articulate or mystify remain intractable. I believe, against Paglia, that the daemonic is not pure nature returning to blast culture apart, but the return of a repressed desire so inextricably bound up with history it is impossible any more to distinguish between the two.[4] And even if it were possible to tell them apart, I suspect the most recalcitrant kind of desire might be more socialized than 'natural'. I could put this differently, in the form of a familiar paradox explored by artists (for example Mann, in *Death in Venice* and Joseph Conrad, in *Heart of Darkness*): only the highly civilized can become truly daemonic. Renaissance and Enlightenment sceptics observed that corrupted reason was capable of an intensity of evil unknown to the non-rational or irrational. Lilies that fester smell far worse than weeds. Freud once remarked that the superego could be a gathering place for the death instincts and, as such, 'as cruel as only the id can be'. In a state of repression this destruction and cruelty is masochistic and directed at the self; in sexual desublimation it can find expression as a sadism which complements rather than replaces the masochism.

Shakespeare's *Measure for Measure* is a compelling dramatization of what I mean. The city of Vienna is perceived by its rulers to be on the verge of anarchy. Although the sources of the problem are complex[5] they decide to target illicit sexuality. The Duke deputizes Angelo to take his place when he ostensibly goes abroad, but actually remains in the city in disguise, observing at close hand both the low life and Angelo's attempts to control it. Angelo is 'A man of stricture and firm abstinence' who 'scarce confesses / That his blood flows' (I.iii.12, 51–2), one who has hitherto been sublimating his own sexuality into strict government not just of himself but of his society, such that the opportunity to suppress illicit sexual desire in the community in his new capacity as deputy is a self-realization more than usually charged with libidinal energies. But this is also why the executing of this power, initially a compensation for repression, becomes the occasion for its return.

In Act II, Scene ii we witness Angelo being torn apart by illicit sexual desire for the chaste Isabella who is aspiring to enter a nunnery. The man who was immune to the 'double vigour' of the strumpet (l. 188) becomes sexually obsessed with the passionately virtuous, and, in order to possess her, embarks upon a reckless course of blackmail, betrayal and would-be murder. In Angelo we see how desublimated desire has a virulence which is not the opposite of civilization but its inversion. This is not unfettered pre-social libido indifferent to the civilizing restraint it has escaped. On the contrary this is desire returning via the 'civilizing' mechanisms of its repression, mechanisms it is still inseparable from, even as it violates them. This is Angelo in agonized soliloquy:

> Having waste ground enough,
> Shall we desire to raze the sanctuary
> And pitch our evils there? . . .
> . . .
> Dost thou desire her foully for those things
> That make her good?
>
> (ll. 175–80)

Because Angelo is violating the civilized world which has made him what he is and cannot at some irreducible level cease to be, he is therefore also violating himself. Which means that the intent here is and is not Angelo's; it is hardly conscious. We see too in Angelo how his 'desire' is a pressure not so much for fulfilment, but to be free of something in itself which it cannot fully understand, something which, in effect, it does not desire. 'Angelo', devastated by the ferocity of his own vicious passion, is doubly mutilated: first by the repression, and then by its return.

To generalize the situation here dramatized is to realize that it is when we believe we have comfortably and completely left the past behind that it returns to haunt and wreck us and it does so not via the old but via the new. That's to say, older ways of thinking and feeling emerge precisely from within the discourses which we thought had superseded them. This is a situation I earlier described in terms of the radical continuity. It is the reason why I advocate an intellectual history over the pseudo-radicalism of a postmodernism forever claiming that the present has made a radical and irreversible break with the past, and that we cannot ever really know the past anyway. Correspondingly, the daemonic is not only a question of desire, libido or drive but, as we'll now see, of structure, identity and dialectic.

6

Dangers Within

An individual identity is composite, a partial organization, more or less complex, and based in part on exclusion: identity, as we saw earlier, is constituted by what something is not as well as by what it is. So too are cultures and civilizations, albeit inconceivably more elaborate in both their organization and their exclusions. The more complex the organized unity, the more vulnerable it is to being destabilized, especially by, or in relation to, its exclusions. Further, what is excluded remains inseparable from what is included, which means it is never fully outside. This is one reason why the most potent threat to something operates internally, in terms of its structure and organization. Ruin is an internal not an external process: disintegration from within rather than destruction from without. There are other terms for the same or related processes: to degenerate, decompose, dissolve (dissolution, dissolute), unravel, unbind, regress. The foregoing are, in the first instance, anthropological propositions, not ethical ones – although they are crucial to ethical as well as aesthetic understanding and judgement.

A traditional word for that process of internal ruin as typically conceived in monotheistic religion is 'evil', and it derives from Satan's relationship to God. Satan is expelled from Heaven, but the power of his evil derives from his ability to pervert God's creation – pervert in the sense of disrupt from within – and to do so in terms both of what it is, and what it isn't (the two being inseparable). Satan can unravel the unity and turn it against itself not least because he was once interior to it, being originally God's left-hand (and doubtless left-handed) man.

This, 'in essence', is what evil is – not a reality essentially different to creation, but the forces which can undo it: forces of decreation internal to creation. No lesser an authority than St Augustine confirms this. God, says Augustine, created man from nothing. Evil is not some-thing, but a turning away from God, a perverse regression back to originary nothingness. No-thing that exists is intrinsically evil; it is only this turning away, this perversion, that makes it so. This means that evil could not exist without good, a realization which, as Augustine readily admits, has worrying implications:

> Since every being, insofar as it is a being, is good, when we call a defective being an evil being, we seem to be saying that what is good is evil, and that only what is good can be evil. . . . Nothing, then, can be evil except a good. Although this seems to be an absurd statement, the sequence of our argument forces us to it. (*Enchiridion*, 44.13)

In a sense then, good produces evil. Which is why Milton's Satan describes his war with God in these terms:

> If then his providence
> Out of our evil seek to bring forth good,
> *Our labour must be to pervert that end,*
> *And out of good still to find means of evil;*
> Which oft-times may succeed, so as perhaps
> Shall grieve him, if I fail not, *and disturb*
> *His inmost counsels* from their destined aim.
>   (*Paradise Lost*, I.162, my emphasis)

Similarly with fallen Man: John Donne, drawing on Augustine, tells us: 'We seem ambitious, God's whole work to undo; / Of nothing he made us, and we strive too, / To bring ourselves to nothing back' (*An Anatomie of the World*, II.155–7). Elsewhere within orthodox Christianity, the disintegration of creation hardly needs even the active agency of evil; all that is required is for God to withdraw his providence. It's as if there exists within creation an innate, primordial pressure to return to nothing, a pressure only prevented by the sustaining inner support of God:

> God hath his influence into the very essence of all things, without which influence of Deity supporting them their utter annihilation could not choose but follow. (Richard Hooker, *Laws*, vol. 2, p. 226)

In other, pagan-influenced myths, the primordial reality is a 'chaos' both more and less than 'nothing':

> in the wide wombe of the world there lyes,
> In hateful darknesse and in deepe horrore,
> An huge eternall *Chaos* . . .
>
> (Spenser, *Faerie Queene*, III.vi.36)

What is interesting about this mythical chaos as conceived here by Spenser, is that it is 'eternall' and, as such, the source of life and being: everything that lives, says the poet, is formed from it and returns to it; chaos is nothing less than the 'substance' (III.vi.37) of life itself.

The nothing or the chaos which precedes creation is the primal, originary state to which the immeasurably complex unity of creation is always susceptible to being reduced. Let us briefly look at another influential antecedent for this idea. Lucretius (*c.*99–55 BC), in *On the Nature of the Universe* had described a universe made up of atoms, and the void in which they ceaselessly move. When unrestricted by each other, the atoms remain in perpetual movement in the void. Life forms arise when atoms clash and restrict each other's movement. But this is an arrested movement which can only be temporary. Literally everything which exists derives from the conflict, collision and conjunction of atoms. Lucretius describes a world in which the motions which make atoms collide into being are ceaselessly countered by other motions which unbind and disintegrate those same atoms. So, while Lucretius' universe is astonishingly fecund, it is also 'blind', in the philosophical sense of being without an inner essence, sanctioning universal or teleological design. Additionally, there is a destructiveness at the very heart of creation which is reproduced in human desire itself: we ceaselessly crave but are never satisfied (pp. 75, 128–9, 163–6).

So the idea that when Satan tempts us to disintegration, he is working with a tendency innate to creation, isn't exactly new. But in Christianity it becomes an insuperable problem since the unavoidable implication that evil is ontologically interior to creation is unacceptable in monotheistic – as distinct from dualistic – theology. It gives rise to the central problem of theodicy – how to reconcile God's omnipotence with the reality of evil: simply, if God is all-powerful then he must have created evil; if he didn't create it, then he isn't all-powerful.

More immediately, these older ideas find expression in the idea of individual identity as a fragile unity susceptible to being disintegrated because of its very nature. If it survives today in remarks like 'it breaks me up' or 'pull yourself together', it was a more compelling commonplace in earlier periods. William Drummond describes the human body as 'a Masse of discording humours . . . which though agreeing for a trace of tyme, yet can never be made uniforme'. This very discord is at once natural and the agency of death – it is an *'inward cause of a necessarie dissolution'* (my emphasis). Man is an entity so inherently and radically unstable, so contradictory, both psychically and physically, that 'wee should rather wonder how so fragill a matter should so long endure, than how so soone dissolve, and decay'; if the 'Frost of Life bindeth together', death is the great 'Thaw' which unbinds (*Poems and Prose*, pp. 152, 155, 156).[1]

Lest it be thought that this mythology of ruin as radically internal has become obsolete in a 'post theological' world, I here briefly chart its survival in influential strands of psychoanalytic, and then dialectical, thought, and (in chapter 8) nineteenth-century degeneration theory. I take psychoanalysis first, looking in turn at Freud's theories of repression and the death drive.

As we've already seen, for Freud, the relationship between instincts and civilization is deeply conflicted. Civilization is created only by the repression of instinctual desire. But the desire which is repressed never goes away; it can't be eliminated, dissolved or transformed. Which means that it always remains as that which can wreck psychological and social equilibrium. Whether it be an individual identity or some larger human organization, all such 'unities' remain vulnerable to being destabilized from within by the return of the repressed. And, as we saw earlier, repressed desires return because they never disappeared in the first place; they continue to make their demands on consciousness from the unconscious:

> the process of repression is not to be regarded as an event which takes place once, the results of which are permanent . . . repression demands a persistent expenditure of force, and if this were to cease the success of the repression would be jeopardized. . . . in obsessional neurosis the work of repression is prolonged in a sterile and interminable struggle. ('Repression', pp. 151, 158)

Neurosis is one symptom of failing or imperfect repression, and everyone is neurotic to a greater or lesser degree. I said just now that the repressed instincts cannot be successfully dissolved or transformed. This is not quite true. To a degree they can be sublimated, that is, their *aim* can be redirected towards other objectives which civilization draws upon and in fact requires. A typical example would be the authoritarian, predominantly male-bonded disciplinary structures which bind religious and military organizations. Sublimated desires, especially sexual ones, can, says Freud, put astonishing amounts of energy at the service of social organizations like these because the aims of such instincts can be altered without diminishing their intensity. Repressed desire – what in its original form would wreck society – becomes instead the opposite, a force of social cohesion. This means that repression and sublimation are hard to distinguish from each other. Civilization becomes dependent upon what it represses, protecting itself against anarchic desires not only by directly repressing them, but also by tapping into them as a source of ordering energy. But this means that the repressed instinctual energy is relocated at the heart of civilized activity, and dangerously so, because, as and when it is desublimated, it has the potential to wreak even greater havoc: it returns not from the outside but the inside.

But it is in his account of the death drive that Freud drives the principle of disintegration even deeper into life itself. Kant had made rational thought the force which unites and integrates. Freud, eventually and implausibly, gives this task to eros. Whereas (for the later Freud) eros binds together and unifies, the death drive unbinds with the aim of restoring the organism to the stasis of the inanimate: the stillness that passes all understanding. And the death drive, at least initially in Freud's thinking, is prior: truly primordial. It is the first instinct, inseparable from, if not the lifeforce itself. As life flickered into being, says Freud, it 'endeavoured to cancel itself out. In this way the first instinct came into being: the instinct to return to the inanimate state. It was still an easy matter at that time for a living substance to die' (*Beyond the Pleasure Principle*, p. 311). This death drive seeks to 'dissolve' life back into its 'primaeval inorganic state'; it is an instinctual reaching towards an originary state where there was a complete absence of excitation, a state of zero tension characteristic of the inorganic and the inanimate (*Civilization and its Discontents*, p. 310).[2] The peace which passes (annihilates) all understanding. Let's be clear about what Freud is saying: the most basic instinctual drive for satisfaction is a regressive reaching towards the absence of all tension: ' "*the aim of all life is death*" ' (*Beyond the Pleasure Principle*, p. 311; both the emphasis and the quotation marks are his). As he wrote to Albert Einstein in 1932, the death instinct is 'at work in every living creature and is striving to bring it to ruin and to reduce life to its original condition of inanimate matter' ('Why War?', p. 357).

Contradiction

It wasn't only Freud who understood modern society as inherently repressive; other ways of thinking equally influential for the twentieth century did so too, although a major difference is that with them the repression is no longer thought to be the necessary corollary of civilization but a pernicious and eliminable aspect of it. Diverse ethically and politically engaged kinds of thinking have focused on the ways culture represses and exploits its cultural, sexual and racial 'others'. Freud remains influential here, but so do Hegel and Marx, and it is via them that the emphasis becomes not only on repression working subjectively, within the individual, but in society as well – in, for instance, the formation of national and racial identity. But here too forces of disruption are dangerously internal.

Capitalist society repressed and exploited people on such a vast scale that, if their repressed potential could be liberated, educated, and organized against capital, those people had the power to effect nothing less than world revolution. Drawing on Hegel, Marx developed this idea of revolution with the concepts of dialectic and internal contradiction: simply put, something evolves in a way at once unavoidable *and* destabilizing, if not self-destructive. Thus what made capitalism vulnerable to revolutionary overthrow was partly the contradictions internal to it: as it evolved, its very exploitation of the working class gradually began to empower that class. The requirements for ever more efficient production and greater profits meant workers were concentrated together in factories and cities. When that same social proximity enabled them to organize and resist the economic system which brought them together, there emerged a contradiction between the means of production and the relations of production. Generalized, this suggests how a powerful system inevitably develops internally the conditions for a challenge to it: in this case it comes from that upon which, or those upon whom, the system is dependent. That was the theory, notoriously contradicted by the fact that in practice capitalism proved immeasurably more adaptable than Marx realized. But he was not wrong to identify the principle of contradiction and the dialectic by which it evolved. Marx's error was to teleologically contain the principle of contradiction, to halt, as it were, the movement of the dialectic at the point at which it was convenient for the emergence of his own utopian political vision: communism.

Betraying in this its origins in a literary education, political criticism has never been much concerned with economic realities. But it has appropriated the principle of contradiction for one of its most persistent concerns: individual identity (or, in more theoretical language, identity formation). As we saw earlier in relation to sexual identity, there has been a recurring concern in recent decades with the vulnerability and breakdown of identity, the way it is eventually undone by the exclusions which constitute it. The fundamental cause of breakdown can be put thus, if somewhat over-simply: to be *this* is *not to be that*. But by the same token *not being that* is part of what it is to be *this*. In trying to be exclusively *this* we are haunted by what we exclude because it is already a part of what we are. Because we are dependent upon our others, our dependence upon them typically intensifies with time: the difference needs to be insisted upon but in ways which increasingly complicate and betray the dependence. This is just the most recent version of this long preoccupation with a force of unbinding which is the more dangerous for being ineradicably internal.

By making the death drive primary, Freud theorized something else which had long been apparent in artistic treatment of intense passion, namely the fact that unbinding can be intensely desired. Whether we call it the death wish or something else, its seductiveness is one of the subdued scandals of art. We'll see later how pervasive suicide is as a literary theme; but that is by no means the full story. It's much more to do with what we encountered earlier in relation to Bataille: a passionate, reckless reaction against civilized restraint; a bid for freedom from restraint which is inherently destructive of self and society. It's the regressive impulses so feared and policed by F. R. Leavis, so idealized by, among others, Shelley, Keats, and Brontë (to name some of those discussed later), and to be found in the music of Wagner, Mahler and Richard Strauss. A descendent of several of the foregoing is Thomas Mann's character Aschenbach in *Death in Venice*: burnt out with repression, anxiety and effort, but still, fatally, drawn to travel. Dreaming of 'escape from the demanding complexity of phenomena', Aschenbach experiences 'a forbidden longing deep within him that ran quite contrary to his life's task and was for that very reason seductive, a longing for the unarticulated and immeasurable, for eternity, for nothingness' (p. 224). But then Aschenbach experiences a return of repressed libido which shatters him back into an intensity of being which in turns leads inexorably back to death.

Forbidden knowledge: perversion and hubris

Most of the writers and musicians just mentioned were fascinated at some stage with what their cultures regarded as pathological or perverse. In the longer perspective of intellectual history, perversion becomes more revealing than our earlier encounter with it in the context of queer theory (chapter 1), might suggest. Let's recall what, in this longer perspective, perversion was. We've seen already that it worked internally to the normality it threatens: something is perverted from the inside not the outside. Because and not in spite of this, the normal will demonize the perverse, trying to refigure it as utterly alien. But the same original intimacy may enable the perverse to track back to the normal, returning along the same demonizing trajectory whereby it was ejected. I've called this process the perverse dynamic.[3] My focus here is the way perversion can be a resistance working in terms of desire *and* knowledge: the pervert desires deviation in a way inseparable from knowing what he or she should not know.

As Roger Shattuck has shown, forbidden knowledge has always been a feature of human cultures, most clearly perhaps in the concepts of taboo and heresy (*Forbidden Knowledge*, *passim*). Speaking generally we can say that in the west injunctions against such knowledge have progressively weakened since the Enlightenment. But in all periods there is ambivalence: to observe the injunction not to know has been seen to be the very condition of social and psychological well-being, and the survival of civilization itself (a position we will encounter later, in the study of censorship in Part III). Against that, the breaking of the injunction has been regarded as necessary for progress and liberation – for, again, the very survival of civilization. Straddling that opposition are some of the great transgressive figures of myth and literature, including Prometheus, Faust/us, Mary Shelley's Frankenstein, and of course Adam and Eve. Others, like Robert Louis Stevensons's Jekyll/Hyde embody the realization that evil is nearer to genius than bestiality, while those like Shakespeare's Macbeth, Dostoyevsky's Raskolnikov and Nietzsche's fantasy of the creator as supreme amoral artist (see chapter 10), chillingly confirm Pascal's observation that there is a kind of evil which often passes for good because 'it takes as much extraordinary greatness of soul to attain such evil, as to attain good' (*Pensées*, p. 215). If most of these figures carry a sense of the dangerous, as distinct from the liberatory, potential of the forbidden, this is because once again the knowledge that is forbidden reveals the proximity of evil to good.

In proverb and myth, in theology and philosophy, one human language after another tells us there are things we should not know, do, or see,[4] places we should not go, and of course desires we should not satisfy. Ignorance is bliss, we say. In *Paradise Lost* Milton gives us this picture of Adam and Eve, sleeping innocently after having made love:

> These lulled by nightingales embracing slept,
> And on their naked limbs the flowery roof
> Showered roses, which the morn repaired. Sleep on
> Blest pair; and O yet happiest if ye seek
> No happier state, and know to know no more.
>
> (IV.771ff.)

In a phrase, 'Be lowly wise', Adam and Eve disobey, and their transgressive desire for forbidden knowledge brings death and disintegration into the world – and into desire.

Other myths tell how gods literally disintegrate mankind as a punishment for hubris. In the story of the Tower of Babel God dislikes the fact that mankind is united as one community and with one language: 'And the Lord said, Behold, the people *is* one, and they have all one language . . . and now nothing will be restrained from them, which they have imagined to do' (Genesis 11.6). One thing they have 'imagined to do' and are now actually trying to do is build a tower reaching to heaven. God checks their hubris, scattering them across the face of the earth and confounding their one language into many. In Plato's *Symposium* there is an even more compelling myth of original dis-integration. Aristophanes tells a story of the origins of human desire. Originally human beings comprised three sexes, each of which was self-sufficient. As such 'their strength and power were terrifying, and they were also highly ambitious'; so much so that they 'tried to mount up to heaven to attack the gods'. Zeus responds by splitting human beings in half. Thereafter each half yearned for the half from which it had been severed. This is how 'our innate sexual drive arose': sexuality is an attempt at reintegration and to heal the wound which humanity suffered (*Symposium*, pp. 25–7, 189c–191d).[5] God splits humankind but this fragmentation only intensifies the restlessness which leads once again to the quest for completion in the illicit. The experience of incompletion and lack is subjected to the persistent repression of which Freud speaks, but never successfully; repeatedly it returns to torment consciousness.

It is not enough for modern perverts to trace their history back to, and then repudiate, the abject identities created within sexology and some strains of psychoanalysis. They should go back further to the archetypal perverts – the heretic and the wayward woman, Satan and Eve – whose crimes were, inseparably, crimes of desire and of knowing. In addition to these perverts' vicious, unregenerate desire, there was this question of their knowing too much, or being infected with heresy. That's why, theologically, perversion is the opposite of conversion. The pervert precisely defects/deviates/errs. Thus Satan. And Eve too, who after all desires the apple not from any old tree, but rather the tree of knowledge, which is of course the one forbidden her. Mythologically desire, death and knowledge were all born in the first transgression. In the creation of the modern pervert this connection of perversion with dissident knowledge was largely but not entirely eradicated. Here is Kenneth Burke's dramatization of this, *circa* the eve of creation. Discussing the pros and cons of the project, Satan asks God if the new earth creatures will possess 'a deviant kind of "freedom" '. The Lord replies: 'You would ask that, my lad! I see why I love you so greatly. If my negative ever broke loose from me, I'd know where to look for it.' Satan can only say, 'Milord, I blush!' This is followed by a noted pause (*The Rhetoric of Religion*, pp. 279–80). Never was a pause more pregnant with desire *and* knowing; indeed, one might say of perverse desire that it was born in that pause, on the eve of creation, when Satan, because he already knew more than he should, wanted to 'fuck with' God. Here we see well enough what it is that Satan as pervert knew: among other things, that the other is always somehow within the same; that what a culture designates as alien is never actually so, never entirely other; that in a paradoxical and complex way the other is integral to the selfsame. There's more to learn about what it is to be a pervert from the mythological history of Satan and Eve than anything in queer theory. But what we also discover is that the perverse dynamic is also a violent dynamic; there is no instant subversion, only long and terrible struggles.

Perverse desire lives across a separation of same and other which is also a proximity. As we'll see in the next chapter, the history of homosexuality across the last century epitomized this. Homosexuality is imagined, positioned or represented as utterly alien and simultaneously, mysteriously inherent within: so alien that any healthy, normal person finds it repulsive, so familiar that a homosexual can corrupt healthy and normal youngsters in an instant. But we are talking here of a process at once psychic and social; brutally material in its effects, mercurial and contradictory in its representations.

*

This section has explored several powerful, recurring, and related themes: daemonic desire, dangerous and forbidden knowledge, the intrinsicality of evil to good, the way the repressed returns ineradicably marked by the cultural history of its repression. And linking all of them, the actual and/or feared instability of all cultural unities: their acute susceptibility to being undone, and, the inverse of that, the intense desire for them to be undone.

It hardly needs saying that the creative intelligence is fascinated with all of this, exploring the always inadequate repression of the forbidden, and the inevitable breakdown of 'successful' repression, in ways which range from unequivocal identification through ambivalent realization, to resolute attempts at containment.[6] In important respects the last of these is just as interesting as the other two, as I suggest in relation to Milton's *Paradise Lost* (chapter 8). Whichever, that fascination is never free from an irreconcilable tension between the aesthetic and the ethical.

PART III

Desire and Art

Iseult stood by herself in the Dickens room in Bleak House, Broadstairs . . .
All-in-all, what a literature – of what? Longing. The lyricism of forgetfulness. The nightmare of the frustrated passion. The jibbering self-mockery of the 'comic'. The abasements of love. The unplumbable panic of the lost man, the incurable damnation of the forsworn one. Helplessness. Hair fetichism. The turning of persons into pillars of salt. A bunch of roses despairingly cast on to a river, to be carried away. A sickening scene with a schoolmaster in a City churchyard. This was the man they lived for, the man they died with. Commemorated in ashtrays, cream-jugs. 'He took our nature upon him' – *no*, that was Christ. What a blasphemy; or rather, how nearly!

Elizabeth Bowen, *Eva Trout*

Those who Love Art the Most also Censor it the Most

'More than half of modern culture', remarks Algernon in Oscar Wilde's *The Importance of Being Earnest*, 'depends on what one shouldn't read' (I.131). And the other half, he might have added, on benign interpretations of what one should read. Which is the more effective in keeping the peace: blunt state censorship of 'dangerous' texts, or safe interpretations of supposedly 'respectable' ones?

One wants to say the former, and with good reasons, not the least of which is that overt censorship of art tends to be the symptom or forerunner of more insidious and brutal censorship. At the same time, in a 'democracy' nothing more effectively gives a platform to the voices of the enlightened like state censorship; to ban a book is to guarantee its place in cultural history. In certain democratic contexts censorship is a gift on a plate limpingly delivered by someone who's just shot themselves in the foot. Even establishment critics are likely to cautiously dissent from censorship, even though privately they avow that the work in question is of little or no literary merit (this being the case with Radclyffe Hall's *The Well of Loneliness*, as we'll see shortly).

I sense then that more effective censorship arises with the benign interpretations. Consider how often we find such criticism from the past striking us now as myopic; either missing the truly significant, or just looking the other way, full of censorship by omission. And yet in its time it seemed otherwise, the height of good judgement delivered from the seat of wisdom, the Oxbridge chair. It's customary in literary criticism to disregard such voices from the past, or cite them in passing as instances of individual stupidity, preliminary instances of how not to read. Yet this might be to remain complicit with the same institution of criticism, since such voices must remain significant precisely because they once seemed obviously right and sensible.

Behind the problem of censorship is the scandal of influence; quite simply, it cannot be predicted or controlled. With reason Yeats asked:

> Did that play of mine send out
> Certain men the English shot?
> Did words of mine put too great strain
> On that woman's reeling brain?
> Could my spoken words have checked
> That whereby a house lay wrecked?
>   ('The Man and the Echo')

That powerful influences can be effected by the most fleeting of contacts, the most blatant of misreadings, the most partial and incomplete of interpretations,[1] is one reason why art has the power to challenge both conservative and progressive social agendas. Establishment critics respond by legislating for responsible ways in which art should be approached. If this is the basis of their kind of censorship, it also produces an irony they can never acknowledge: the most influential interpretations have usually violated whatever 'responsible' criteria of viewing or reading currently obtained.

More interesting than the establishment critics of the past were the voices of those off-centre: those who were unconventional enough not to get the establishment jobs – the Oxbridge chairs, grammar school headships, editorial positions in the broadsheets, and more – but who were sufficiently of the same cultural formation to be heard, and who might still have been educated at Oxbridge, still be avid readers of the arts pages of some broadsheet, and still be keen to send their children to the local grammar school and hopefully Oxbridge thereafter. These are the enlightened voices, quick to contrast themselves with establishment complacency. It used to be the case that such voices were of a liberal or left persuasion. Not much perhaps, but somewhat so. Which is one reason why it was they who would want to rescue books like *The Well of Loneliness*, or D. H. Lawrence's *Lady Chatterley's Lover* from the censor, and help confer eventual respectability upon them. It's they who made the 'dangerous' book safe, if not for the whole culture, then for its liberal constituency. The establishment and the enlightened critics perform complementary tasks in the medium run. Establishment critics are, in retrospect, easy targets – though, as I just remarked, not insignificant ones. My argument is with the enlightened, for whom I also have more respect.

It's customary for these enlightened voices to ridicule state laws against obscenity, and to regard others who support such laws as not merely authoritarian, but stupid as well. But these opponents of obscenity know, albeit perhaps in a stupidly authoritarian way, something about the power of art which the enlightened often do not. To take art seriously – to recognize its potential – must be to recognize that there might be reasonable grounds for wanting to control it. Some artists, like certain intellectuals, seek out and embrace the dangerous knowledge which potentially conflicts not just with reactionary social agendas, but progressive, humane and responsible agendas as well. An inability to acknowledge this leaves art lovers in an impasse resonating with ironies: their belief that true art is intrinsically incapable of damaging or 'corrupting' us is one which does not take art seriously enough, and its corollary, their conviction that true art should not of its very nature be subject to censorship, actually produces a censorship of its own. In fact, as we will see, in the celebrated censorship trials of *The Well of Loneliness*, *Lady Chatterley's Lover*, and James Joyce's *Ulysses*, the subtler censorship emanates from the defence rather than the prosecution. In short, both in and out of courts, some of the most effective censors of art have been its most earnest defenders. As a result we find ourselves in a position today where significant dimensions of literature are avoided or persistently misrecognized by those who claim literary critical expertise. I believe that a refusal of the naive faith in art's cultural efficacy is now a precondition for being fully receptive to the significance of art. We accord it the seriousness it deserves by trusting it less.

Literature and obscenity

In 1933 Judge John M. Woolsey ruled that James Joyce's *Ulysses* (1922) was not legally obscene, thereby ending a thirteen-year ban on the novel in the USA. As Paul Vanderham shows in his recent study of the history of the censorship of *Ulysses*, Woolsey based his judgement on a range of significant criteria since characterized as 'well-intentioned lies'. They drew on the aesthetic defence of art, which can be summarized in two claims: first, that the truly literary work cannot, by its very nature, be obscene or pornographic; second, that its effect – at least upon those who have read it properly – is always and only aesthetic; in other words, the true work of art does not influence its readers politically, morally or whatever. This second idea had been put by others before, including Oscar Wilde and Joyce himself. This is Wilde in 1890: 'No artist has ethical sympathies. . . . There is no such thing as a moral or an immoral book. Books are well written, or badly written. That is all.' (Preface, *The Picture of Dorian Gray*, p. 5). Joyce's version also comes from a work of literary fiction, *A Portrait of the Artist as a Young Man* (first published in 1916):

> The feelings excited by improper art are kinetic, desire or loathing. Desire urges us to possess, to go to something; loathing urges us to abandon, to go from something. The arts which excite them, pornographic or didactic, are therefore improper arts. The esthetic emotion (I use the general term) is therefore static. The mind is arrested and raised above desire and loathing. (pp. 204–5)

Wilde's disreputable or 'decadent' version was not thought to help the cause, whereas Joyce's austere philosophical one was. There is indeed a significant underlying difference between the two views. Joyce is voicing the aesthetic defence of art as it will be enshrined in law; Wilde is voicing the decadent crede of art for art's sake which was always cunningly tendentious: by liberating art from morality it was also liberating illicit experiences and desires; to licence, in other words, a view of art the opposite to that expressed in the Joyce passage. In that the Wildean aesthetic made art a place to explore the illicit, 'art for art's sake' is a misdescription of it, and one which has subsequently helped to evade its implications, as the aesthetic defence of art does more generally.[2]

Joyce's *Ulysses* could not have been elevated to its status as one of the greatest modernist masterpieces without the aesthetic defence of art.[3] With variation and greatly differing degrees of sophistication, it has been, and remains, an influential defence against censorship. When in 1992 Iranian intellectuals in exile publicly defended Salman Rushdie's *The Satanic Verses* against the censorship of it by the government of Iran (which included a notorious death sentence upon its author), their statement proposed that 'in judging a creative work of art no considerations are valid other than aesthetic ones.'[4]

Vanderham is surely right in thinking that the logic of this defence is not only counter-intuitive and implausible, but also tends to rob art of its power, suggesting as it does that essentially art affects nothing, least of all its readers, who, in Joyce's terms, find themselves in an arrested, static and transcendent mode of apprehension. Neither the true work of art, nor its correct aesthetic reception, will endorse or challenge anything. And yet we know that literature does have the capacity to influence readers for better or worse, and a theory of art must account for this fact, not eliminate it by definition from consideration. In practice of course the aesthetic defence is always invoked selectively: we often allow art to challenge the things we think need challenging, rarely those we don't. Dissident art is rather like the dissident sexuality discussed earlier (chapters 1 and 2): it always challenges someone else. If a work of literature does seem to challenge our own cherished beliefs there are two main ways of dealing with it: we may invoke the aesthetic defence to neutralize the challenge (considered as art, the book isn't really about that) or, if that seems impossible, we disqualify it as not 'true' or great art. Most recently the aesthetic defence has also been invoked to combat political criticism *of* literature; arguably, in the culture wars of recent decades, that defence becomes as active in relation to criticism of art as of art itself (see Part III).

It is a historical fact that what has been generally agreed to be art, just like almost any kind of representation, has the potential for kinetic effect, and literary theory since Longinus has recognized as much. Both history and theory would justify a use of 'kinetic' which included more than Joyce's 'pornographic or didactic' arts; here I mean it to include responses to art which are political, moral, religious and philosophical, as well as explicitly erotic and phantas-matic. Whether we invoke theoretically sophisticated notions like 'aberrant decoding', or just the common sense one of reading against the grain, we know it has always happened. And, ironically, the very sophistication of high cultural artefacts far from pre-empting the 'incorrect' readings, facilitates them.

'The more dangerous because of its literary character'

In 1928, the British Government wanted to ban Radclyffe Hall's *The Well of Loneliness*. Despite 'enlightened' testimony to the contrary, those against the novel feared it would encourage or legitimate lesbianism. In the long term, and probably the medium if not also the short term, their fears proved to be justified. To avoid misunder-standing, let me say at the outset that the trial and subsequent suppression of this book was engineered through a contemptible establishment conspiracy fully prepared to 'pervert' the course of justice to achieve its end.[5] The eminent men involved in this con-spiracy, initiated by the then Home Secretary Sir William Joynson-Hicks, loathed and feared the very idea of sex between women.[6]

That notwithstanding, the Chief Magistrate, Sir Chartes Biron, said something during the trial that is true, but which the aesthetic defence of art would subsequently deny:

> The book may be a very fine piece of literature and yet be obscene. Art and obscenity are not disassociated. This may be a work of art. I agree it has considerable merits, but that does not prevent it from being obscene. (Souhami, p. 205)[7]

Biron used this as a conclusive reason to prevent an array of literary experts giving evidence at all: if a book could be great literature *and* obscene, then evidence as to its literary merit was irrelevant to the question of its obscenity. One can see then how urgently were the well-intentioned lies needed as a defence in censorship trials.

A similar opinion to Biron's had already been put by James Douglas, editor of the *Sunday Express*, in an editorial which precipitated the trial. For Douglas sexual perversion was a 'pestilence . . . devastating the younger generation'. He would rather give 'a healthy boy or a healthy girl a phial of prussic acid than this novel. Poison kills the body, but moral poison kills the soul.' This editorial displays the extreme contradiction in the anti-homosexual position remarked earlier, one evident in the Wilde trials, and which reappears throughout the twentieth century: on the one hand homosexuality is so self-evidently 'hideous', 'loathsome', a 'degeneracy', a 'degradation', a 'debasement' (all terms which Douglas uses) that any right-thinking and healthy person would avoid it like the plague. On the other hand it has this extraordinary capacity to seduce precisely the 'healthy', right-minded boy or girl; to devastate the entire younger generation, in fact. More than that: for Douglas it has the capacity to destroy Christianity and 'the civilization it has built on the ruins of paganism'. That last remark inadvertently suggests the reason for the panic in those like Douglas: 'paganism' is still underneath or latent within Christianity, and capable of being reactivated. Worse still, Radclyffe Hall brilliantly appropriates Christianity to validate lesbian love – Stephen, the hero/ine of the book is a Christ-like figure, full of suffering integrity and martyrdom. Douglas half realizes what Radclyffe Hall has done – that's why he, like Biron in court, also finds that the book's aesthetic virtues make it more dangerous, not less:

> It is no use to say that the novel possesses 'fine qualities' or that its author is an 'accomplished' artist. It is no defence to say that the author is sincere or that she is frank, or that there is delicacy in her art.
> The answer is that the adroitness and cleverness of the book intensifies its moral danger. It is a seductive and insidious piece of special

pleading designed to display perverted decadence as a martyrdom inflicted upon these outcasts by a cruel society. It flings a veil of sentiment over their depravity. (Souhami, p. 177)

Douglas's position becomes even clearer from another of his reviews, written thirteen years earlier. This one, which appeared in October 1915, was also influential in the legal suppression of the book it was castigating, D. H. Lawrence's *The Rainbow*. And here too lesbian love was singled out, in court, as an especially disgusting and subversive aspect of the novel. Douglas in his review insists that it's the job of the artist not to tell the truth but to uphold civilized values – even more so at that time, in the midst of the First World War. The danger of 'decadent' art like Lawrence's is that it leads us in the direction of forbidden knowledge, it 'open[s] all the doors that the wisdom of man has shut and bolted and double-locked'. Whereas the power of art should be on the side of beauty, wholesomeness and health, Lawrence uses it to 'express the unspeakable and to hint at the unutterable. The morbidly perverted ingenuity of style is made the vehicle for saying things that ought to be left unthought, let alone unsaid.' In this review, read out in court, Douglas finds *The Rainbow* pernicious not because it tells lies, but because it tells the truth about a reality which civilization necessarily and rightly represses. There are echoes here of degenerationist philosophy (which I shall examine in chapter 8), as when Douglas insists that life must 'go on climbing up and up' to put as much distance between its evolved forms and the 'nethermost deeps', and when he acknowledges the inherent instability of those evolved forms.[8] But Douglas is drawing on a very old belief, affirmed with new vigour in the late nineteenth century in relation to novelistic realism, that the artist is potentially dangerous because of seeing, saying and knowing too much. This was Walter Bagehot's view of Thackeray. Comparing him unfavourably with Dickens in this respect, Bagehot describes Thackeray as a writer who frequented 'the borderline that separates the world that may be described in books from the world which it is prohibited so to describe'. What made Thackeray particularly worrying was his power of suggestion, his 'hinting with subtle art how thoroughly he is familiar with . . . the interdicted region on the other side'; and although he never explicitly violated conventional rules, 'the shadow of the immorality that is not seen, is scarcely ever wanting in his delineation of the society which is seen' (*Collected Works*, vol. 2, p. 98). The question being: whose shadow is it? That of course is one question asked implicitly by the artist who knows too much and goes where she shouldn't.

Returning to the censorship of *The Well of Loneliness*, those who were to speak in defence of the novel, had they been allowed to, argued that it would not encourage perversity. A. P. Herbert was representative when he said that if he'd found a healthy girl of twenty with the book he'd tell her to read on because she'd be bored. And if he found an 'unhealthy' one reading it he'd still say read on, because it would be a warning to her. This claim about the effects of the novel was another well-intentioned lie, as subsequent history has shown. Long after this trial gay liberation fostered, perhaps necessarily, the belief that homosexuality cannot be nurtured (another well-intentioned lie): one simply is or isn't gay. But the increase in gay and bisexual people in more liberal climates isn't just a consequence of those who are 'already gay' and bisexual coming out; it's also because many people are exploring homosexuality who otherwise wouldn't have. Without in any way underestimating the extent of the virulent homophobia around these trials, we can allow that there is more than 'phobia' involved: those like Douglas, Biron and the Home Secretary believed literature could contribute to homosexuality becoming more widespread, along with many other things which they believe equally deplorable. And they were right. Just before the unsuccessful appeal against the banning of *The Well*, the Home Secretary triumphantly addressed the Authors' Club in London; the degenerationist rhetoric is clear:

> The tone of the Empire comes from you the authors of our land. If the tone is pure, the blood will go on pulsating through the whole world carrying with it purity and safety. If the stream of the blood is impure, nobody can tell the effect it will have right through our Empire.[9]

Not even this Home Secretary could believe that lesbian literature could destroy the Empire, but he made it a focus of, a surrogate for many of the things that could and would, and about which people like him could do little. And Joynson-Hicks' worst fears were, after all, realized: the Empire would go, lesbianism would become acceptable, and the censorship of literature would be relaxed, to then unthinkable degrees. Maybe there were connections after all?

Radclyffe Hall's defence as author was a dangerous mixture of outright defiance and high moral purpose. Yes, she wanted to plead sympathy for those who were condemned to be inverts. But this was a problem of abnormality, not evil. Inverts were no better or worse than normal people, but 'when they are good they deserve more praise because from their birth nearly every man's hand is against them. Hopeless outcasts are a social danger, and persecution is as harmful to the persecutors as to the persecuted' (Souhami, p. 199). It was evident she was not ashamed of, or apologizing for, her own sexuality, and reading between the lines of her defence as well as the novel it was evident too that she thought some inverts *were* morally superior to some normal people. And nothing more enraged the normal than that.

This was her compromise position, the one she would have put to the court had she been called. But as it became clear that the case was going against her, she became more defiant still. When her counsel, Norman Birkett, claimed in court that the relationships between women in the book were romantic and sentimental, and had nothing to do with sex, Hall was furious. She told him that unless he retracted this statement she would get up and tell the magistrate herself. So retract it he did, and the case was certainly lost then, if it wasn't before. In a way, and as I've argued elsewhere, her compromise position was as disturbing as her uncompromising defence of explicit sexuality (*Sexual Dissidence*, chapter 3). In respect of sexual inversion Radclyffe Hall was a radical; in most others she was deeply conservative. That combination constituted her challenge: with magnificent hubris she appropriates for lesbianism a religious ethic of the martyr and crosses it with a romantic ethic of the outsider. The lesbian is identified with Christ; the 'pagan' re-emerges in place of the Christian. Those like Douglas and Biron realized what was happening: if one reason for condemning the book as obscene was because it showed lesbian sex to be good – in Biron's revealingly perceptive words, 'giving these women extraordinary rest, contentment and pleasure; and not merely that, but it is actually put forward that it improves their mental balance and capacity' – another was that it used a religiose and romantic ethic to make lesbians attractive and objects of admiration. The judgement that the book was obscene was upheld in an appeal. Summarizing the proceedings, the Director of Public Prosecutions, Sir Archibald Bodkin, highlighted again the perceived threat: 'the book was regarded as a subtle and insinuating one and the more dangerous because of its literary character' (Souhami, p. 217).

Whether in relation to her compromise position, or her more radical one, the aesthetic defence of art, had it been available to her, was as irrelevant for Hall as it was for Magistrate Biron. From opposing positions, both realized the potentially radical kinetic influence of a work of literature, an influence which worked through a conversion which is, inseparably, a perversion of culture's most sanctified images.

And yet, the aesthetic defence would become victorious against exactly the prejudice which led to the suppression of *The Well*. Much to the chagrin of those on the far right, the claim that art is essentially apolitical has won the day for broadly progressive political positions. In doing so, however, it instigates a subtler and arguably more effective kind of censorship of its own, one which was already apparent in the defence solicited for Radclyffe Hall's novel. Clearly their denial that the novel would encourage lesbianism was strategically necessary, but for the most part it was also what they wanted to believe; these testimonies for the defence – Birkett said 'a more distinguished body of witnesses have never been called' – wanted art to be safe.

Burning out the shames

In the trial of D. H. Lawrence's *Lady Chatterley's Lover* in 1960, the prosecution alleged that the book exalted adultery and promiscuity, bad enough in themselves but doubly so here because occuring between a woman and her husband's employee (his gamekeeper – property, power and class perfectly meshed).[10] The growing influence of the aesthetic defence of art is reflected in the Obscene Publications Act of 1959,[11] under which Lawrence's book was prosecuted. But the actual defence was as ethical as it was aesthetic. In practice this is usually so: the aesthetic defence can't operate effectively without an implicit or explicit moral appeal. Distinguished witnesses queued up to defend Lawrence as a great literary moralist with a puritanical zeal to reform human sexual relations, and now they *were* allowed into the witness box. Some even argued that Lawrence was implicitly criticizing the anti-social and promiscuous practices he described. Again this was strategically necessary, but there was a large measure of agreement between those witnesses and many literary critics, most influentially F. R. Leavis, who, unhampered by the exigencies of the courtroom, helped make Lawrence one of the most respected writers of the post-war period.[12]

Significantly, the novel's notorious episode of apparently ecstatic sodomy was overlooked by both prosecution and defence. Sodomy is one thing which makes Lawrence's work dangerous, not just because he was writing approvingly of a practice that would then have undoubtedly rendered the book obscene, but because anal intercourse is complicatedly central to Lawrence's own sexual ethic. It is, for instance, the focus for his ambivalent attitude to homosexuality. Sometimes for Lawrence an idealistic homoeroticism offers the possibility of redemptive escape from the degeneracy of western culture;

more often *actual* homosexuality is felt to manifest that very degeneracy. Likewise with anal sex: if, in the homosexual embrace, it is imagined as the sterile desire for dissolution and death, in the heterosexual embrace it seemingly becomes the transgressive search for life at its most searingly intense – a shattering of the self into a vulnerable, receptive authenticity:

> Burning out the shames, the deepest oldest shames, in the most secret places. It cost her an effort to let him have his way and his will of her. She had to be a passive, consenting thing, like a slave, a physical slave. Yet the passion licked round her, consuming, and when the sensual flame of it pressed through her bowels and breast, she really thought she was dying: yet a poignant, marvellous death.
>   . . . And necessary, forever necessary, to burn out false shames and smelt out the heaviest ore of the body into purity. With the fire of sheer sensuality.
>   . . . She would have thought a woman would have died of shame. Instead of which, the shame died . . . routed by the phallic hunt of the man . . .
>   . . . the last and deepest recess of organic shame. The phallos alone could explore it. And how he had pressed in on her![13] (*Lady Chatterley's Lover*, pp. 258–9)

But is it the case that this is exclusively 'heterosexual'? Might there not be displaced homoerotic and/or bisexual fantasies here also? Elsewhere in Lawrence the male yearning towards the male is occasionally expressed explicit, as in the suppressed prologue to *Women in Love*, but more often it is expressed through the eyes and desires of women. He not only merges the male homoerotic gaze with the female heterosexual one, but he exemplifies the bisexual fantasy described earlier: he desires the male from the position of, and even as, a woman; a homoerotic fantasy is articulated in the form of the heterosexual one which it fuses with. This suggests something about human sexuality which might be even more disturbing than ecstatic sodomy, but which also suggests why the latter is excoriated. I've expressed elsewhere[14] my belief that this makes Lawrence a writer of greater not lesser significance, someone who was exploring aspects of human sexuality which the trial prosecution apparently couldn't see, and which the humanist defence could not afford to acknowledge even if it suspected them. If, in Lawrence's most intense imaginings, the perversity of sexuality is found at the heart of the 'normal', this is something few of his admirers or detractors have been able to acknowledge. For some, like Leavis, he becomes the prophet of mental and social health: 'There is no

profound emotional disorder in Lawrence . . . intelligence in him . . .
is not thwarted or disabled by inner contradictions' (*D. H. Lawrence:
Novelist*, pp. 15, 28). In fact, the remorseless expression of 'inner
contradictions', his own and others', is exactly what makes Lawrence
such a courageous and significant writer. Even those more insightful
than Leavis as to the sexual obsessiveness of the novels, like Norman
Mailer in *The Prisoner of Sex*, would celebrate Lawrence's vital
heterosexuality at the expense of a 'deathly' and 'sterile' homosexuality, thereby also suppressing Lawrence's own obsession with death.
In the feminist criticism which so influenced the reading of Lawrence
after the publication of Kate Millett's *Sexual Politics* in 1969, a
gender politics gains plausibility only through a misrepresentation of
Lawrence (and sex) as complete as anything that went before. As
Rachel Bowlby has remarked, even Millett, this most unforgiving of
Lawrence's critics, seems to share his conception of 'wholesome' sex
(*Shopping With Freud*, pp. 42–3). Not despite, but because of her
radical sexual politics, Millett shares something with the aesthetic/
moralistic defence of art: a truly great novel cannot be pornographic,
perverse or unhealthy. I am persuaded to the contrary. A not
inconsiderable virtue of Camille Paglia's *Sexual Personae* is the way
it finds the western artistic canon to be pornographic and perverse at
its heart. Time and again she finds a disturbing knowledge in the
texts which have been tamed by those academics and critics who
continue to censor literature even as they fight furiously to speak
authoritatively on its behalf.

8

Critical Wars and Academic Censors

In the last couple of decades the censors have indeed been fighting furiously, especially in the universities where battle lines have been drawn up between traditionalists and diverse others. The struggles have occasionally been vicious: splitting departments, ending friendships, producing interminable correspondence in letter columns, and – when happening at Oxbridge – even making headline news. Beyond the universities the culture wars have raged in the media, and been sufficiently important for politicians of the highest rank to get involved. Since a significant feature of these battles has been the reductive way each side defines the other, my categories here of 'traditional' and 'anti-traditional' must be regarded as provisional. My concern isn't to demarcate schools of criticism, but to try and identify some of the significant cultural issues being fought over.

One kind of traditionalist, especially active around canonical figures like Shakespeare, subscribed to what is often called an 'idealist' aesthetic, which finds the profundity of literature in its ability to transcend what is merely local or relative, especially political concerns specific to a particular time and place. Of course they recognize that great literature deals with the particular and the political, but its ultimate meaning has a higher aim – a quasi-spiritual realm of eternal verities and values which actual politics and specific histories contaminate and betray. On this view great artists translate temporal disturbance into spiritual/aesthetic harmony. The idealist wants art to transcend politics because only then can it compensate for, and overcome, the failures of the latter – failures regarded as more or less inevitable in a postlapsarian world, or indeed a postmodern one, the latter being after all only a chronic manifestion of the former. The idealist view partakes of the aesthetic defence of art described earlier but, to distinguish itself from aesthetes like Oscar Wilde, roots it in firm moral criteria. Actually the criteria at issue might more accurately be called moralistic, since the enduring truths which idealist critics found in literature have all too often turned out to be the conservative social and political values one would expect someone of their time and class to hold. If their belief in eternal verities was often intellectually embarrassing it was nevertheless acceptable in the culture at large because it was what many wanted to believe, and what others had – and still have – a vested interest in propounding. In so far as such critics were also academics, their version of those values suffered additionally from the complacency and narrowness characteristic of academic life. Some who have taught in conservative academic institutions will testify to the way that teachers and students use idealist aesthetic criteria to ignore or repudiate whole areas of culture and experience. This limitation has been blatant with regard to sexuality. In 1990 I described traditionally-minded critics of Shakespeare as, too often, 'upmarket moral hacks'[1] and was reprimanded for doing so. A decade further on their writing on the subject of sexuality seems to me to merit more than ever that description. And I would record my surprise now at a situation which has not changed much: I mean the way intelligent students were so resigned to being taught literature by people of limited life-experience who, for that reason and others, often couldn't teach anyway.

With remarkable complacency, idealist critics have turned canonical writers into spiritual Civil Servants even more tedious than their real-world counterparts. But Leo Bersani is surely right to detect in this tradition something more insidious than complacent, especially in so far as it advocates what he calls a 'culture of redemption'. By this Bersani means a view of art which celebrates its supposed capacity to repair or 'correct' experience which in real life is damaged or seemingly worthless. This attitude derives from a wish to redeem the catastrophe of history and the pain of being human, and ultimately perhaps from a horror of life, and a deep fear of being. Furthermore, argues Bersani, such a theory is intellectually symptomatic of the very process it purports to identify in art. I believe Bersani is right when he says that at heart the culture of redemption is a culture of death because it 'denies the historical reality that it attempts to redeem [and] represses the suicidal impulse that is its very motivation'. In other words, the culture of redemption 'presents itself as making the civilization intelligible – as a philosophically and aesthetically superior version of the reality that society lives historically.' But in attempting to do that it actually helps to repress the destructive impulses for which it is also meant to compensate ('Conversation', p. 5). In the work of a number of writers including Baudelaire, Bataille and Genet, Bersani identifies a different kind of art, one which repeatedly risks – though in very different ways – the always dangerous encounter with being.[2]

Idealist critics tame literature and either fail to see, or actively censor, whatever challenges it might have for them and us. In a letter of 3 May 1818 John Keats reflects on the respective merits of Milton and Wordsworth. He wonders whether 'Miltons [sic] apparently less anxiety for Humanity proceeds from his seeing further or no than Wordsworth'. And of the latter he asks: 'whether or no he has an extended vision or a circumscribed grandeur – whether he is an eagle in his nest, or on the wing' (*Letters*, pp. 93–4). Whatever the truth about Milton and Wordsworth, some artists have indeed censored themselves, and for various reasons, by no means all of which would be reprehensible. My concern is with those critics who have been more than willing to do it for them, containing any suggestion of an extended vision with their own aesthetic version of circumscribed grandeur. The strategy, though long established, is not necessarily reactionary in the obvious sense of the word. Susan Sontag once described something similar as an aspect of literary modernism: an 'outrageous, essentially forbidding author' is made respectable by being described in a way which overlooks or conceals the real nature of the work itself 'which may be, among other things, extremely boring, or morally monstrous or terribly painful to read. Certain authors become literary or intellectual classics because they are *not* read' (*Antonin Artaud: Selected Writings*, p. lix).

In truth the idealist critic I have described is these days an extreme case – an extrapolation of tendencies which in practice overlap with yet other positions including one which I shall call, more respectfully, humanist. This is a much more interesting view: that the truly great creative intelligence is fundamentally on the side of humane values, and is driven by conscience, sincerity and ethical responsibility. The humanist is less concerned to release the text from its historical context than to reconcile it with the most humane values discernible in that context and in the critic's own. A case in point is the Leavisite notion of a great literary tradition which is the storehouse of humane values and the measure of cultural and psychological health.

F. R. Leavis and Max Nordau

F. R. Leavis is widely regarded as the most important single influence in establishing the direction of English studies in the mid-twentieth century.[3] Leavis was censorious of attitudes, emotions and desires which he regarded as bad for cultural and mental health. In this he has been seen as the product of a specifically English tradition which is anti-intellectual, moralistic and empiricist. But this kind of moral aesthetic extends far beyond England's borders and beyond Britain's too, for that matter. Leavis was one of the most engaged critics of his time, and deserves respect for being so. By the same token, what Leavisism censored becomes the more significant. In the last quarter of the twentieth century the school of criticism he largely created was widely rejected. But with the turn of the new millennium interest in him revives, and with good reason, since, as I hope to show, in underlying respects, Leavis remains much more representative than his reputation would suggest. Some of the explicitly ethical demands he made of literature were widely shared within nineteenth- and twentieth-century thought, and remain influential today, especially in literary education – albeit in a more overtly liberal guise. The newly revived commitment to ethical criticism is indebted to Leavis, as Andrew Gibson acknowledges with the assertion that 'It is time to go back to Leavis' (*Postmodernity, Ethics and the Novel*, p. 1). Leavis's ethical relationship to literature was shared even by those who became vociferously anti-Leavis or ignorantly post-Leavis. So it is not surprising to find Terry Eagleton, a political critic once regarded as opposing everything Leavis stood for, then offering a spirited defence of him ('F. R. Leavis').

For Leavis the supreme virtue was 'Life', a word which, as Francis Mulhern observes, evokes two equally important things – a human totality and actual lived experience (*The Moment of Scrutiny*, pp. 170–1). Generalized, normative judgements about what life should be are affirmed in and through the intensity of the specific, hence Leavis's high valuation of 'concreteness' and 'particularity' in literature. But what counted as 'Life'? Notoriously, this affirmative word became, in practice, controlling and delimiting. Leavis was against much more than he was for, finding most things in the modern world to be anti-life – but then so did many others, including one of the far-reaching intellectual influences on the twentieth century, Friedrich Nietzsche. For Leavis, some of the things on the side of 'Life' were robust good sense, unflinching outward awareness, honest perception, self-awareness tempered by a refusal of self-

indulgence or unhealthy introversion, and the effort to remain emo-
tionally responsible and self-controlled. All this was epitomized in
the aesthetic/ethical ideal of *a firm grasp of the actual.*

It was not the first time that 'realism' of this kind was invoked in
the service of a socio-political critique of the 'realities' of contemporary life. Only a few decades earlier there was the hugely popular
degeneration theory of Max Nordau, someone else who found much
that was anti-life in modern culture.[4] His *Degeneration* was published in 1892 and proved a best-seller. An English translation was
published in 1895. I suspect that, via Leavis and others, Nordau's
Degeneration is a major though indirect and unacknowledged influence on twentieth-century criticism. Nordau was not alone in arguing
that modern civilization was threatened by disintegration and
exhaustion, but degeneration was a pseudo-scientific explanation of
why this was so, and how it was happening. Essentially, degeneration
was evolution reversed and accelerated. Instead of steady ascent to
ever more complex forms of life, degeneration threatened enervation,
regression and possibly even extinction. Physical and social organ-
isms were regarded as essentially composite, highly sophisticated
unities terrifyingly susceptible to – once again – internal mutiny.
Degeneration could undo the existing, arduously achieved forms of
civilization in much less time than it had taken them to grow. Nordau
discovered signs of this everywhere. Modern art was a major symptom of degenerate tendencies – intellectual, imaginative and sexual.
(As we saw earlier, James Douglas's diatribes against Hall's *The Well*
and Lawrence's *The Rainbow* echoed degenerationist fears.)

For all their manifest differences,[5] Nordau and Leavis share
important criteria of judgement – aesthetic, ethical and epistemolo-
gical. There is the same demand for health and integration at both
the psychic and social levels, with the latter being indispensable for
the former; the same insistence that great artists will display (in
Leavis's description of Wordsworth) an 'essential sanity and normality' (*Revaluation*, p. 174).[6] Both believe in the power of the will and
self-control, and both share a deep anxiety about regression and the
influence of perverse sexuality. Leavis's advocacy of a firm grasp of
the actual is anticipated in Nordau's argument that a vital and
healthy art depends on vivid and accurate sense-perception –
'attention, observation, and knowledge' (*Degeneration*, p. 560). Only
then can the dangerous instincts and emotions which obscure, con-
fuse and confound reality be controlled: 'In a healthy and sane poet
even the mood pure and simple is united to clear presentations, and
is not a mere undulation of fragrance and rose-tinted mist.' That is
Nordau (p. 128), but it could have been Leavis.[7] For Nordau, the

causes of this dangerous turning away from reality are manifold but include atavism and 'a madly inordinate eroticism' (*Degeneration*, pp. 110–11, 120). To be vital, desire must be rigorously controlled.

With this in mind we can see that the 'realism' advocated by both Leavis and Nordau is only partly about limiting access to the real. As we'll see shortly in relation to Shelley, it is, even more crucially, a measure and contributor to psychic health. The mentally balanced have a strong (selective) grasp of reality, the infirm a weak (inclusive) one. We've already remarked how for Leavis one of the things that made Lawrence a great writer was his freedom from inner contradictions. That this is implausible to say the least is not, at the moment, my point; what's significant is the apparent conviction that to be free of contradictions is a precondition of greatness in the writer. Leavis had earlier made much the same point about Shakespeare, strongly defending him against any suggestion that he was the victim of 'unresolved contradictions, of mental conflict or uncertainty'. In fact, adds Leavis, it is Shakespeare's great triumph in *Measure for Measure* to have expressed a complexity of attitude distinguished from contradiction, conflict and uncertainty ('The Greatness of *Measure for Measure*', p. 240). Nordau says the same of Dante: he was free of 'internal contradictions' (p. 91). For Leavis and Nordau to be anything else was to succumb to the corrupting tendencies of one's times – degeneration, neurasthenia, perversion and much more. Quite recently, Brian Vickers, echoing Leavis's and Nordau's faith in the sanity of the artist and the coherence of his product, declares: 'Either texts have an integrity constructed by a writer with definite aims in mind, or they are truly random collections of signifiers which critics are free to arrange in any pattern that serves their own obsession' (*Appropriating Shakespeare*, pp. 289–90). Vickers' claim, proffered as a defence of art against nothing more degenerate than literary post-structuralism, nevertheless perpetuates the same reductive strategy to that found in Nordau and Leavis: a false opposition is set up whereby one either subscribes to a naive critical tenet (in this case the contention that a text will always have an integrity deriving directly from a writer's definite aim) *or* chaos is come again.

It's evident that the creative process, with all its imaginative achievements, is often (though not invariably) riven with uncertainty, conflict, and contradiction. A writer is frequently led to deviate from 'definite aims in mind' by many things, including his or her imagination, unconscious, frustrations, intelligence, fantasies and contradictions. In other words, what diverts them is inseparable from what makes them creative in the first place. Not surprisingly then, some of the most engaging texts become so because of just that deviation.

Most obviously there is the compromised didacticism in Milton's *Paradise Lost*, that most powerful dramatization of the most resonant of all human myths, the Fall. Of this work Blake famously said, in terms that are clearly 'Freudian', that Milton was of the Devil's party without knowing it. But one could maintain the point differently, in terms which are not Freudian: the sincerely held theological framework enables and even invites an imaginative exploration of what opposes it; one might even say that a certain strength of conviction can't resist the exploration of what resists it. Perhaps what we encounter in *Paradise Lost* is the courage – or arrogance, and perhaps paranoia – of the most formidable kind of theology, that which believes it can and must experientially embrace the contradictions and paradoxes which threaten it. In Milton's case such a confrontation would be intensified by the fact that he was writing from the experience of Revolutionary defeat. Additionally, in *Paradise Lost*, the damage to didactic intent is done not by this strategy per se, but by performing it not only as theology but as tragic literature – arguably the definitive expressive medium of defeat. It therefore becomes productive to think of the subversion of didacticism in *Paradise Lost* as a consequence of a consciously deployed genre as well as of barely conscious contradictions. In truth it probably derives from elements of both.

There is something else which may contribute even more powerfully to the undermining of 'definite aims': identification. Georges Bataille, comparing Emily Brontë's *Wuthering Heights* with Greek tragedy, says of the latter: 'The tragic author agreed with the law, the transgression of which he described, but he based all emotional impact on communicating the sympathy which he felt for the transgressor' (*Literature and Evil*, p. 21). Of Greek tragedy possibly, and of literature closer to us certainly, it should be said that this description is only accurate if 'sympathy' carries its full (and now largely lost) potential for profound identification. That this was true of Greek tragedy is suggested by the fact that tendency to identify, in artist and audience, was something Plato feared about drama. And where identification with the transgressor does occur, neither the law, nor the artist's 'agreement' with it, is safe, especially when, as we saw earlier, identification is complicated by desire (see, chapter 2). In this respect Freud, drawing on Aristotle's theory of catharsis, has some interesting if unflattering things to say of identification on the part of the audience. He is speaking mainly of drama, but also of lyric and epic poetry. As spectators, says Freud, we are people who experience too little, who feel nothing of importance can happen to us. We have learned to suppress or displace our ambitions and desires but still yearn to act in accord with them. So we live them vicariously by identifying with rebellious heroes, thereby giving way 'to such suppressed impulses as a craving for freedom in religious, political, social and sexual matters'. This includes masochistic identification with the suffering of heroes ('Psychopathic Stage Characters', p. 122). It's a familiar position which goes back to Aristotle: this identification produces catharsis, or, in Freudian terms, enough vicarious pleasure to keep the repressions in place.

But those like Nordau and Leavis (with unmistakable echoes of Plato) feared the reverse might be true. That is why Nordau is even prepared to compare the artist with the criminal: 'The artist who complacently represents what is reprehensible, vicious, criminal, approves of it, perhaps glorifies it, differs not in kind, but only in degree, from the criminal who actually commits it' (p. 326).

The trauma of loss

For Leavis, another serious threat to psychological health was something which drives the narrative of *Paradise Lost*, namely the wounding, debilitating sense of loss. In fact, this most obsessive theme of western literature is often expressed in terms which echo the Fall. But this hardly makes it a safe subject; on the contrary, for Leavis it's a positively dangerous one, and the occasion for some of his most influential comments on the nature of poetry. In two seminal essays, ' "Thought" and Emotional Quality' (1945) and 'Reality and Sincerity' (1952–3),[8] he compares several poems on 'that most dangerous theme, the irrevocable past' and 'irreparable loss'. Why so dangerous? First because here above all there is the temptation for regressive emotion to overpower thought and thereby subvert the quest for 'emotional hygiene and moral value – more generally (there seems no other adequate phrase) of spiritual health' (*A Selection from Scrutiny*, vol. 1, pp. 214, 215, 248).

Again, this is Leavis but it could have been Nordau. Leavis (p. 216) refers approvingly to the contention of D. W. Harding in his essay, 'A Note on Nostalgia' that 'the fact of experiencing the tendency towards regression means nothing. It is the final attitude towards the experience that has to be evaluated.' And (continues Harding) whereas some poets submit to the pleasure of regression, D. H. Lawrence in his poem 'Piano', is by contrast 'adult, stating the overwhelming strength of the impulse but reporting resistance to it and implying that resistance is better than yielding'. To consult Harding's article directly ('A Note on Nostalgia', p. 70) is to discover something Leavis does not make clear, and perhaps does not want to, namely that the regressive impulse in question is nothing less than the death wish.

Regression involves an erotic drive. Leavis goes on to criticize Shelley for writing a poetry of 'passive submission' not only divorced from, but opposed to thought. Passivity and submission drown intelligence and encourage surrender to regressive pleasure – especially inappropriate, apparently, in the masculine gender, and especially visible in a poem like Shelley's 'Ode to the West Wind' (Leavis, p. 218). But if Leavis is even half right, how come Shelley is able to so effectively eroticize, adulate and *identify* with an imagined potency?

> A heavy weight of hours has chained and bowed
> One too like thee: tameless, and swift, and proud.
> . . .
> Be thou, Spirit fierce,
> My spirit! Be thou me, impetuous one!

From this intense cathexis arises a memorable expression of the 'active', identificatory impulse in sexual passivity:

> to pant beneath thy power, and share
> The impulse of thy strength.

At the risk of labouring the point, these lines suggest the reductiveness of the active/passive binary as deployed by Leavis; his inability to acknowledge the complicity between the 'passive' sensibility and the 'active' poetic one which results not just in the transgressive fantasy, but the insight, concentration and control of such lines.[9] In short, this expression of passivity is as thoughtful and controlling as it is erotic – like passivity itself. There's 'control' here all right, but it's not of the kind Leavis wants, nor where he wants to find it.

It is Shelley's eroticism which is the real problem for Leavis. There are dark remarks about him being a genius, but a dangerous one in whom we can discern a 'spiritual malady' (*A Selection from Scrutiny*, vol. 1, p. 219). This recalls Nordau's notion of the 'higher degenerate', an individual who is dangerously brilliant because endowed with an intelligence which has evolved too far and at the expense of the ethical faculty which has become correspondingly atrophied. (One of the most famous fictional higher degenerates is Kurtz, in Joseph Conrad's *Heart of Darkness*). In *Revaluation* (first published in 1936), Leavis went further. Again 'Ode to the West Wind' is reproved, and in terms which resemble Nordau even more closely. In Shelley's alleged immaturity and narcissism, excessive emotionalism, lack of critical intelligence, and preoccupation with dissolution, Leavis detects 'viciousness, corruption . . . radical disabilities and perversions, such as call for moral comment'. The problem, he decides, is one of pathological eroticism, a dangerous 'surrendering to temptation' which derives from bad habits and 'truly corrupt' gratifications including a radical lack of self-knowledge, and an identification with the feminine (pp. 216, 221–3). Once again we encounter the disturbance generated by the bisexual fantasy in which the male identifies with the woman[10] (rather than the more comfortable bisexual fantasy of being midway between – and above – sexual difference). For Leavis all of Shelley's supposed deficiencies are, somewhat implausibly, rooted in his inability to be empirically precise – 'his weak grasp upon the actual' (p. 206).[11] A more robust epistemology could have saved him from sexual perversion. Ostensibly it is this which justifies Leavis's charge that Shelley is 'almost unreadable'. In fact, it is clear even from Leavis's own account that Shelley is all too readable; far from being unintelligible, he articulates the reprehensible.

Leavis wants 'a clear, disinterested and mature vision', rooted in 'a profoundly serious concern for reality' (pp. 229–30). But *in reality*, this vision of the real is selective to the point of censorship and repression. To have 'concretely grasped' something (*A Selection from Scrutiny*, vol. 1, p. 217) is all too often to have eliminated from the vision some reprehensible aspect of it. And when that reprehensible aspect remains – as in Shelley – it constitutes a failure of the mature vision and becomes symptomatic of psychic and sexual unhealth. Leavis is fond of the word 'disinterested' as a way of describing the mature vision and the valuation it entails (cf. p. 215), but what he is describing is anything but.

Turning to Tennyson, Leavis contends that his 'Tears, idle tears . . .' (from *The Princess*) contains similar shortcomings, being indulgent, specious, and offering emotion for its own sake; in short it is, in the words of W. B. Yeats, 'sentimental for lack of thought' (p. 218). Yet this poem, like Shelley's, can be read for a complexity of thought inflected by an erotic 'perversity' which is anything but thoughtless and sentimental. It too expresses an aesthetic intelligence made possible by passivity and submission. Here is the 'sentiment' of Tennyson's last stanza:

> Dear as remember'd kisses after death,
> And sweet as those by hopeless fancy feign'd

> On lips that are for others; deep as love,
> Deep as first love, and wild with all regret;
> O death in Life, the days that are no more.

The poetic mode is conventional enough to be read as an expression of loss whose emotions remain within agreeable bounds. But the relatively comforting 'Dear as remember'd kisses after death' shifts via deceptively smooth syntax into the jarring recollection of unrequited desire alleviated only by fantasy. When we realize that this fantasy is 'hopeless' but also pleasurable, 'sweet' becomes too sharp for cliché. To the extent that this unrequited desire refers to the 'love' of line 4, it explains the precise, wonderful qualification in 'deep as love, / Deep as first love'. This is not lazy hypnotic repetition; nor is it, *pace* Leavis, emotion washing away precise thought, but precise memory arising – following on – from emotion. And then 'hopeless fancy feign'd / On lips that are for others'. *Are*, not *were*: this is an impossible desire still alive within a nostalgia which, 'wild with all regret' provides the excess of frustrated desire which nostalgia cannot contain – hence loss surges back as 'death in life'. And that is the crux: not just death in life but death in eroticism. It is this experience – one could say poetic tradition – which Leavis is censoring. If the foregoing sub-Leavisite exposition of these lines has any plausibility at all, it suggests that the complexity of response which Leavis declines to consider can be revealed through just the kind of close reading he insisted on.[12] It suggests too the extent of the censorship of the experience of loss within the Leavisite tradition, and why it is neither surprising nor unprecedented for a critical intelligence committed to health, harmony and normality to be preoccupied with their apparent loss. As Francis Mulhern remarks of the writers who contributed to *Scrutiny*: 'the leitmotiv of their writings was *loss*: the loss of order, wholeness and certainty in every cell of modern English society' (*The Moment of Scrutiny*, p. 269). The trauma of loss: always we try to forget this, and especially in times of cultural or personal optimism, but nothing is more stubbornly constitutive of the human psyche, and of its creative or intellectual expression.

Leavis approves in Emily Brontë's 'Cold in the Earth' an attitude of mind which holds in check 'dangerous temptations'. It has a 'controlling strength' expressed via a 'tough prose rationality . . . a resolute strength of will' which gives us 'an attitude, nobly impressive, of *sternly controlled passionate desolation*' (*A Selection from Scrutiny*, vol. 1, pp. 248–9, 252; my emphasis). For Leavis this stoical fortitude in the face of loss is 'quite opposed' (p. 250) to regression and the death wish – what Brontë, in the last stanza of this poem, calls 'memory's rapturous pain'. But the death wish is not the opposite of stoicism, so much as its suppressed source of energy. Brontë says as much in the very lines which Leavis endorses:

> Then did I check the tears of useless passion,
> Weaned my young soul from yearning after thine;
> Sternly denied its burning wish to hasten
> Down to that tomb already more than mine!

So it is not surprising that Leavis overlooks another poem by Brontë, written just one month earlier (February 1845) and entitled 'The Philosopher's Conclusion', in which this eroticized death wish surfaces with a fierceness greater even than (and because of) its suppression. Betraying everything Leavis has attributed to her, the poet yearns for the oblivion which releases us, inseparably, from the pain of desire and the pain of individuation:

> O, for the time when I shall sleep
> Without identity –
> And never care how rain may steep
> Or snow may cover me!
> No promised Heaven, these wild Desires
> Could all or half fulfill –
> No threatened Hell, with quenchless fires
> Subdue this quenchless will!

Leavis reserves his highest praise for Hardy's 'After a Journey'. Its power and meaning are conveyed through specific fact and concrete circumstance. Its emotion is thereby held and controlled, and 'an essential effect of the poem is to constate, with a sharp and full realization, that we *cannot* go back in time' (pp. 252–3). The temptation to regress is overcome and the poet holds to life despite the terrible sense of loss (pp. 255–6). The general position advocated by Leavis in relation to Hardy closely resembles the one put by I. A. Richards in *Poetries and Sciences*; a firm grasp of the actual now includes a firm grasp of death:

[Hardy] is the poet who has most steadily refused to be comforted in an age in which the temptation to seek comfort has been greatest. The comfort of forgetfulness, the comfort of beliefs, he has put both of these away. Hence his singular preoccupation with death; because it is in the contemplation of death that the necessity for human attitudes to become self-supporting, in the face of an indifferent universe, is felt most poignantly. Only the greatest tragic poets have achieved an equally self-reliant and immitigable acceptance. (pp. 68–9)

Literary critics who subscribe to this stoic ethic have always had most difficulty with the romantic poets, tending either to reproach them for their regressive tendencies, or deny that they had them. Jean Hangstrum in *The Romantic Body* disputes the 'common illusion' that Keats had an instinct for, and an 'erotic attachment to non-being' which is glossed as 'that perverse type of feeling' associated with the 'infertile'. Indeed, 'Keatsean love did not drive inexorably toward death but toward life.' And Keats, 'in his last great poem ["To Autumn"], far from being in love with death, is amid growing tribulations invincibly in love with life' (pp. 67–9). By contrast Benjamin Kurtz declares that 'in Keats's poetry, though not in his life, the special stamina of the moral victory over "death" is lacking.' Unsurprisingly Kurtz finds this moral victory in the subject of his own critical study of Shelley, who, in the last five years of his life allegedly overcomes a self-indulgent romanticizing of death in favour of a threefold victory over it, moral, aesthetic and mystical (*The Pursuit of Death*, pp. 82, 209). Shelley's biographer, Richard Holmes, isn't so sure, and complains of *Adonais* that while the poem ostensibly celebrates the indestructible life of the creative spirit, 'its personal drive and its most intense images tend always towards consummation and death' (*Shelley: the Pursuit*, p. 657). The point here is that in one important respect Hangstrum and Kurtz (and probably Holmes) agree: if this attraction to death *is* present it severely damages a poet's claim to greatness. They thereby continue to censor and censure one of the most significant themes in western literature, and one which never goes away.[13] Keats's own lines are famous:

> for many a time
> I have been half in love with easeful Death
> . . .
> Now more than ever seems it rich to die,
> To cease upon the midnight with no pain.

Academics are anxious to reassure us that Keats's insertion of the word 'half' means this is not really the death wish. They overlook the more significant phrase which precedes it: 'many a time'. Here are more contemporary, less ambiguous lines: 'It seems kind of funny, it seems kind of sad / The dreams in which I'm dying are the best I've ever had' (Tears for Fears).

Beneath his increasingly reactionary confrontations with the modern, Leavis was trying to save literature for 'life'. On the question of contradiction in the creative process his opponents have rightly shown how productive it can be for the creative process. In relation to the other issues discussed here, Leavis's opponents have for the most part followed him, censoring or downgrading anything that remotely resembles the death wish, especially if it has an erotic component. Leavis is right to detect in Shelley, Tennyson and others a pain of loss strangely crossing with thwarted desire, a yearning for release, and an eroticism flirting in fantasy with death, or at least oblivion; an acute sense of loss which leads to a fantasized loss or dissolution of the self. Such desires have always been at odds with civilized endeavour, and as my readings have tried to suggest, they are inextricably fused with what they threaten. The articulation of such experience disturbed Leavis and he was not wrong to be disturbed. Leavis, like Nordau before him, wanted literature to be a robust ally of psychic, social and cultural health: 'Discrimination is life, indiscrimination is death'.[14] It was to his credit that he was explicit if dogmatic about this. While justly criticizing him for having a restricted sense of culture, we shouldn't lose sight of the fact that he and Nordau were right in realizing that culture has always survived and progressed through rigorous exclusions and repressions.

But Leavis was too intelligent, and too off-centre from the cultural establishment, to go along with those like Douglas, who said quite clearly that certain artists are dangerous because they see and say too much. Leavis reworked this view by liberalizing its terms somewhat. But his real achievement was to rehabilitate its ethical and political imperatives by giving them a quasi-vitalistic grounding. Leavis's great achievement was to enclose the ethical and political explicitness of those like Douglas in a vitalistic epistemology; instead of having to say that decadent artists see too much or too far, Leavis reconstituted the limited vision as a robust grasp of actuality. Thus a poet like Hardy is said to have 'a great advantage in *reality*', which translates as 'quiet presentment of specific fact and concrete circumstance' and corresponds to – almost guarantees – 'a profounder and completer sincerity' than other poets (in this case Emily Brontë – p. 252).

After Leavis, Wilbur Sanders spoke for a later generation of critics when he declared that the function of criticism is 'to stand for health in the broadest sense of that term'. In critical practice this means discriminating between the maturity, genius and imaginative power of Shakespeare on the one hand, and the merely neurotic intensity, perversity, and imaginative malfunction of someone like Christopher Marlowe on the other (*Dramatist*, p. 140–2). As with Leavis's assessment of the poets, it's the difference between, for example, tragedy and melodrama, mature emotion and hysteria, healthy sex and perverse sex. But I suggest, the most significant difference is the belief that unrestrained intelligence threatens mental health and social stability, a view by no means the province only of anti-intellectual philistines; in different ways it is also a recurring preoccupation of modern philosophy (e.g. Nietzsche) and modern literature (e.g. Thomas Mann), and one which the Anglo-American critical tradition has been unable to confront. After Leavis's death his ethical-epistemological aesthetic was pragmatically softened rather than abandoned. The day I write this a reviewer speaks of Thom Gunn's *The Man with Nightsweats* as one of the outstanding poetic volumes of the decade because 'elegiac, beautiful, rigorous and resolutely affirmative even in the face of grief'.[15] And if it were not resolutely affirmative even in the face of grief? The idea that literature in and of itself is life-enhancing has to be one of the most enduring delusions of humanist culture.

A more interesting instance of how the Leavisite commitment to art as the defender of psychic and social health survives, now aided very clearly by the aesthetic defence, is provided by Dennis Walder. In an engaging book on Ted Hughes, Walder argues that this poet gives us his own vision of 'what he perceives necessary for minimal human survival' in the modern world (back cover). To this end Walder points up the humanity of Hughes's verse whenever he can. Notoriously though, this poet's attitudes to violence and death conflict with that humanity. Finding some of these attitudes disturbing and reprehensible, Walder follows the familiar strategy of discrediting them. First as bad perception (incorrect history), second as expressions of the poet's apparent attraction to machismo (with just the hint of a hang-up), third, and most damningly, by designating as aesthetically inferior the poetry in which these attitudes occur. Once again the aesthetic defence of art becomes more accurately a defence against art. A case in point is 'A Motorbike', a poem about boredom and failure which confronted those who arrived home after the Second World War:

> The men surrendered their weapons
> And hung around limply.
> Peace took them all prisoner.
> They were herded into their home towns.

In such a life 'the morning bus was as bad as any labour truck' and 'the sameness of the next town / . . . as bad as electrified barbed wire / The shrunk-back war ached in their testicles.' A quiet young man buys a motorbike which has languished in the poet's family home throughout the war. Kicking it into life he comes alive too and,

> A week later, astride it, before dawn,
> A misty frosty morning,
> He escaped
>
> Into a telegraph pole
> On the long straight west of Swinton.

For Walder this is 'alarming' but 'unimpressive as a poem', and 'betrays the worst of Hughes' (*Ted Hughes*, pp. 41–2). For me it shows Hughes writing perceptively about the betrayal of men returning from war (an eternal verity if ever there was one); about how one of the many consequences of war experience is an even more intense sense of the boredom and built-in failures of routinized (civilized?) living; about a yearning for libidinal freedom at all costs, including at the risk of death, and the growing significance of the motorbike in relation to such yearning, and such risk, throughout the twentieth century. *Pace* Walder, 'He escaped / Into a telegraph pole' is compelling poetry, violently absurd, even blackly comic, in a way which doesn't undercut the romanticism so much as make it contemporary.

Leavis felt it necessary to strengthen his ethical humanism by injecting it with a dose of diluted vitalism, thereby suggesting its origins in the life force with which, in reality, it was in permanent tension. The truth is that the ethical order which we all live by and utterly depend upon, requires a repeated turning away from life's energies. A profound, as distinct from a facile, humanism knows this. The achievements of ethical humanists need no advocacy, unless it is to say that as art, they too can be self-challenging (rather than simply self confirming). In different though connected ways, a novel like George Eliot's *Middlemarch* (1871–2), a play like Arthur Miller's *Death of a Salesman* (1949), a film like *The Last Picture Show* (directed by Peter Bogdanovich, 1971) – to pick arbitrarily from three different genres – movingly explore the humanizing influence of the experience of loss, disappointment and failure; the humane necessity of submitting to limitation, ethics and law; maintaining personal integrity within a corrupt society; knowing how to love even or especially when it is not reciprocated. But humanism is most compelling when it honestly acknowledges the price, in terms of repression, renunciation and control, of adhering to humane values; when, in other words, it takes upon itself the responsibility for limiting human aspiration and acknowledging that humane values and human desire will always be in tormenting conflict.

There is a memorable picture of Leavis taken in June 1973.[16] Looking austerely fragile, still indomitable yet deeply exhausted, he recalls Mann's Aschenbach, burnt out by the unsustainable effort of speaking on behalf of civilization. Wrecked by discrimination.

9

Shakespeare at the Limits of Political Criticism

In recent decades so-called political criticism has been in dispute not just with the descendents of Leavis, but with most other kinds of traditional criticism and often some of the recent theoretical developments too, including postmodernism.[1] Political criticism does not align tidily with any of the diverse new critical movements but is more readily identified with some than others – with, for example, cultural materialism, feminism, gay studies, post-colonialist criticism.

It earns its name for several reasons: by insisting on regarding literature, especially the work of canonical figures like Shakespeare, as deeply political; by bringing to criticism an explicit social and political agenda of its own; by arguing that the idealist separation of art and politics rests on metaphysical ideas of transcendence and essentialist notions of an unchanging human nature which are contradicted by the historical realities which artists and audience alike actually live. It also attempts to recover for our understanding of art the historical conditions of its creation and interpretation, conditions which are invariably marked by conflicts and contradictions which the art work sometimes addresses, sometimes effaces, but never escapes. In relation to some kinds of literature – for example that of the English Renaissance – some political critics have gone further, finding in it a version of the dangerous knowledge which is my concern here: not just an ambivalent revealing expression of political anxieties, but a challenging insight into what was provoking anxiety in the larger culture (see Dollimore, *Radical Tragedy*, esp. Introduction to the Second Edition). And, along with that, an emerging sense of historical complexity and cultural contradiction. In relation to later periods it has identified in some kinds of art a realism which deliberately confronts the mystifications of authoritarian power.

I have been associated with political criticism and want to be, still. If it has sometimes advanced the above claims crudely, it has on other occasions done so with intelligence, insight and commitment. Undoubtedly it has helped liberate literature from the dreary pieties of some traditionalists, and in ways which were desperately needed. At its best political criticism has never succumbed to the self-serving fictions of wishful theory; it has always tried to make 'theory' – an umbrella term which, incidentally, has long outlived its usefulness – serve a historical perspective, and has tried to subject unhistorical theory to historical scrutiny.

Even so, political criticism has found new ways of taming the literature of the past – by, for instance, always having a historical explanation of it. Sometimes that historical explanation dovetails neatly into its own political perspective. And even when it does not, the entirely valid historical explanations can still neutralize the challenge of literature; it's as if, by restoring a work of literature to its appropriate conditions of production and reception we not only discredit anachronistic interpretations of it, but also foreclose on further thought about its challenge to us now. The injunction 'always historicize' has become a truly worthy one, so much so that the urge to disobey it is now irresistible, not least because of its a priori assumption that explanation via historical context is always possible. The idea that anything can be explained if a full enough historical context for it can be recovered, may become, paradoxically, a way of disengaging from the past. At its worst, political criticism has allowed some to read literature reductively or dismiss it altogether (as patriarchal, misogynist, homophobic, racist and more). Criticism of this kind encourages the reader to be just as defended against the challenge of literature as any traditionalist, although in a very different way. It too fails to recognize art as often – not invariably – a medium of dangerous knowledge. Or if it does see this, it forecloses on that recognition by designating the art in question as reactionary or obsolete: the product of social conditions which can and should be changed, or which already have been.

Political criticism recognizes the importance of fantasy in art, but defensively. The return of the repressed is a welcome topic for political critique when it is someone else's repression and not threatening to us. As Stephen Greenblatt notoriously and rightly said in another context – and he has been punished through repeated misrepresentation for doing so – 'There is no end of subversion, but not for us' ('Invisible Bullets', pp. 29, 45). It is here that the mind-set of political criticism can be at a considerable remove from the artistic one, and in being so is continuous with a wider difference between the artist and the philosopher (which is the subject of chapter 11).

With laudable political intent, and real insight into the ideological underpinning of supposedly natural and inevitable inequalities, political critics, like philosophers, rationalize reality. For instance, human violence is regarded not as the unavoidable manifestation of an innately violent human nature, but as the product of unjust social conditions: by altering these conditions we can control the violence. This works. Yet if doing that leads us to believe it is only a question of social conditions, we deceive ourselves. In the broadest sense, that belief derives from rationalist philosophy, even where it shares the modern political distrust of the rationalist tradition. In the sense that it believes the world, or at least society, to be in principle controllable, political criticism of literature has become more rationalist than its subject.

In this chapter, I argue, against traditionalists, that ethical distrust is a precondition for realizing the insights of Shakespeare. Against a reductive kind of political criticism I argue that, because their socio-political judgement of Shakespeare may foreclose on those same insights, it too is not to be trusted. I seek to rehabilitate for cultural criticism a way of reading which borrows freely from other perspectives, including intellectual history and Brechtian dramatic theory, in which keeping a distrustful distance is not only compatible with intellectual and aesthetic respect, but enabling of it.

Shakespeare: conservative, radical – or decadent?

In 1908 S. P. Sherman published an interesting but now hardly known article on the relative merits of Shakespeare and John Ford (1586 to c.1640). The comparison resembles that made by Bagehot between Dickens and Thackeray (see chapter 7, above). In 'Forde's Contribution to the Decadence of the Drama' Sherman conceived of decadence as a 'crumbling and dissolution of the established order' under the pressure of 'untrammeled desire' and deviant excess in all areas of life (p. xviii). Ford is a decadent because he is a romantic in revolt against the real world and 'subversive of the established order', especially conventional morality. In particular he abandons 'muscular and intellectual activities of the rugged and virile sort' in favour of the sentimental, the emotional, the effeminate and the sexual; he shifts attention from the council chamber and the battlefield to the boudoir. It is this which makes Ford relevant to the twentieth century: 'across the centuries Forde clasps hands with the most modern of the moderns.' Nowhere, says Sherman, is this more apparent than in his treatment of incest in *'Tis Pity She's a Whore* (pp. ix–xii).

Sherman, like Leavis, Douglas and many others in the last century, was influenced by ideas of degeneracy, especially the suspicion that someone like Ford is a degenerate not in spite of being a genius but because of it. He is one of the 'higher degenerates' mentioned in the last chapter. By contrast Shakespeare is a traditionalist:

> the very sanity of his genius limited its scope; whatever a wholesome mind may perceive, or a sound heart feel, came within the range of his observation and his sympathy. But beyond his boundaries lie the Bad Lands of human experience on which he seldom trespassed. (p. xiii)

Shakespeare was, furthermore, 'an ardent and headlong conventionalist. He stood, in the main, for the established order. His mind was very little touched with anarchy' and therefore able to avoid the 'fog-hung moral quicksands infesting modern decadent literature for this plain reason, that he sticks to the broad highways and the wellbeaten paths' (p. xiv). By not deviating from the straight and true, he avoids the perverse. But for Sherman there is another, related, reason for the decadence of the drama, namely 'the intellectualizing influence of the drama itself, the intense mental stimulus afforded by the production, in one little centre, year after year, of hundreds upon hundreds of plays.' Sherman also assumes, rightly, I believe, that the Elizabethan drama had an immense and direct influence upon the intellectual and moral ideas of the public. The audiences of these plays were enabled to live an imaginatively extended life which focused upon the undermining of the established order: princes deposed, power demystified, the strangeness of other cultures. The effect was something like 'cosmopolitanism, than which no more powerful dissolvent of standards has been discovered. . . . Familiarity with a variety of standards differing greatly and conflicting among themselves leads pretty surely to scepticism concerning the authority of any one standard.' The effect is anarchy – moral, political and religious, and Ford was one of its 'more thoughtful contributors' (pp. xvi–xvii).

It's usual to ridicule or ignore such views. But as we've already seen, Sherman's idea of the great artist as being on the side of spiritual, moral and social health, even at the expense of intellectual insight and/or a certain economy with the truth, was widely shared even if not explicitly acknowledged. Degenerate and decadent artists see too much, not too little. Sherman acknowledges what most later critics of his persuasion cannot, namely that the 'decadent' artist may have a deeper insight than his 'healthy' counterpart. And this becomes especially dangerous when, as with the early modern theatre, these views are being promulgated to the population at large. Sherman would probably have agreed with Keats's distinction: the decadent has the extended vision rather than the circumscribed grandeur of the conventionalist.

I believe Sherman to be wrong about Shakespeare, for reasons I'll come to, but in a sense right about Ford. In fact, what he says of Ford applies also to Shakespeare and numerous other writers.

For the most part the vision attributed to Shakespeare by Sherman, (and by Leavis and Sanders and many others for that matter), one which is mature, healthy and conflict-free, is a myth. In truth, Shakespeare could be as 'decadent' as Ford, but was rather more strategic with it. That's to say, he seemingly subscribed to the conventional order while simultaneously disrupting it. Shakespeare's apparently conventionalist political stance is repeatedly damaged by an 'irresponsible' imagination and intellect that animates its representation. As perversely curious as Ford, he was more cautious in its expression. Shakespeare was one of the most successful practitioners of something widespread in the Elizabethan and Jacobean theatre: a conformity to the letter of the law, precisely in order to express a corrosive intellectual curiosity about what compromises the spirit of the law. For example, the ending of an Elizabethan or Jacobean play is often didactic – the villains get their just deserts and some kind of conventional and/or providential moral order is vindicated. In the mid-twentieth century a generation of critics tried to convince themselves that this didactic denouement effectively discredits or at least neutralizes the subversive questioning and thought which preceded it. Unfortunately for them, from an intellectual and a theatrical perspective, the didactic denouement is not a closure of, but precisely the enabling precondition for, that questioning. It is enabling in that it subscribes to the law's letter in order to challenge its spirit: a conforming framework licences a subversive content. This was a strategy familiar not only in the theatre of this period, but for writers much more generally.[2]

Sometimes the subversive questioning was motivated by cautious and 'responsible' political or intellectual dissent. But it was also motivated by 'irresponsible' intellectual or erotic curiosity. Such curiosity is more than apparent in Shakespeare's comedies when theatrical convention (e.g., role-playing and disguise) gets cross-aligned with gender roles so as to suggest that the latter are equally conventional. At one level this is a very challenging thing to do, and critics have made much of it in recent years. But then, of course, at the end of the comedies everything gets put back in its natural place. Or does it? In fact, a delicate but far-reaching irony re-presents nature as itself an artifice; nature is wrapped up in and by the same formal ending which 'contains' the questioning: normality becomes a formality. But that doesn't make Shakespeare a gender radical; it is more likely that he is conveying a contemporary realization that orthodox gender divisions are conventional – they do not have the sanction of God or Nature – *and* an accompanying conviction that this is a very good reason why they should be protected, even, or especially, to the point of pretending they are natural. Such knowledge is ironically conservative rather than politically oppositional and aligns with the contemporary argument (via Machiavelli and others) that those in the know, which means those in charge, need to be accurately aware of the artificial basis of society in order to protect it most effectively.

And with that argument comes another, namely that it is more necessary than ever to inculcate upon the ruled the belief that the existing social order *is* the will of God and/or is natural. Successful conservative rule depends upon the ruled being mystified and the rulers not; in other words, the masses have to be God-fearing, the rulers closeted cultural materialists. Except, that is, in times of rapid social change, when over-passionate attachment to the mystifications on the part of the ruled may hinder their more 'enlightened' leaders from moving with the times. Then the ideal conservative becomes like the Victorian bishop's wife who, on hearing that Man might be descended from the apes declared: 'let us hope that it is not true; but that if it is, let us pray that it will not become generally known' (quoted in Shattuck, *Forbidden Knowledge*, p. 2).

One of the differences between this lady and Shakespeare would include the latter's ironic, flirtatious relationship with dangerous knowledges, his inability to resist making them, if not generally known, then half known. But never so far as to ferment social disruption. Thus Shakespeare on class: in plays like *Henry V* and *Coriolanus* it's clear that his knowledge of the social order as conventional rather than God-given generated a real sympathy for the oppressed *and* a horror and condemnation of insurrection. The two things go hand in hand: sympathy for the starving (it doesn't have to be this way) and fear of disorder (it could so easily happen) both derive from that realization of the contingent basis of social order. What strikes us now as hypocritical, then seemed politically sensible.

The artist and the malcontent

We can be fascinated by Shakespeare's powers of representation, his insight and intelligence, his articulation of social and psychological complexities – all this and much more – without necessarily trusting or revering him. After all, we can find contemporaries of his like Francis Bacon equally fascinating, and for not dissimilar reasons (and I for one definitely wouldn't have trusted him). We might go further: one good reason for not trusting Shakespeare ethically, even as we learn from his insights, is that he, like so many of his artistic contemporaries, resembles a figure in his plays and his society with whom he was greatly fascinated – with whom, perhaps, he identified: the malcontent. The malcontent is someone who is complicit with what he condemns: whose astute, disruptive insights into social corruption arise partly as a consequence of surrendering to it; whose fascination with evil is often veiled and sometimes intensified by the language of morality; whose satirical expressions of sexual disgust are animated by intense sexual fascination.

One of the most intriguing and enigmatic of all Jacobean malcontents is Shakespeare's Iago in *Othello*. As has been remarked before, Iago is a consummate artist in the way he destroys Othello by both deceiving him and playing upon his insecurities. These insecurities are by far the most important factor in his destruction and the deception could not work without them. One of the most compelling of all scenes in Shakespeare is that where Iago convinces Othello that his wife, Desdemona, has been unfaithful to him. As a result Othello kills her. He is black, she is white. Additionally he is older than her, and his cultural history is very different. Early on in the play, Desdemona's father, Brabanzio, is appalled when he discovers that she has secretly married Othello. He had been sufficiently impressed with Othello's military prowess and social prestige to invite him to his house. But for his daughter to marry such a man is terrifying beyond belief. He rages against and abuses Othello who, at that time, appears immune to his insults. But he has subconsciously registered them, and one in particular. Brabanzio says – and sincerely believes – that the union between his daughter and Othello is deeply unnatural; for her to so 'err / Against all rules of nature', she must have been seduced with potions; only then could she have been persuaded to desire what she 'feared to look on!' (I.iii.98–101). Later, in the pivotal scene just alluded to, Iago undermines Othello's confidence. He knows that if he can break through Othello's defences, deep social and psychological insecurities will erupt as sexual jealousy, with devastating consequences. Othello, increasingly paranoid, finds himself recalling Brabanzio's remarks. As he does so, Iago pounces:

OTHELLO: And yet how nature, erring from itself –

IAGO: Ay, there's the point; as, to be bold with you,
         Not to affect many proposèd matches
         Of her own clime, complexion, and degree,
         Whereto we see in all things nature tends.
         Foh! one may smell, in such, a will most rank,
         Foul disproportion, thoughts unnatural!
                                    (III.iii.232ff)

The economy of these lines is extraordinary. If poetry is, in essence, language at its most powerfully concentrated, this is pure poetry. It is also pure evil of a remarkably modern kind: here in just a few lines racism, xenophobia and misogyny are imaginatively fused. Some would say that these terms – 'racism, xenophobia and misogyny' – are the ugly, anachronistic currency of political criticism. But they are also things manifestly there in Shakespeare's text and his culture. Iago is saying that for a woman like Desdemona to spurn the advances of men of her own country (clime), colour and race (complexion) and class (degree) in favour of one who is none of these things, is unnatural. A misogynistic conception of the woman is continuous with a racist and xenophobic view about who she should 'naturally' desire. And somewhere inside himself, Othello agrees. And he does so because he has come to identify unconditionally with the society he serves.

Racism, xenophobia and misogyny: the tragedy of Othello is steeped in these things. If it were established that they are precisely *not* transcended in this play, and that the deaths of Desdemona and Othello are inextricably bound up with them, the idealist critic would find this aesthetically regrettable and probably sufficient to disqualify it from being of the greatest tragic power. To a political critic on the other hand the tragedy is the greater for their not being transcended, and their full extent remorselessly exposed. Such a critic might then contain his own insight by believing that the racism is entirely down to Iago. In fact, Desdemona's desire for Othello, and his for her, are both inflected with racial idealizations. Each romanticizes the difference of the other by way of escaping the limitations of their own lives. We can reprove them if we like; alternatively we realize again that desire is an effect, as well as a refusal of its own history.

Only a very intelligent and highly imaginative writer could articulate the fusion of racism, xenophobia and misogyny with such economy and in such psychically plausible terms. For Othello and Iago, though differently, those terms are sexual. Both experience sexual disgust, underpinned by racial and/or social insecurity, manifested as sexual jealousy. Additionally Iago can't help imagining the sexual union of Othello and Desdemona, even while he's disgusted by it. Desire and revulsion: both are there, each feeding the other. That is one of the things which gives this scene its intensity. The disgust is concentrated in the multiple meanings of 'will' – which could mean volition, sexual desire and sexual organs – and 'rank' – which could mean lust, swollen, smelling, corrupt, foul: 'one may smell, in such, a will most rank.' Such words make for an imagery which is intensely voyeuristic even as it is so dense as to be beyond visual realization. Compressed in the next line is a pornographic fantasy of 'Foul disproportion': the monstrously phallic black man violating the white woman. Again there is an allusion here to Iago's earlier taunt: 'an old black ram / Is tupping your white Ewe' (I.i.88–9). If Shakespeare dramatizes a pornographic imagination through Iago, it is also as dramatist that he reveals how central is that imagination to a certain kind of ambivalent racism in which disgust and desire escalate dialectically. Sexual disgust is central, not only to this play, but others by Shakespeare: *Hamlet* and *King Lear* being the most obvious. It has led some to attribute to Shakespeare a lurking psycho-sexual neurosis. Call it what one will, its experience and articulation here is devastatingly insightful for that sexually charged racism violently triangulated between the black man the white man and the white woman, and which will become increasingly widespread in later centuries (see David Marriot, *On Black Men*). The lynched, castrated black man is prefigured here, in this scene from Othello. Might it be that this 'neurosis' of Shakespeare's, rather than an unfortunate character weakness essentially irrelevant to his creative insights is, in fact, central to them?

One kind of political critic is inclined to say that Shakespeare is complicit with the racism of *Othello*, another that Shakespeare is clearly repudiating the racism he represents. Either view is too comfortable, and each ignores the element of fantasy in this scene. It seems bizarre to think of a play, performed on a stage, as a sexual fantasy: the one is overtly public, the other essentially private. But the language of the play at this point is steeped in fantasy. And anyway, fantasies, like plays, are typically visualized; they are enacted in a scene. Here the scene is what Iago/Shakespeare imagines. Fantasies of the kind being expressed here are not for-or-against attitudes, and nor are they free-reigning expressions of desire; rather they are wish-fulfilments struggling to escape frustration, disturbance and ambivalence. In relation to Iago/Shakespeare, we might say, following Stallybrass and White, that disgust bears the imprint of disturbed desire (see chapter 4). If it is disgust which licenses him to imagine – to 'smell' – the scene of sex between Othello and Desdemona, it is frustrated identification with that scene which leads him to demonize both Othello and Desdemona, and get him to kill her.

10

The Aesthetic Attraction
of Fascism

The wished-for separation of literature from politics is strong in literary criticism, and never more so than around canonical figures like Shakespeare. However, beyond Shakespeare studies if not beyond English studies, there was always a more powerful account of how art and politics connect, one based not upon their ultimate separation, but, on the contrary, their fusion in the form of a radical aestheticizing of the political. Some postmodernists have flirted with this attitude, but its most significant historical moment was in the last century, in the context of fascism. This aesthetic was most seductively evolved by Nietzsche, and then by Futurists like Filippo Marinetti, and proved irresistible for modernists like Lawrence, Yeats and others.[1]

Interest in the aesthetic dimension of fascism has been considerable and continues to grow.[2] Writing in 1936 Walter Benjamin made some remarks on the subject which eventually inspired more sustained study.[3] The importance of recent studies like David Carroll's is to show how aspects of fascism are logical if extreme developments of aesthetic concepts. In the case of the fascist writers and intellectuals Carroll studies, their aesthetic sensibilities, far from saving them from fascist dogma, led them to identify with it. Carroll's study surely vindicates his claim that the notion 'that art and literature are in themselves opposed to political dogmatism and racial biases and hatred, constitutes nothing less than a mystification of art and literature as well as of the artist and writer' (*French Literary Fascism*, pp. 7–8). So maybe it is time to forget the idealist critic with those genteel universal values and equally genteel essentialist human subject: it's the aestheticizing of politics, rather than the aesthetic escape from them, that constitutes the greater challenge.

What I've elsewhere called an aesthetics of energy figures in fascism, futurism, and strands of modernism, but is not to be exclusively identified with any of them. It is a complex sensibility with a wide appeal.[4] In *The Birth of Tragedy* (1872) Nietzsche suggests that existence can only be justified in aesthetic terms, as exemplified by a creator whom he imagines as 'the supreme artist, amoral, recklessly creating and destroying, realizing himself indifferently in whatever he does or undoes, ridding himself by his acts of the embarrassment of his riches and the strain of his internal contradictions' (*Birth*, p. 9). The cost in suffering of such violent self-realization is necessarily considerable, but justified by the beauty, purity and power of its expression. Liberation is found not in the immorality of evil but in the vitality of amorality and the exhilarating inhumanity of beauty. This is Lawrence in 1926, in *The Plumed Serpent*, as it were 'humanizing' Nietzsche's fantasy of recklessly creating and destroying: 'what do I care if he kills people? His flame is young and clean' (p. 354). Thus, though only in part, the erotics of Lawrence's notorious blood consciousness. In the novel this is the thought of the main female character. Without claiming that women are incapable of this kind of attitude, I would suggest that this is another instance in Lawrence of what I alluded to earlier: a thwarted homoerotic perception 'liberated' through identification with the woman's position.

In Yeats too the aesthetics of energy are a fantasy resolution of the experience of thwarted energies. Many a critic has avowed that Yeats's politics are irrelevant to an appreciation of his verse. But common sense, if not critical consensus, is surely on the side of those like George Orwell who concluded his 1943 essay on Yeats with the remark that this poet found his way to fascism via the aristocratic route. He adds that the attraction of fascism for the literary intelligentsia was something badly in need of investigation, not least because 'a writer's political and religious beliefs are not excrescences to be laughed away, but something that will leave their mark even on the smallest detail of their work' (*Collected Essays*, p. 201). It was another twenty-two years before Yeats was given the kind of reading which Orwell advocated. In a major essay Conor Cruise O'Brien argued that Yeats's politics deserved to be taken more seriously than they had been previously, and were, in his maturity and old age, 'generally pro-Fascist in tendency, and Fascist in practice on the single occasion when opportunity arose'.[5] O' Brien then puts the question so often evaded by professional literary critics: how is it that those like himself who loathe such politics, can 'continue not merely to admire but to love the poetry, and perhaps most of all the

poems with a political bearing?' In trying to answer that question
O'Brien cites Yeats's own note to 'Leda and the Swan' (1923):

> I wrote 'Leda and the Swan' because the editor of a political review
> asked me for a poem. I thought 'After the individualist, demagogic
> movement founded by Hobbes and popularized by the Encyclopaedists
> and the French revolution, we have a soil so exhausted that it cannot
> grow that crop again for centuries'. Then I thought 'Nothing is now
> possible but some movement from above preceded by some violent
> annunciation'. My fancy began to play with Leda and the Swan for
> metaphor and I began this poem; but as I wrote, bird and lady took
> such possession of the scene that all politics went out of it, and my
> friend tells me that his 'conservative readers would misunderstand the
> poem'. (A. Norman Jeffares, *A Commentary on the Collected Poems
> of W. B. Yeats*, p. 296)

O'Brien seeks to answer his first question by asking another of this
passage: 'how can that patter of Mussolini prose "produce" such a
poem? How can that political ugly duckling be turned into this
glorious Swan?' His answer is not that the connection between the
political prose and the poetry is irrelevant, but that both are 'cognate
expressions of a fundamental force, anterior to both politics and
poetry'. That fundamental force is Yeats's profound and tragic
awareness of the violence at work in Europe and which was to
culminate in Hitler and the Second World War ('Passion and Cunning', pp. 273–5). In support of this claim O'Brien compares Leda
with the famous lines from another Yeats poem, 'The Second Coming', written three years earlier:

> Things fall apart; the centre cannot hold;
> Mere anarchy is loosed upon the world,
> The blood-dimmed tide is loosed . . .
> . . .
> And what rough beast, its hour come round at last,
> Slouches towards Bethlehem to be born?

Whereas the mundane politician in Yeats settles for fascism, the poet
in him, free of such 'calculated practical deductions', achieves a
'purity and integrity' of insight into the tragic reality sweeping
Europe – 'of what is actually happening and even, in a broad sense,
what is about to happen' (p. 278). The poem was written in 1923;
Yeats died in 1939. For O'Brien then, 'Leda and the Swan' is a
quintessential expression of this profound poetic/historical vision.

If, as I want to suggest, O'Brien's attempt to answer his own two questions falters and slides towards some of the same evasions as those he criticizes, this is surely a measure of the extent of the problem rather than a failure of nerve on his part. O'Brien is right in thinking that the poem escapes immediate political concerns. Yeats, in his note, says as much: 'all politics went out of it'. Any thought of pleasing the conservative readers or the editor of that political review disappears in the creative articulation of something more profound. But I disagree with the claim that the poet transcends the political. Rather, it is when the poet is free from politics in the narrow sense that he can be most effective in articulating some of the deeper fantasies which drive those like him to certain political identifications and affiliations. That, I believe, is what is happening here: 'Leda and the Swan' is an extraordinary fantasy articulation of the aesthetics of energy. Far from being an imaginative warning against violence, this poem is a seductive aestheticizing of it. To grant it that kind of effect isn't, as the idealist would claim, to desecrate poetic language, but to take it more seriously than the idealist ever could. Here is the poem:

> A sudden blow: the great wings beating still
> Above the staggering girl, her thighs caressed
> By the dark webs, her nape caught in his bill,
> He holds her helpless breast upon his breast.
>
> How can those terrified vague fingers push
> The feathered glory from her loosening thighs?
> And how can body, laid in that white rush,
> But feel the strange heart beating where it lies?
>
> A shudder in the loins engenders there
> The broken wall, the burning roof and tower
> And Agamemnon dead.
>
>   Being so caught up,
> So mastered by the brute blood of the air,
> Did she put on his knowledge with his power
> Before the indifferent beak could let her drop?

Against O'Brien's wish to see this poem as an intimation from Yeats's better poetic self of the terrible political realities beleaguering contemporary Europe, a more recent kind of political critic would now dismiss it as a hateful, fascistic rape fantasy. Both responses are evasions of the challenge which this poem poses, but the second is nearer the truth. And, in truth, political critics are no longer in the business of quick, reductive and judgemental dismissal, being more often than not ready to execute a careful historical critique. Even so, no matter how responsible it is, this very commitment to historicizing keeps the poem at a distance, and with it the kind of challenge it has. What is that challenge?

The poem re-enacts the myth of Leda being raped, by Zeus disguised in the form of a swan. The violence is as much in the detail of the fantasy as in its substance; I'm referring to the fact that the girl is imagined to half respond:

> How can those terrified vague fingers push
> The feathered glory from her loosening thighs?
> And how can body, laid in that white rush,
> But feel the strange heart beating where it lies?

She submits to the coercions of a creature whose beauty and potency are, in both senses of the word, *irresistible*; this conflation of the two senses – unable, and not wanting to, resist – being also an aspect of fascist fantasy. It is a beauty instinct with sexual potency, amoral omnipotence and sheer physical power. Again, the detail is crucial: hovering, it yet has strength to spare to stagger the girl into submission; in other words its beauty is an effect not just of power, but of *effortless* power:

> A sudden blow: the great wings beating still
> Above the staggering girl, her thighs caressed
> By the dark webs, her nape caught in his bill,
> He holds her helpless breast upon his breast.

Recall that O'Brien, in arguing that Yeats the poet is offering a tragic metaphor for the violence and irrationality sweeping Europe, makes a comparison with 'The Second Coming'. But recall too that the swan in this poem could not be more removed from the slouching rough beast of that other poem.

The third stanza of 'Leda' suggests that, because history begins in this act of sexual aggression, it can only unfold as a 'heroic' repetition of the 'beautiful' violence of its conception. Further, in these remarkable lines, history is 'seen' omnisciently; as if from a vast height and distance, its temporal sweep is telescoped into the definitive moment and resonant image, the metaphoric distillation of the idea of history being generated in the moment of climax:

> A shudder in the loins engenders there
> The broken wall, the burning roof and tower
> And Agamemnon dead.

There could hardly be a more extreme fantasy of potency than when a single orgasm engenders an entire violent sweep of history with its own final death. Never before has the 'little death' so momentously prefigured the larger. The poem ends with another question:

> Being so caught up,
> So mastered by the brute blood of the air,
> Did she put on his knowledge with his power
> Before the indifferent beak could let her drop?

Yet another creation myth: history 'begins' in an act of sexual violence, of rape. Zeus inseminates Leda with his 'power' but not his 'knowledge'; in effect the race is abandoned in its inception, dropped by the 'indifferent' god, incompletely created. And so history is tragic: that is, heroic yet always inherently self-defeating, expressing divine power devoid of divine knowledge. Perhaps that is what it means to be half-divine: condemned to heroic defeat. But if Yeats is here interpreting an ancient myth to explain human suffering, he is also, from the position of post-creation limitation, identifying with a full pre-creation omnipotence.

This poem about Zeus disguised as a swan is a poetic articulation of Nietzsche's fantasy about the creator cited earlier.[6] It is worth repeating since in the context of Yeats's poem, it comes to seem even more distinctly sexual:

> the supreme artist, amoral, recklessly creating and destroying, realizing himself *indifferently* in whatever he does or undoes, ridding himself by his acts of the embarrassment of his riches and the strain of his internal contradictions. (*The Birth of Tragedy*, p. 9, my emphasis)

The challenge of 'Leda and the Swan' is that it allows us to understand a fascist fantasy. Drawing on myth and allegory helps Yeats to sanction what is at heart an adoration of beauty and potency arising from a deep frustration. In 1937, in 'A General Introduction for my Work', Yeats gives a 'political' expression of that frustration. Its focus is the ugly incoherence, anarchy and dissymmetry of the modern world:

> When I stand upon O'Connell Bridge in the half-light and notice that discordant architecture, all those electric signs, where modern hetero-

geneity has taken physical form, a vague hatred comes up out of my own dark and I am certain that wherever in Europe there are minds strong enough to lead others the same vague hatred rises; in four or five or in less generations this hatred will have issued in violence and imposed some kind of rule of kindred. I cannot know the nature of that rule, for its opposite fills the light; all I can do to bring it nearer is to intensify my hatred. (*Essays and Introductions*, p. 526)

'A vague hatred come up out of my own dark . . .' Though it includes it, the frustration of which I am speaking goes much deeper than the political, and it requires much more than a political consciousness to articulate it. Perhaps only the 'poetic' voice can express it; if so I am partly in agreement with the idealist critic. Where we differ is in our sense of the range of that voice. Here, it expresses the frustration at the heart of a certain kind of fascist sensibility. When Yeats the poet is, in his own estimate, least interested in politics in the narrow sense, he is articulating most powerfully a sensibility animating politics in a deeper sense. It is fundamentally a desire which dreams of mastery:

> A bloody, arrogant power
> Rose out of the race
> Uttering, mastering it
> ('Blood and the Moon', 1927)

But this is a sensibility in which an urgent desire to control derives from intense frustration. It is shadowed by an equally powerful wish to submit. Peter Nicholls argues that a strong emphasis on mastery enabled certain modernists to reject the way their 'decadent' precursors were preoccupied with weakness, impotence and masochistic desire, and to an extent 'which barely concealed a death-drive within the aesthetic itself'.[7] What makes Yeats especially interesting in this respect is that his sadistic mastery remains shadowed by masochism. Thus the poetic voice in 'Leda' makes a double identification, with the swan and the girl; it identifies with mastery, omnipotence and omniscience, but also yearns to submit to them, not least perhaps because it is from that position that heroism and tragedy, the more viable options for human frustration, are created. To fail is one thing; to fail heroically half redeems failure.[8] The poetic voice of this poem fantasizes, in the swan, an erotic beauty whose attributes include amorality, potency, indifference – a kind of highly exalted, seriously straight, rough trade. But, just as they can be both masochistic and sadistic, so the aesthetics of energy can be heterosexual or homoerotic, or both at once. Certainly the gender coordinates of this aesthetic are not straightforward, as can be seen from one of Yeats's earlier poems, 'No Second Troy' (1908). Here the Nietzschean superman becomes a woman, before whom the male poet prostrates himself abjectly, reminding us again that, with due respect to a new orthodoxy of gender politics, the so-called 'mobile subject' is not necessarily a progressive one. The focus of this remarkable poem is Maud Gonne, a woman for whom Yeats experienced an intense, unrequited passion:

> Why should I blame her that she filled my days
> With misery, or that she would of late
> Have taught to ignorant men most violent ways,
> Or hurled the little streets upon the great,
> Had they but courage equal to desire?
> What could have made her peaceful with a mind
> That nobleness made simple as a fire,
> With beauty like a tightened bow, a kind
> That is not natural in an age like this,
> Being high and solitary and most stern?
> Why, what could she have done, being what she is?
> Was there another Troy for her to burn?

Again the aesthetics of energy are celebrated, not just energy itself but its formal, tensioned beauty: 'beauty like a tightened bow',[9] to which our appropriate attitude is submissive, admiring, even abject. But once again the poet is on both sides at once: he is speaking from the position of adoring submission to potency, but still identifying with that power through his own mastery of the language which expresses it; he achieves potency himself not by embodying or even appropriating it, but through its articulation at a remove.

To lead a lesser humanity into violent engagement – 'had they but courage equal to desire' – is the *raison d'être* of this kind of being; it is what they were made for, again recalling Nietzsche's 'God', recklessly expending himself regardless of the cost. Yeats would remark later, again following Nietzsche, that heroism negates morality as conventionally understood: 'People much occupied with morality always lose heroic ecstasy' (*Letters*, p. 836). There is passing scorn for the inferior classes who desire beyond their courage; and yet isn't inferiority what the speaker himself feels in relation to the female subject of this poem, and if so, isn't this charge of cowardice also a displacement of his own felt inadequacy? Another aspect of fascism: the identification with potency is also a revenge on those too close to, too like, the self in all its impotence.

At the time 'No Second Troy' was written, Maud Gonne was engaged in a violent anti-colonial struggle, though you would hardly know it from the poem. Yeats is interested in a kind of purified, 'disinterested' violence, unsullied by political – that's to say, human – concern. In this poem the actual anti-colonial struggles of Ireland are important only as a platform for the same link between amoral beauty and erotic violence as in 'Leda'. The aesthetics of energy typically invite this fantasy purification and erasure of history in a way which tends to feed directly into nationalism and racism. Beauty is as much about an abstract sense of purity as actual embodiment. And the obverse of this desire for purity – is disgust. Again, Nietzsche is the influential antecedent. He tells us in *Ecce Homo* that he can '*smell*' the ' "entrails" of every soul . . . all the *concealed* dirt at the bottom of many a nature. . . . *Disgust* at mankind, at the "rabble", has always been my greatest danger' (pp. 18–19).

From his various pronouncements, Yeats apparently believed violence was not just inevitable in historical progress, but, as for Nietzsche, a purifying force to be positively encouraged; that way we release the vital principle of history. The squalid masses, full of ignorance and cowardly desire, really should exist only for Helen to burn – except she can't, because one thing these degenerate modern democracies suppress is the heroic impulse to go around destroying whole cultures and cities in the name of heroic 'power'. Yeats was of course proved wrong by the fascism he once admired.

Nietzsche thought western culture had been corrupted by the fear of the primal power which this poem celebrates, and in particular a fear of the radical impermanence which is its essence. That is why philosophers and theologians, in labouring for the knowledge of how to escape impermanence, have turned us away from life itself, towards the eternal. Yeats was influenced by Nietzsche in this as in other respects, but in another poem written four years later, 'Sailing to Byzantium', he seemingly empathizes with the very philosophers Nietzsche repudiated:

> That is no country for old men. The young
> In one another's arms, birds in the trees
> – Those dying generations – at their song,
> The salmon-falls, the mackerel-crowded seas,
> Fish, flesh, or fowl, commend all summer long
> Whatever is begotten, born, and dies.

Turning away from this mutable world, the poet yearns for its opposite:

> Consume my heart away; sick with desire
> And fastened to a dying animal

> It knows not what it is; and gather me
> Into the artifice of eternity.

So we should say that Yeats as poet identifies with the religious desire for eternity as well as the aesthetics of energy. But that is my point: the poet here speaks with a deep sense of failing power – 'An aged man is a paltry thing' – and as one who is still 'Sick with desire'. It is the alternative expression of that same frustration – a frustration so deep it may lead us to embrace either renunciation – the stasis of eternity; or the fantasy of libidinal freedom in conquest – the aesthetics of energy. Yeats as poet reveals how frustrated desire knows the attractions of both renunciation and conquest rather than one or the other, and he does so because they are neither opposites nor alternatives.

In Yeats's earlier verse frustration had tended towards erotic dissipation; it was, as it were, the poetry of entropy rather than energy, even when energy and desire are its explicit subjects. A case in point is 'He Bids His Beloved Be at Peace', written in 1895, and, incidentally, a fine example of the enervated aestheticism Nordau, Nietzsche and Leavis regarded as decadent. It enacts an imaginative reduction of frustrated desire – 'endless Desire' – to a tolerable mood of erotic ennui. That is less remarkable than how, in the process, it manages to do the same to the object of desire. In this mood there is little difference between desire and object. In a kind of passive aggression, the object of desire is reduced to fit the onanistic mood; a painful reality is filtered, dissolved and attenuated until it can be accommodated to that mood. Energy, power, yearning are blanketed and muffled in the poetics of entropy:

> O vanity of Sleep, Hope, Dream, endless Desire,
> The Horses of Disaster plunge in the heavy clay:
> Beloved let your eyes half close, and your heart beat
> Over my heart, and your hair fall over my breast,
> Drowning love's lonely hour in deep twilight of rest,

The death wish haunts such eroticism, as is clear from another poem by Yeats, 'The Travail of Passion':

> We will bend down and loosen our hair over you,
> That it may drop faint perfume, and be heavy with dew,
> Lilies of death-pale hope, roses of passionate dream.[10]

Nietzsche regards the death wish of Christianity as rooted in a morality which was anti-life, not least because it involved 'a fear of beauty and sensuality' (*Birth of Tragedy*, p. 11). Reading Yeats we realize that it is not just morality which is allied to death, but beauty too.

Yeats would react strongly against the erotic enervation of his own 'decadent' poetics in favour of the aesthetics of energy. An argument of Leo Bersani's in relation to Freud is also suggestive about this change. Bersani contends that Freud's most original speculative move was to regard:

> sexual excitement as both a turning away from others and a dying to the self. The appeal of that dying – the desire to be shattered out of coherence – is perhaps what psychoanalysis has most urgently sought to repress. But the compulsion to eliminate from life the incomparable pleasure of dying has led to the infinitely more dangerous idealizing of that pleasure as moral masochism. (*The Culture of Redemption*, p. 45)

'He Bids His Beloved Be at Peace', like other so-called decadent verse of the 1890s, seems to me to contain elements of both the stages Bersani describes. That is to say, this poem expresses, somewhat preciously, an experience of sexual excitement as a dying to others and to the self, but in a form whereby it is already implicated in the moral masochism which, in Bersani's schema, should arise only with the repression of such experience. The 'incomparable pleasure of dying' and moral masochism are not different states, the one pre- and the other post-repression, but inextricable aspects of a single state. Correspondingly, when Yeats embraces the aesthetics of energy, believing now it is imperative not to 'sink unmanned / Into the half-deceit of some intoxicant/From shallow wits' ('Nineteen Hundred and Nineteen') it is not the straightforward shift into mastery which the new dislike of being 'unmanned' might imply. In that he reveals, wittingly or otherwise, how masochism haunts the desire for mastery, Yeats is a greater not a lesser poet. His wanting to be involved in a poetic movement towards 'something steel-like and cold within the will, something passionate and cold' (*Letters*, pp. 836–7) expresses not a leaving behind of the experience of thwarted energies, but a sublimation of it into something more aggressive, something indeed steel-like and cold within the will; that's to say, something pressured by renunciation and compensatory fantasies of mastery. In Yeats we discern again how the lifting of repression is always partial: what is 'freed' remains ineradicably marked by the cultural history of its repression.

Consider, finally, some comparisons with 'Leda'. First Gerard Manley Hopkins's 'The Windhover: to Christ our Lord', in which the exhilarating poetic enactment of a kestrel in flight becomes a very different occasion for the aesthetics of energy. If there is the same libidinal identification, it is only half admitted. But still, in Hopkins's own word, it is 'dangerous' (l. 11); sure it's all for Jesus, but the poet's yearning toward the 'Brute beauty and valor and act' (l. 9) of this creature is not so far from the erotic, liberatory amorality of Nietzsche, Yeats or Lawrence:

> My heart in hiding
> Stirred for a bird, – the achieve, of, the mastery of the thing!

Or, later, of Ted Hughes, one of the greatest aesthetes of energy. Hughes' apparent amoral acceptance, if not immoral celebration, of 'violence' (it's hardly the right word) has been a point of contention among his readers. The destructive forces which Hughes depicts in breathtaking visual realizations of the natural world is at one level an attempt to disclose that reality which the humane necessarily represses, namely a life force indifferent to life itself. But it is complicated by a projection onto nature of a specifically human violence deriving in part from that first-order repression. Consider Hughes's 'Hawk in the Rain', a poem which bears more than passing resemblance to Yeats's 'Leda' and Hopkins's 'Windhover'. It begins with the poet struggling through the mud of ploughed fields, winter mud which feels like the primal 'mire' of the last line, resisting every step, sapping his energy and dragging him down into its own indistinction. The elements too relentlessly, indifferently wear him to death: 'banging wind kills these stubborn hedges, / . . . . / Thumbs my eyes, throws my breath, tackles my heart, / And rain hacks my head to the bone.' It is the futile struggle against the inevitable elemental reduction to the primal 'mire': 'I drown in the drumming ploughland, I drag up / Heel after heel from the swallowing of the earth's mouth.' In contrast to his own frustrated, death-haunted physical struggle, the hawk

> Effortlessly at height hangs his still eye.
> His wings hold all creation in a weightless quiet.

The poet makes a futile attempt to identify with the potency of the bird: 'I . . . / . . . strain towards the master- / Fulcrum of violence where the hawk hangs still', only to then make another identification, now with the elements, by imagining the hawk's own eventual ruin, hurled to the ground by the same wind it now masters: 'the round angelic eye / Smashed, mix his heart's blood with the mire of the land.' There is a distinctively human vengeance here. If the potency of the bird cannot be reached let alone shared, its death can at least be imagined, and in a way which enables the poet momentarily to shift from being death's victim to its aide, signalled by the impotent, angry imperative ('mix'). Perhaps too this is a failed vengeance, even in imagination, since hawks, while alive, don't misjudge the wind.

11

Desire: Art against Philosophy?

Earlier I invoked, against the safe radicalism of the new bisexual politics, the susceptibility of all to the experience of being wrecked by desire. This hardly needs saying, not least because literature and philosophy, even back to the beginnings of recorded culture, have been telling us as much, time and again. But they do so rather differently: if in literature the seductions of desire prove most compelling, in philosophy, at least up until the last century, it is the warning against desire.

It has been said often enough that we would never fall in love if we had not first learned the language of love. Literature, along with some other arts, notably film, are places where we learn this language, and thereby may earnestly desire to be in the position of the lover and/or the beloved, whatever the cost. For some at least, there is something risky in even reading about, and watching, lovers. The question is: Who is at risk, and who decides that they are? Women and children, servants and the lower orders generally have usually been thought to be most at risk. Thus the poet Robert Montgomery, in 'On the Effects of Indiscriminate Novel Reading':

> E'en sluttish housemaids crib a farthing light,
> To whimper o'er the novel's page by night;
> And then, like heroines, scorning to be wed,
> Next night make John the hero of their bed.[1]

Accounts of women's reading have variously identified it as an addiction resulting in insanity, unchastity and family breakdown. The novel especially has been suspect, as Jacqueline Pearson and others have shown.² Because here, just as in the censorship trials described earlier, such views are rife with sexual, class and every other kind of prejudice, it is easy to dismiss them as that alone. In fact, as political critics have shown, they are more accurately regarded as a displacement and refocusing of wider cultural, economic and sexual fears in terms of reading and female transgression. And, as feminist writers have shown, such displacement makes art a place of potential contest and dangerous knowledge. Madame Bovary is one of literature's most famously 'immoral' lovers. When Flaubert made her an avid reader of romance literature, he may not himself have been free of prejudice, but that did not preclude insight into the relationship between reading, imagination and transgressive desire – for her, him and his readers.

Madame Bovary is also one of literature's many suicidal sacrifices to desire. Georges Minois has written a short history of suicide – or what, until around 1700, was called self-murder – in western culture. The overall story he tells is familiar: a gradual if uneven movement from unequivocal condemnation to greater tolerance. Throughout, Church and State have condemned it as severely as was possible at the time. One wonders incidentally whether this is despite or because of the fact that religion itself articulates profound suicidal tendencies. Minois explores these tendencies in the seventeenth-century spiritual texts where the thirst for the annihilation of the self is vividly apparent. In contrast to the spokesmen for Church and State, philosophers have been more tolerant, and in the vanguard of demystifying and helping to decriminalize suicide by arguing that it is not evil, against nature, a denial of God's providence, or whatever. The rational deliberations of the philosopher confirm what the distressed have always known in their pain: suicide is an attractive option when things get very bad. That said, most philosophers have been on the side of life, not so much advocating suicide, as cautiously acknowledging it as a regrettable last resort.

It is in literature that dissident and transgressive attitudes to suicide are most fully explored. This is consistently so across the period that Minois mainly addresses, from the sixteenth to the eighteenth centuries. This is especially significant given the emphatic condemnation and criminalization of it by the dominant culture throughout this period. Minois offers the safety-valve explanation: literary suicide is a 'symbolic liberation for a troubled society'; literature plays 'a therepeutic role by helping a troubled generation get through difficult times and by limiting the number of real suicides'. One suspects though that it invites a more anti-social involvement than this allows, particularly since more often than not literature generates sympathy for, and even glorifies suicide. In the English drama between 1580 and 1640 we find more than 200 suicides in around 100 plays; Shakespeare has no less than 52. And, as Minois himself remarks, 'characters in eighteenth-century literature kill themselves by the hundreds with not a word of authorial reproach.' Goethe's *The Sorrows of Young Werther* is only one of the most notorious instances of those works which 'inspired' actual suicides. The book was banned in some areas and denounced by many. Towards the end of his life, when the Bishop of Derby reproached him for writing a work of such devastating influence, Goethe apparently replied that politicians send millions of men to their deaths with a clear conscience (Minois, pp. 110–11, 223, 268).

For Church and State, theologians, and most other hacks on the side of authority, the official cause of suicide was despair generated by the active intervention of the devil; it was a diabolic act. So perhaps the main interest of John Donne's *Biathanatos* (written around 1610, published 1647), is not its tortuous rehabilitation of suicide, but the fact that he arrives at his conclusions through recourse to Christian theology rather than the example of the ancients. By implying that the death of Christ was one of the noblest suicides, Donne commits a daring blasphemy; the kind that could only come from someone whose theological and philosophical concerns are supplemented by aesthetic ones, including (as Donne's verse clearly shows) the seductions of death, melancholy and masochistic sacrifice. Minois observes a situation which remains unchanged today: we admire suicides in literature, while at the same time regretting the increasing numbers of ordinary suicides whose motives do not seem noble – unless of course they match the literary ones, in which case we admire them perhaps, if secretly.[3]

Whereas literature seductively dramatizes the experience of being suicidally wrecked by desire, much philosophy offers rational advice on how not to be. This is in part what Plato means when he refers to the, by then, already 'long-standing quarrel between poetry and philosophy' (*Republic*, p. 339, 607b); certainly it is a difference between say, the Greek love lyric or Greek tragedy on the one side, and Plato's own philosophy on the other, reminding us that the social and political distrust of art originates not from the most obvious of philistines, but the most famous of philosophers.

Plato and censorship

Plato's views on art have always been found worryingly unacceptable and in need of careful rebuttal. And with good reason since no society to date has escaped censorship, and in recent times many have felt an increasing need for it. If Soviet-style censorship proved to be as counter-productive as it was oppressive, it was nevertheless based on the sound realization that in the modern world knowledge was more than ever before a form of power, not as immediately effective as more coercive forms like the military, but effective nevertheless. I devote space to Plato here not to follow the usual practice of respectful rebuttal, but to agree with him, at least in certain respects. Like other would-be or actual censors of art, he had reason on his side.

Plato wanted to exclude artists from the commonwealth on grounds which included the following: they don't tell the truth; they are concerned with appearances, not reality; they appeal to the emotions in a way which undermines rationality; they corrupt 'even [or was it especially?] men of high character' (*Republic*, p. 337, 605c). It seems to me that all three criticisms are plausible given the kind of society Plato wanted. And in fundamental respects what he wanted, many still want today. That is why censorship of art continues to be an issue: Plato was only the first of many to correctly infer that art can threaten ideals of rationality and civilized human conduct. I for one agree with him, with the proviso already registered, namely that this is true not of all art but only of a certain kind – for me the most interesting kind.

I disagree with Plato when he says art does not tell the truth about reality (the deep truth). The kind of art I am describing might be said to undermine reason precisely because it searches for the deeper truth. Put another way, Plato wanted to ban art not because it told lies about reality, but because it refused his own censorship of the real. That censorship took two related forms, metaphysical and rational. His ultimate reality/truth – the world of the ideal Forms – is metaphysical in the sense that it transcends, and compensates for, the inadequate world of 'appearances': the form is more real than the appearances to which is gives meaning. But if we believe that Plato's ultimate reality serves, like God, to repressively organize mundane reality, then the art which makes the latter its subject is, directly if insecurely, on the side of truth – i.e., it doesn't accept a philosophical/religious mystification of the real. In practice, much art since Plato is attracted by such mystifications, but also refuses them.

Plato's censorship is rational in a more direct sense: he believed we are subject to a dangerous conflict between reason and passion, and like most philosophers he was confident about which needed to triumph. His ideal society is based on rigorous control of all that is disruptive in human desire. Art appeals to the passions, including sexuality, and is in need of such control. Fairly obviously, our understanding of the 'passions' has become more complex since Plato's time and not only because of Christianity, later philosophy, and psychoanalysis: literature itself, for example, has also influenced that change. But the Greek notion of the passions was anything but naive. By 'mimesis' Plato meant different things, one of which was the ability to imitate to a degree which involved identification; this is what the actor does, but also the audience. He realized that in drama we are not just moved by what we see, but that we 'passionately' identify with it. Yes, there is a prima facie difference in that the actor's identification is active, the audience's passive; and yet in a deeper sense the identification of the viewer (and, we might add, for the reader of a novel) is just as active. Identification encourages mobility where there should be stability.[4] That is one reason Plato believed that drama had the power to do great harm:

> As a country may be given over into the power of its worst citizens while the better sort are ruined, so, we shall say, the dramatic poet sets up a vicious form of government in the individual soul. (*Republic*, p. 337, 605b)

Explicitly political comparisons like this suggest Plato's assessment of art and psychology is formed inseparably from the experience of social disorder, and a belief that art contributes to that dangerous state of affairs.[5] Sometimes he allows that they can say profound things but this is almost as bad as saying untrue things, in that poets can be inspired without being responsible. In that he is surely right.

So for Plato it was imperative that the ideal ruler, the philosopher, and those in charge of educating the young, enforced a rational control of the passions. Exclusion, control and censorship are necessary in all aspects of social life. Only then can we minimise the danger that our guardians will:

> grow up among representations of moral deformity, as in some foul pasture where, day after day, feeding on every poisonous weed they would, little by little, gather insensibly a mass of corruption in their very souls. (*Republic*, p. 90, 401c)

People, guardians included, but especially the young, are presented in *The Republic* as overly susceptible to corruption. That is why they need to be brought up in a rigorously controlled social environment in which they will be imperceptibly drawn into 'sympathy and harmony with the beauty of reason, whose impress they take' (*Republic*, p. 90, 401d). Artists will contribute to such an environment by becoming little more than ideological hacks, hymning the praises of the two principle sources of law: the gods and great men. Like many of the more interesting censors since, Plato knew that dissident art had to be excluded from his 'well-governed society' (p. 339, 607c) not for representing too little reality, but too much. This is perhaps hinted at in the occasional nice irony in his description of the dangers of the artist; as, for instance, when he imagines a gifted actor visiting from abroad. This actor, 'clever enough to assume any character and give imitations of anything and everything', is given this welcome: 'we shall crown him ... anoint his head with myrrh, and conduct him to the borders of some other country' (*Republic*, p. 85, 398).[6]

Plato's account in the *Symposium* of Socrates' refusal to be seduced by Alcibiades, is a memorable instance of reason triumphing over passion. Socrates was ugly but brilliant, Alcibiades the most beautiful young man of his generation, and arrogant with it. *The Symposium* describes a party where Socrates is present and which Alcibiades later joins, drunkenly and disruptively. He describes himself as a passionate lover of Socrates. But this is a love nurtured and sustained by the latter's apparent indifference to Alcibiades' sexual charm. Alcibiades tells his listeners that he several times offers himself sexually to Socrates – even getting into bed with him – but each time is politely refused. As a result Alcibiades becomes infatuated with Socrates in a way he never would have been otherwise (*Symposium*, pp. 60–70, 215a–222b). Here is the philosopher renouncing desire, or rather empowering himself by being seen to renounce desire. But he is also defending himself against the treacherous seductiveness of the beautiful: by the time Plato is telling this story, Alcibiades is remembered as one who betrayed Athens. In more ways than one he was an exceedingly beautiful, walking tragedy.

After Plato, literary theory increasingly tended to defend art, but did so by stressing its social responsibilities and didactic function. The Horation view that art should instruct as well as delight became especially influential. But the alternative view of art as potentially anti-social never disappears. It is invoked in order to be refuted, though rarely plausibly. Sir Philip Sidney tries to refute it in *An Apology for Poetry* (*c*.1579–84), one of the most famous defences of art. Sidney sets out to answer the charges that art (or 'poesy') is 'the mother of lies' and 'the nurse of abuse, infecting us with many pestilent desires', seducing us 'with a siren's sweetness' into 'wanton sinfulness and lustful love'. In answering these charges Sidney has recourse to some fanciful arguments: poetry doesn't lie because it never tries to tell the truth. Rather than making falsifiable claims about an actual fallen work, art depicts an ideal world in which virtue reigns and sin is punished (poetic justice). And the fact that some poets contravene this idealist aesthetic and arouse libidinous thoughts shouldn't be allowed to damage art as properly practised. Sidney's defence, though not uninfluential, was not an accurate account of contemporary art but a didactic reaction to it, and later remarks in the *Apology* about plays in the theatre of the time indicate that he knew as much (pp. 247ff.). The theatre of the time was to become, increasingly, the focus of what might be called 'modern' censorship – that is, under direct control from the state, but also under attack from observers (especially puritans) who saw it as a grave threat to political and sexual health.[7] The constituency of art's enemies is wider, but the terms of its opposition were anticipated, if not established, by Plato.

Conclusion

Artistic culture is said to be under threat from philistinism. Maybe it is; and it probably always has been: certainly the protests that it is go back a long way. I've been arguing that artistic culture is equally under threat from the limited vision of those with a cultivated taste who speak earnestly on its behalf.

We are told, in Britain and from abroad, that cultural standards on British radio and television are the best in the world. But across the last couple of years the media has been full of charges that these standards are threatened by capitulation to populist pressures and mass audiences. 'Dumbing down' – has become the new buzz-phrase for declining standards everywhere but especially at that revered meeting point of cultural *gravitas* and the populace, the BBC. And yet even at their supposed best, most arts programmes on British radio and television are comfortably undemanding. Stripped of the presentational gloss most are little more than a chatteringly articulate diversion for the educated: essentially forgettable encounters with Culture delivered in the urbane cadences of the metropolitan lovers-of-art, and framed to the second by culture-journalists. With their anodyne agendas, such programmes are not opposed to, but dovetail with, the forces of dumbing down. Likewise with coffee-table/television 'philosophers' like Alain de Botton, who purvey high culture as the route to health and wisdom if not wealth.[1]

So it isn't just those who collect paintings for whom art becomes a mode of cultural capital, safeguarded and safeguarding, essentially cumulative. Shakespeare has never before been so persistently if crudely exploited as a form of national and cultural capital. Politicians cynically appropriate him for party-conference rhetoric, as do heritage hacks for tourist currency. In doing so they often invoke the idealist version of culture: Shakespeare as the supreme instance of cross-cultural, universal human values. The irony here, still largely lost on idealist critics, is that their vision of Shakespeare is comfortably exploited by the same vulgar culture and politics they spurn.

But the problem is deeper than cynical politicians, heritage management and naive literary critics. It's no secret that as they evolve, modern societies, especially but not only capitalist ones, produce cultural disruption, conflict and insecurity on a large scale. And 'high' culture, often in the form of the western tradition generally, and Shakespeare particularly, is wheeled on to provide a compensating sense of continuity, coherence, tradition, timeless values and so on. And it is hardly surprising if we are susceptible to this in some degree; we turn to art (among many other things) to find meaning and value which our own lives apparently lack. But what this also means is that the greater damage is done not by cynical politicians – who trusts them anyway? – but by those who give academic authority and cultural respectability to this conservative version of Shakespeare. Most have an academic base. The academic Shakespeare industry is for the most part an intellectual embarrassment, full of well-trained, mediocre minds climbing professional ladders. The contradiction that defines their professional existence – promoting a timeless, unchanging Shakespeare, while at the same time having to find something new to say about him in order to justify the industry's existence – is painful to behold. And those in this industry who are its media spokespersons are politicians in their own right.

The effects of heritage-compatible high culture go far beyond the national capital of Shakespeare. In the summer of 1998, the British actor Ian McKellen caused a stir, by remarking that there are no black faces in the audience at the National Theatre, and leaving London for provincial Leeds. Soon after, outrage is expressed at Bryan Appleyard's incisive attack on the shallowness of British theatre. Appleyard attributes this shallowness to several causes, including the catastrophic collateral damage inflicted on British culture by Shakespeare's genius, encouraging as it did the erroneous conviction that theatre is an art form specially suited to our national talent. He is surely right in claiming, in passing, that the television play often has more depth than the stage play. But his most telling criticism concerns the theatre as a place where a naive trust in art now verges on stupefaction:

> So determined are theatrical audiences to join the luvvies on the high aesthetic ground that they laugh when it's not funny and cry when its

not sad. To be present at a bad night at a highly-rated production . . . is to be enlisted in a deranged community of contrived, misdirected emotion.

The commercial London West End stage is propped up by tourists who, 'thanks to the success of the publicity formula that says Britain equals theatre troop solemnly into the stalls to stare at the actors in carefully concealed bewilderment'. Observing that the national Arts Council gives over £27 million to theatre annually, while those in the theatre whine continuously about the lack of public funding, Appleyard concludes that a big contraction in British theatre would not be much of a disaster.[2]

Perhaps the Arts Council paid heed? Well, shortly after that its Chairman, Gerry Robinson, did complain of middle-class elitism and superciliousness in the arts in Britain. But Robinson also believes in the social, political and spiritual efficacy of the arts (how could an Arts Council Chairman claim otherwise?). In the same speech, delivered, significantly enough, to the Royal Society of Arts, he commends art with a religiose and missionary zeal of the kind which must remain immune to its real challenge:[3]

If we believe that experience of the arts can inspire, can lift the spirit, can add a third dimension to our lives, surely it is nothing less than our duty to spread what can be a life transforming experience. (*Independent The Monday Review*, p. 4)

Robinson realizes that if its audiences aren't to go the same way as church congregations in Britain, high culture will have to hang on to the audiences it's got while at the same time hooking in those who at present are largely indifferent to it. So he complains that middle-class artists and art lovers do not sufficiently care about sharing the cultural heritage; they complacently hope that 'one day enlightenment might descend semi-miraculously upon the rest'. Actually, this is not quite fair. For example, against the background of frequent laments that young people are becoming less and less interested in Shakespeare, we encounter many well-intentioned attempts to re-engage their attention. It's no longer permissible to openly bowdlerize Shakespeare to this end, so the emphasis falls heavily on accessible interpretation and diverting theatrical production. But what emerges is an embarrassingly tamed Shakespeare, typically a production for a family day out, full of stage 'business' even more boring than the theme park in which it is probably being performed (open-air of course). There is no more banal version of the efficacy of high culture than this: if we can package Shakespeare attractively enough to get even a bit of him to rub off on the young they (and therefore we, their guardians) will be better off for it.

If the lovers of Shakespeare really wanted to revive his popularity with the young, they would do better to alert the latter to everything in his work which compromises their own good intentions – of which there is enough. If we want young people to read Shakespeare, let's attach to him a warning to the effect that he can damage psychic and moral health. The *reductio ad absurdum* of the Shakespeare lovers' educational strategy came to me in the form of a dissertation written by a trainee primary school teacher who had summarized the plots of Shakespeare's main tragedies for infants. Try as she might she could not make them read, in this stripped-down form, as anything other than the deranged musings of someone obsessed with sex and violence. But, in a way, this version of Shakespeare, at least to the extent that it unintentionally blew open the pious one, was the truer: the return of the repressed still distorted by the pieties muffling it. In a similarly distorted way the bowdlerizers of Shakespeare had a truer sense of what he might mean, at least in the context of the education of their own times. And there, of course, is the rub: to become a benign force and take a central place in a liberal education, art, especially literature, has to be tamed and censored. And that, in the longer term, is also what threatens its survival with the young (and, as time will have it the not so young): the selfsame pre-condition for its cultural authority becomes a guarantee of its demise.

Nothing excites the censorious more than the prospect of the young hearing and seeing what they shouldn't. Of the vulnerable groups censors have obsessed about the most – women, the lower orders and children – the first two have been emancipated, but not children, or even adolescents. We saw in relation to the literary censorship trials how concerned were both the prosecution and the defence with the possibly harmful effects of literature upon the young. It was an obsessive theme during the Wilde trials on the eve of the twentieth century, and remained so right up to the Section 28 legislation in Britain on the eve of the twenty-first. This legislation, passed in 1988, forbade the 'promotion' of homosexuality in schools. The attempted repeal of the law in 1999 and after, was met with considerable resistance, especially in Scotland, provoking even more dispute than the initial legislation. As so often before, the battle lines are drawn up with reference to the young. And it's no coincidence that the original legislation was precipitated by a book, for children, about a child living with gay parents. Anxieties are most explicit in relation to children but remain acute in relation to adolescents, hence the repeated frustration of the British government's attempts to reduce the age of consent for homosexuals. In fact, concern about adolescents is often displaced onto children because it's the latter who can still be legally controlled. It's hardly surprising then that the price of installing literature at the centre of our liberal educational agenda is both explicit censorship and even more far-reaching censorship by interpretation. The latter becomes still more important now that higher education is governed by market pressures.

One last instance of how completely Shakespeare has been tamed and the extent to which the cultural establishment is now dependent upon its business counterpart, with all the self-censorship which that entails. In the Spring of 1999 we learned that a University School of Management had teamed up with the new Globe Theatre in South-wark to offer courses on what Shakespeare can teach today's corporate executive. The course, reputedly costing £1000 per two days, had the ultimate seal of authenticity in the form of its organizer: Richard Olivier, director son of Lawrence Olivier. He is reported as saying that the rationale of the course derives from the fact that those who run the multinational corporations of today face the same problems as the kings and dukes of 1600. Additionally, they will learn from the theatre some acting skills which will help them get their way in the boardroom (Hamilton, 'The pay's the thing for business Bard', p. 9). Hot on the heels of this news there appears a book by Paul Corrigan, *Shakespeare on Management: Leadership Lessons for Today's Managers*. Academics sneer at this, and yet if we're not yet in quite the same boat it's not for want of trying: as successive governments urge us to be more and more self-financing, I'd say we're queueing for exactly that kind of ticket. After all, what *wouldn't* we be tempted to do with Shakespeare for one grand per student across two days? Already we entice fee-paying foreign students to take our higher degrees, some of whom are without even the qualifications for admission to a first degree. Still, there are degrees of complicity, and while I'd defend any university from the arsonist, I'd definitely step aside were he or she to have the Globe Theatre in prospect. In fact, when it happens – history always repeats itself – I'll be looking for an alibi.

Whose fault?

John M. Ellis laments the threat to a humanist education posed by political critics and their emphases on gender, race and class. His account of them is often inaccurate and always reductive, but what concerns me here is not that, so much as his sympathetic representation of the traditional humanist agenda. Ellis pines for a humanities education which enabled us to become 'enlightened citizens'; which produced a society of people educated 'for full and intelligent participation in a modern democracy'; which helped us 'develop a richer understanding of human life and to train the mind'; which taught us to enjoy and to love literature; which taught the still viable classical precept that poetry 'delighted and instructed', and so on (pp. 3–4, 33, 49, 51). This is exactly what one might expect of an Ivy League educational strategy, but as an approach to art it adds up to the same censorship observed earlier; it is the soothing rationalization of literature not for life, but a life of professional respectability, US-style.

At its best the humanist engagement with literature has been ethically sincere in a way which demands respect. But the pedagogical situation which it produced in the penultimate quarter of the twentieth-century was characterized by ethical complacency which in turn led to a blunting of political and ethical sensitivities in students. Roger Shattuck, writing in 1996, tells of how he became increasingly worried by the ethical naivety of his students in relation to a text like Albert Camus's *The Outsider*. He acknowledges that these students are sincere in their response to the book. The problem is that they empathize with the protagonist of the novel and therefore forgive (or simply forget) that he has murdered, as the saying goes, 'in cold blood'. Shattuck reprimands them for 'a grave misreading leading to moral myopia' (*Forbidden Knowledge*, p. 147). My first point would be to point up the irony that the responses of his students derive *not* from brainwashing by radical political critics (e.g., their supposed tendency to promote the outsider at all costs), but from the humanist tradition of criticism which Shattuck defends. Revealingly, he tells us that even he, initially, partly agreed with his students' attitude, later shifting his position after considering its moral implications. From what Shattuck says I cannot be sure, but I suspect these students have inherited a humanist perspective whereby they have been led naively to over-trust artists and their 'characters' – to identify and sympathize with them at the cost of other critical responses, and thereby to find 'sincerity' more seductive than political and ethical discrimination. My second point is that the possibility remains that students encouraged to exercise such discrimination might still empathize with the outsider who murders: such is the risk of literature.

The situation that perturbed Shattuck was in the first instance encouraged by an uncritical and trusting notion of creativity which goes well beyond the humanist. Denis Donoghue, writing about Yeats, observes:

> The single article of faith which goes undisputed in the Babel of modern criticism is the primacy of the creative imagination. It bloweth where it listeth, indisputable and imperious, it gives no quarter. . . . It is strange that we have accepted such an authoritarian notion in aesthetics while professing to be scandalized by its equivalent in politics. (*Yeats*, p. 121)

Donoghue wrote this in 1971, before the scepticism about the creative imagination which came from theoretically and politically inclined critics. But again, that scepticism is not my concern here. Rather I'm asking whether that kind of naive faith in the artist ever did amount to giving priority to the unrestrained creative imagination. It depends I suppose on who Donoghue's 'we' are. Certainly most literary critics across the last half-century have not, and especially not in the case of writers like Lawrence, Yeats, Artaud, Genet, and numerous others. Because of selective blindness, censorship-by-criticism, not to mention limited life-experience, they have managed by and large to avoid being scandalized by the unrestrained creative imagination. And the corollary is the ethical naivety of Shattuck's students.

That is part of the story. It's also true that art itself can encourage this situation: creative deceptions facilitating critical ones. It is the great merit of Yeats's verse that it often is imaginatively unrestrained in just the way described by Donoghue. But this is not, of course, the same as saying that its meaning is self-evident. Persistently, Yeats creates, from the experience of thwarted desire, verse of great power and seduction. To a degree it deceives us as to its origins and therefore, to some extent its nature. That is hardly cause for concern: everyone knows, or should do, that deception is integral to art. But one of the things which makes it so interesting is that perfect deception in art is rarer than the perfect crime. The experiential origins of the artistic work may be transmuted beyond recognition without ever being entirely transcended; their effects remain. Many artists use language to its full to acknowledge exactly that. They know and want to half-acknowledge that their bid for aesthetic resolution is only ever a fragile internal distancing, a temporary internal resolution always unstable because pressured by an unrest which formal discipline can never fully sublimate or compensate for. Even Yeats in a poem like 'Byzantium' acknowledges that. So does Philip Larkin's poem 'An Arundel Tomb', in which an earl and countess are seen, equivocally, to 'lie in stone'. This is how it ends:

> Above their scrap of history,
> Only an attitude remains:

Time has transfigured them into
Untruth. The stone fidelity
They hardly meant has come to be
Their final blazon, and to prove
Our almost-instinct almost true:
What will survive of us is love.

Larkin's biographer tells us that at the end of a manuscript draft of the poem Larkin scrawls the following 'cynical graffiti': 'Love isn't stronger than death just because statues hold hands for 600 years' (Motion, *Philip Larkin*, p. 274). Indeed not, and the poem is not scandalized by the graffiti it anticipates. In Larkin's verse affirmations are notoriously muted, and located in moments full, not of life-affirming presence, but a history of absence, loss and failure, and the intense apprehension of impending death. Larkin sees truly when he sees death and failure even in the spinning of a child's top, in 'Tops':

– And what most appals
Is that tiny first shiver,
That stumble, whereby
We know beyond doubt
They have almost run out
And are starting to die.

Larkin is a refined practitioner of the mutability lyric in which, from Shakespeare's sonnets and before, the creative imagination devotes its powers of expression not to human beauty, human value and humane tenderness, but to Time, which destroys them all; put more subjectively, the imagination identifies with what destroys it (Dollimore, *Death, Desire and Loss*, especially pp. xxii–iii).

So how persuasive really is that formalist aesthetic which tells us that art gratifies because it is a triumph of form over matter, the imposition of order upon the chaos of life? I cannot think of any writer who plausibly fits such a theory. Nevertheless, aesthetic formalism, as a theory about art, is interesting in its own right: the detection of a formal 'transcendence' of content is a way of misrepresenting reality by keeping it at a distance. We want to keep it that way because it is indeed 'chaotic' – that's to say, *it wounds us even as it eludes us*. When the aesthetic tries to substitute formal unity for the divisions of experience, it is only as a defence against the real. But the desire for aesthetic transcendence of the real only exists because of having already been wounded by the real. In the most imaginative writing, the wounding reality seeps back into the forms which would formally beautify, rationalize, contain, exclude or transcend it, and the substitution for the real becomes no more nor less than its indirect representation, its defended, half-recognition. We can take formalism seriously without taking it on its own terms; the deceptions and self-betrayals of art, like those of desire, are integral to its meaning. It's to the credit of Oscar Wilde that he wore the deceptions of formalism on his sleeve. His declaration, encountered earlier ('No artist has ethical sympathies. . . . There is no such thing as a moral or an immoral book. Books are well written, or badly written. That is all'), expresses not an indifference to content, but a determination to incorporate a whole load of barely disguised illicit content, and a clear invitation to the initiated to recognize exactly that. And what we now know is that for Wilde the illicit was as dangerous and painful as it was liberating.

We have encountered more than once an idea related to formalism, namely that of 'disinterestedness'. It derives primarily from Immanuel Kant's idea that to contemplate art in the right way is to move from a partial, biased and 'interested' perspective into a more detached and therefore inclusive one. To see deeper and further one must extricate oneself from the limited and limiting entanglements of our immediate lives and consciousness. Involvement implies limitation and, its critics would say, never more so than in the partial perspectives of political criticism. Disinterestedness is often invoked in defence of conventional aesthetic attitudes and has led to some of the most lifeless philosophical reflection on art ever written. But it also facilitated a turning away from the didactic theory of art, and along with other concepts like that of the sublime, allowed an escape from the limitations of who and what we are – from, in other words, the human. Schopenhauer claimed that the profound attraction of the aesthetic attitude is that it released us from the will to live and required the death of the self – an eradication of one's individuality and even of one's humanity (*The World as Will and Representation*, vol. 1, pp. 179, 196–8; vol. 2, p. 371). In modernism a development of the aesthetic of disinterestedness took such aspirations into the realm of amoral or even immoral indifference. Memorable examples abound, including this response of the symbolist poet Laurent Tailhade to a terrorist bomb: 'What do the victims matter if the gesture is beautiful?'[4] The particular interest of this example is that in fact 'beauty' remains anything but politically disinterested.

In conclusion then, not only can we have profound intellectual respect, and great admiration, for a work of literature without trusting it aesthetically, ethically or politically; I'd argue further that a full intellectual/aesthetic engagement is positively enabled by that distrust. For some in earlier generations a trust in art was a way of understanding and changing self and society; for us, in the early twenty-first century, it's a way of standing still amidst the obsolete, semi-mystifying clichés of the culture-industry. More fundamentally, if we approach literature insisting on an alignment of the ethical conscience and the creative imagination, we blind ourselves to the fact that some of the most compelling writing is about the tension between, if not the incompatibility of, these two things.

Sir Frank Kermode is an influential critic who has become increasingly hostile to what Ellis reductively calls the 'race-gender-class' critics. Kermode insists that in the classroom university teachers of literature should be on their honour to show students what it is to love books: 'If they fail in that, either because they despise the humbleness of the task or because they don't themselves love literature, they are failures and frauds' (Kermode, p. 103). Maybe, but I doubt that failure and fraudulence are their prerogatives. When a couple of years ago Kermode lectured (on Shakespeare) to students at my own university they did not think that he conveyed or inspired a love of literature, even though they were prepared to accept that he loved it in his own way. But even if he had been successful in persuading them to love as he loved, I doubt if that would have ensured in them what Kermode wants, namely that we talk about literature in a way which 'will preserve the reading public, and – quite simply – literature . . . from destruction' (p. 103). If we have to have an agenda in the classroom I would rather it be an attempt to inspire in students an attitude to literature of alert, questioning empathy. And by empathy I mean not self-indulgent sympathy, but self-challenging identification. The 'love' of which Kermode speaks hardly encourages the questioning which must be an inseparable part of the empathy. A questioning, empathic *engagement* which would involve a suspension of judgement, while making the notion of a suspension of disbelief simply irrelevant. And then a reawakening of judgement inside, and after, the identification with the work, which the act of empathy has enabled. Judgement and work interrogate each other inside a difficult dialectic. Students can be encouraged into a situation where they are torn between identification with, and a reaction against, a text. In truth, intelligent and sensitive students need little leading into doing this, which is, after all, by no means a new way of reading. But it is a challenging one.

I understand why traditionalists want to protect the aesthetic experience from reductive political criticism, especially the a priori kind which crudely and ahistorically maps a pre-conceived agenda onto the text. That is a criticism in which there is no empathy, no identification, and not even any questioning. But I also think that, in the same move, those traditional critics are protecting themselves not just from the sensitive and sincere ethical demands which political critique, at its best, exemplifies, but also from the very art they love. They passionately smother the thing they love because if they confronted its real nature they could not continue to love it in the sentimental and habitual ways they do. To that extent their objections to a reductive political criticism remain diversionary, even or especially when they are justified: their plausible rejection of reductive criticism enables evasions of their own which are just as significant and sometimes more damaging. We arrive by yet another route to the same irony: those who most love art are often those most responsible for its censorship, and they impose this censorship most effectively when apparently defending art against its 'real' enemies, be they judicial censors or political critics.

Recently there was a new controversy over both the politics and sexuality of Wordsworth. Amusingly, the publisher of the book promoting the argument declares: 'Wordsworth experts are a lethal brotherhood.'[5] If only! Most of them just want him kept as normal as possible. Across recent years one could cite numerous other instances of this kind of stand-off. The game of trying to normalize canonical writers, despite the evidence from their work and their lives, goes right back to those hilarious backs-to-the-wall attempts of scholars, across hundreds of years, to deny the possibility of Shakespeare being bisexual or worse, homosexual.

Earlier I suggested that there was something pornographic in one of Shakespeare's most compelling scenes. Laura Kipnis argues persuasively that the differences between pornography and more exalted forms of cultural expression are less important than their similarities. 'Reading between the bodies' of pornography she find age-old philosophical and political questions – 'about class, aesthetics, utopia, rebellion, power, desire and commodification' – albeit couched in a low idiom. Even more to the point, pornography is 'astute about . . . the discontent at the core of routinized lives and normative sexuality'. Seeking to unravel the opposition between pornography and high art, Kipnis takes her cue from Freud, arguing for the aesthetic complexity of sublimated sexual perversity as a major source of high art (*Bound and Gagged*, pp. viii, xii, 81–6). I wonder though if we even need any more the notion of sublimation to unravel that opposition? To say that a libidinal energy is sublimated implies that it is disguised as something else, and that the elaborate process which achieves this is to a significant extent unconscious in the artist, and that the aesthetic response to the art work also remains largely unaware of it. This may have been half true for the nineteenth century, but was less and less the case as the twentieth progressed. The perverse origins of art are now demonstrable and obvious, as are all kinds of other origins equally embarrassing for a traditional aesthetic.

And with the ever increasing popularity of biography, the deviance, sexual or otherwise, of artists becomes more and more obvious. And despite what critics and others tell us, this deviance is more often than not inseparable from their creativity. Astonishingly, one finds Albert Bermel declaring that Antonin Artaud's agonizing drug addiction and psychosis were not 'even partially responsible for the audacity and unorthodoxy of his ideas'. This opinion, though hardly typical of critical engagement with Artaud, is nevertheless consistent with a moralistic view of creativity which many humanist critics share but rarely admit to as unequivocally as does Bermel: 'If we believed that Artaud had incurred artistic debts to what were evidently grave handicaps, we could not take his writing seriously' (*Artaud's Theatre of Cruelty*, pp. 7–8). By contrast John Calder, Artaud's distinguished English publisher, is willing to acknowledge in passing 'the link between creative energy and abnormal states of mind'. But he then finishes with a typical humanist flourish, speaking of 'the triumph of [Artaud's] life-force over his death-wish' and asserting that 'His prose is always exciting and life-enhancing because it is literature as well as exploration.'[6] That's all right then.

So much for the artist who, like Artaud, suffers from 'insanity'. What of the artist who is sanely immoral? David Lister, commenting on the revelations in 1999 that Arthur Koestler was a 'serial rapist', and the consequent removal from public display of a bust of the writer, responds with one of the oldest and most deluded of all defences against the implications that artists are immoral people: we should consider the artist's work entirely independently of his or her life ('Can Immoral Artists Produce Great Works?', p. 4). But we do not, we cannot, and nor should we even try. That the wish to completely separate life and work only occurs when the former becomes embarrassing, says as much.

Lister's argument is in understandable disagreement with those like Bermel who believe that when an artist is revealed to have been guilty of moral failings and criminal acts, his work is equally and rightly discredited. But this belief derives from the assumption that artistic genius and moral virtue are or should be inseparable. And that assumption derives in turn from the naively reverential and censorious attitudes to art I have been criticizing. My response to the question which Lister's title asks is: Obviously, yes. To say otherwise would be to rewrite history. And the relationship between work and life, where discernible, is as potentially significant as the work itself. In some respects this relationship is comparable to that between what a culture represses and what it is enabled to be as a consequence of that repression.

Such a comparison also suggests that to take art more seriously by trusting it less does not necessarily mean that we replace reverence towards art with a paranoid suspicion of it. If reverence blunts the critical faculties, paranoia sharpens them to a degree which precludes identification. The paranoid gaze is a defended gaze. Tennyson once put a commonplace but profound truth rather succinctly: 'There lives more faith in honest doubt, / . . . than in half the creeds' (*In Memoriam*, XCV). 'Honest doubt': it is a phrase which will serve to describe an attitude of sceptical empathy of which paranoia is incapable. Tennyson is talking of religion a century and a half ago, since which time art, like sex, has become a surrogate religion and just as much in need of honest doubt. And although it may be susceptible to paranoia, it's not the same thing at all.

Art is more often than not the product of the damaged. At the opening of James Baldwin's *Another Country* there is a memorable description of a young saxophonist which I shall cite at some length:

> He stood there, wide-legged, humping the air, filling his barrel chest, shivering in the rags of his twenty-odd years, and screaming through the horn *Do you love me? Do you love me? Do you love me?* . . . This, anyway, was the question Rufus heard, the same phrase, unbearably, endlessly, and variously repeated, with all the force the boy had. The silence became strict with abruptly focused attention, cigarettes were unlit, and drinks stayed on the tables; and in all of the faces, even the most ruined and most dull, a curious, wary light appeared. . . . And yet the question was terrible and real; the boy was blowing with his lungs and guts out of his own short past; somewhere in that past, in the gutters or gang fights or gang shags; in the acrid room, on the sperm-stiffened blanket, behind marijuana or the needle, under the smell of piss in the precinct basement, he had received the blow from which he never would recover and this no one wanted to believe. (p. 16)

Is Baldwin describing himself? No, not straightforwardly, but at heart, via identification, yes, and deeply so. Art is parasitic upon human suffering. The sublime, redemptive harmonies of Thomas Tallis's *Spem in Alium*, could not have been, without the deprivations, violence and disease of the sixteenth century; in the twentieth century some of our most tender aesthetic visions arise inseparably from the brutalities of city life. One difference between the two centuries being that now, as here with Baldwin, the exceptional individual from the underclass becomes beautiful and so qualifies as tragic.

From romanticism to modernism, the creative intelligence is driven by recklessness, neurosis, intense frustration, narcissism, megalomania, anti-social and often murderous fantasies, insecurity, ambition and, yes, paranoia: 'Many poets', declared Philip Larkin, 'are paranoiac bores' (*Required Writing*, p. 136). The case of Larkin reminds us that some of the most compelling art not only grows from diminished or damaged life, but is inseparable from it: critics try and have it otherwise, but Larkin was right to insist that his poetry grew directly from his own life and personal experience. And reading Motion's biography of Larkin one recalls William Faulkner's observation, made via the character of Bayard in *The Unvanquished*, about 'the immitigable chasm between all life and all print – those who can, do, those who cannot and suffer enough because they can't, write about it' (p. 157). Some art, including, perhaps, Larkin's,[7] has its origins in trauma. To say so is not to predict its effect. A novelist whose childhood was wrecked by brutal abuse might write about dysfunctional families, or their opposite; that is, what was so painfully experienced or so desperately wanted. Or both.[8] Another kind of art is driven by what Larkin's poetry knows but studiously avoids: the deepest desire to be irresponsible, to purchase libidinal freedom at all cost.

Even the recklessly creative intelligence is riven by ambivalence. 'Ambivalence' is an over-used word. I mean by it not an oscillation between conflicting attitudes or feelings which, once discerned, is halfway to being resolved, in art or in life; I mean rather an oscillation whose recognition more often than not fails to ameliorate; which may lead to an imaginative resolution which is actually only a displacement and intensification of frustrated energies. Nietzsche, Yeats and Lawrence would be cases in point. They, along with Larkin and numerous other writers, are also described by Faulkner's distinction between those who can and those who can't live. One very significant corollary of this is that those who can live become the objects of ambivalent desire for those who, in Faulkner's sense, can't. One thinks of Yeats's literary treatment of Maud Gonne, Lawrence's of Cipriano in *The Plumed Serpent*, and Nietzsche's comparison of the healthy and the sick man. The healthy man, because and not in spite of his ignorance and limited horizons, stands before us:

in superlative health and vigour, a joy to all who see him; while close beside him a man far more just and instructed than he sickens and collapses because the lines of his horizon are always restlessly changing, because he can no longer extricate himself from the delicate net of his judiciousness and truth for a simple act of will and desire. (*Untimely Meditations*, p. 63)

It is not entirely fanciful to regard Nietzsche's philosophy as inspired by his identification as sick man with his virile counterpart's 'simple act of will and desire'. But, despite or (again) because of the sickness, the identification comes from a position of superiority. In *Human All Too Human* Nietzsche realized that strong communities controlled by these healthy types generate:

gradually increasing inherited stupidity such as haunts all stability like its shadow. It is the more unfettered, uncertain and morally weaker individuals upon whom *spiritual progress* depends in such communities. . . . Degenerate natures are of the highest significance wherever progress is to be effected. Every progress of the whole has to be preceded by a partial weakening. The strongest natures *preserve* the type, the weaker help it to *evolve*. (p. 107)

This is an extraordinary insight, one which makes creative writing (in which I include Nietzsche's philosophy) at once indispensable and socially dangerous, and which suggests why my foregoing description of the creative intelligence isn't meant to represent it as a failure of civilization, but rather one of its most highly developed and compelling expressions. But it also suggests why intellectuals like Nietzsche and artists like Lawrence, Yeats and Larkin are the last people to be trusted with the ethical and political welfare of civilization. What George Steiner has said of philosophers in the context of a discussion of Heidegger is relevant too for artists:

It is an ill-kept secret that cloistered intellectuals and men who spend their lives immured in words, in texts, can experience with especial intensity the seductions of violent political proposals, most particularly where such violence does not touch their own person. There can be in the sensibility and outlook of the charismatic teacher, of the philosophical absolutist, more than a touch of surrogate sadism. (*Heidegger*, p. xxvi)

And what about academic critics, a yet different species from intellectuals, artists or philosophers? I have sometimes thought that one of the several differences between intellectuals and academics is that if the latter can be trusted rather more than the former (and I'm by no means sure) it is only because they are constrained by cowardice and professional self-regard. And literary theorists? It's another ill-kept secret that the radical political credentials with which they travel between continents are not to be trusted.

Intellectuals speculate in a fundamentally irresponsible way and are often in error. Those who express in their lives and work the failings Steiner describes are numerous – Steiner cites, in passing, Plato, Voltaire, Frege, Sartre and of course Heidegger. They remain of profound significance (again) because and not in spite of those failings. (If I have my doubts about Heidegger it is mainly because of the philosophy, not the failings: however, I know they are not separable.) But if we approach such thinkers with the naive trust traditionally accorded to the creative mind, the chances are we learn little and perpetuate those failings. We need a kind of engagement with intellectuals, as with artists, the more serious for being more searching: an engagement whose precondition is precisely that we listen, empathize, identify, take risks and learn in ways we can't when we simply trust.

I have been told that my critique derives from my being too preoccupied with the past; that I am 'Chekovian', the pessimistic product of a tired culture overburdened by its own histories of failure; that even to dwell on such matters is a sign of cultural privilege. I defer to such criticisms with the exception of those that come from the academic conference circuit where the 'radical' alternative is heralded as the 'post-' or the 'after' or the 'beyond' of the most recent brand of wishful theory. I admit to a certain pessimism. It's de rigeur in a certain kind of political criticism to be positive. Not by being reassuring about the future – on the contrary it's required that we predict that things will and must get worse under present arrangements – but by aligning oneself with a politics which, was it adopted by everyone else, *would* change things for the better. Not to end in such a way is to lay oneself open to the charge of having lost faith with the cause. And yet how empty are such positive gestures; they cost nothing and achieve less. The danger of pessimism as bad faith is great. But the greater bad faith is in a facile optimism which misrepresents past and present. We are often told that the anti-humanist tenor of French theory in recent decades was born of the experience of defeat and disillusion in Paris in 1968.[9] If that is true, European intellectuals today should be stunned to perpetual silence if not suicide by the events in Bosnia and Kosovo in the 1990s and the failure of the post-cold-war world to prevent them.

I have not been arguing for the wholesale rejection of theory, nor even of postmodernism. To do so would be to resemble too closely those esteemed public spokespersons who are now reacting against all kinds of literary and cultural theory in a way which endorses the anti-intellectualism from which British culture has always suffered. I am arguing for an intellectual culture which avoids both the 'English' denigration of intellectuals and the French reverence for them (and which especially avoids the naive English reverence for the French); which would be at once more responsive to, and more sceptical of, their work. That would entail a greater effort of historical understanding: one adequate to comprehend, challenge, and maybe even change those recalcitrant, destructive human realities which we inherit and therefore live and perpetuate so stubbornly. An effort of understanding which knows that we always risk misrecognizing the realities we live, and the struggles they imply, and that going back into the past via intellectual history is one way of reducing that risk. For this purpose the materialist concepts of contradiction and dialectic remain, for me, imperative. Arguably they remain significant too for any cultural politics prepared to confront and not evade the complexities of our histories, and which knows, contra postmodernism, the importance of the traditions of intellectual history and philosophical anthropology: which knows, in short, that there is so much more to be learned from the past than either the current reactionary defenders of tradition, or their postmodern critics, allow.

I imagine a critical engagement which strives to understand the contradictions we live and which, after making that effort, does not lack the courage to risk truth-claims about the real; an engagement which knows the difference between human agency and human essence and which recognizes that the feeble relativism of postmodernism only seems viable because those who promulgate it never have to test it beyond internecine squabbles. For all its cosmopolitan affect, much postmodernism thrives on a new parochialism – that self-absorbed, inward-looking and relatively insulated existence characteristic of intellectual city life, and which reminds us once again that material conditions profoundly influence not only the direction of our thought, but what is thinkable and what is not. None of us escapes that limitation. All of our yearnings suffer the limitation of being formed inside the bad histories we want to change. A critique, if it achieves any objectivity at all, probably does so only in terms of an internal distancing[10] – we aspire to get to an outside but rarely succeed; instead we gain some precarious foothold from the inside. Rather than agonizing over this lack of objectivity to the point of becoming silent (or worse, ironic deconstructionists) we should acknowledge those limitations as part of what it is to write, becoming aware of them in a way which contributes to, rather than detracts from, the shared effort to achieve a more adequate critique. Why else write?

I imagine a critical engagement which knows that we have to believe in what we write, but knows also that we might well be wrong. That realization, as much as the engagement itself, is what makes writing ethical in the broadest sense of the word.

Notes

Preface

1 The case has in fact been made compellingly in relation to gothic fiction, by David Punter. See especially his analysis of three of the most significant themes of this fiction. The first two are paranoia and taboo – those areas of human life 'which offend, which are suppressed . . . in the interests of social and psychological equilibrium'. The third is the barbaric: 'time and time again, those writers who are referred to as gothic turn out to be those who bring us up against the boundaries of the civilized.' (*The Literature of Terror*, vol. 2, pp. 183–4). See too Fred Botting, *Gothic*.

2 To a degree this book evolves a critical perspective already explored in my previous ones. Where those books offer fuller elaboration of something, I refer to them rather than repeating the detail here, although nothing in this book presupposes acquaintance with any other. My main focus is literature but I refer to art more generally where it seems justified. I do not mean to assimilate all kinds of art indiscriminately, even when an incautious absence of qualification might be taken otherwise.

Chapter 1   Too Hot for Yale? The Challenge of Queer Theory

1 Although, significantly, it has a precedent in Freud when he speaks of the woman, whose infantile wish for a penis changes in later life into 'the wish for a *man*, and thus puts up with the man as an appendage to the penis' ('On Transformations of Instinct as Exemplified in Anal Eroticism', in *The Standard Edition of the Complete Psychological Works of Sigmund Freud*, Hogarth, London, 1955, vol. 17, p. 129). I am grateful to Rachel Bowlby for this reference.

2 'Unraveling the Sexual Fringe', p. 20; cited from Lynda Hart's important study, *Between the Body and the Flesh*, p. 49.
3 Donald Morton argues at some length that queer values correspond all
   too neatly with modern capitalism; see his 'Queerity and Ludic Sado-
   Masochism'.
4 Anonymous London leaflet, 'Queer Power Now' (1991); cited from
   Alan Sinfield's *Gay and After*, p. 8, itself the most thoughtful account
   of the recent challenges to the gay identity.
5 Carol A. Queen, 'Strangers at Home: Bisexuals in the Queer Movement', *Outlook*, 16 (1992), p. 33; cited here from Elizabeth Wilson's
   provocative and recommended article, 'Is Transgression Transgressive?'
   in Bristow and Wilson (eds), *Activating Theory*, p. 113.
6 'Bareback and Reckless'; see also Michael Warner, 'Why gay men are
   having risky sex'; Tim Dean, 'How Can Psychoanalysis Help Safe-sex
   Education?'; Celia Farber, 'Unprotected'; and Matt Wells, 'Sex on the
   Edge'.

Chapter 2 The New Bisexuality

1 See especially Sue George, *Women and Bisexuality*; Elisabeth Däumer,
   'Queer Ethics; or, the Challenge of Bisexuality to Lesbian Ethics';
   Joseph Bristow and Angelia R. Wilson (eds), *Activating Theory: Les-
   bian, Gay and Bisexual Politics*; Clare Hemmings, 'Resituating the
   Bisexual Body'; Jo Eadie, 'Activating Bisexuality: Towards a Bi/Sexual
   Politics' and 'We should be there bi now'; Nicola Field, *Over the
   Rainbow: Money, Class and Homophobia*; Sharon Rose et al. (eds),
   Bisexual Horizons: Politics, Histories, Lives; Marjorie Garber, *Vice
   Versa: Bisexuality and the Eroticism of Everyday Life*.
2 Cited from Eadie, p. 168 (originally appearing in *Pink Paper*, 18 April
   1993, p. 14).
3 Sukie de la Croix (*Pink Paper*, 23 July 1993), cited by Field, who finds
   in his story a fear of bisexuality which 'to some extent . . . mirrors
   homophobia' (*Over the Rainbow*, pp. 133–4).
4 Freud once wrote: 'But bisexuality! You are certainly right about it. I
   am accustoming myself to regarding every sexual act as a process in
   which four individuals are involved. We have lots to discuss on this
   topic' (letter from Freud to Fliess, 1 August 1899, cited from *The
   Complete Letters of Sigmund Freud to Wilhelm Fliess*).
5 Compare Mandy Merck: 'The Sex Wars have taught us the error of
   attempting to fuse our political and sexual imaginaries, but they have
   also demonstrated the futility of trying to keep them apart' (*Perversions*,
   p. 266).
6 In this the postmodern theorists of bisexuality are little different from
   those 'untheorized' and confessional accounts of bisexual experience
   which the theorists are the first to disparage as inadequate (see *Bisexual
   Horizons*, ed. Rose; especially Section II).

7 Eadie later found this to be a problem for him too: 'I found it very hard recently to acknowledge that I wanted a monogamous relationship because I was so committed to myself as "a person who has multiple relationships".' This occurs in a perceptive piece describing Eadie's misgivings about the way the bisexual community, as it becomes stronger, seems to be deploying the same discriminatory tendencies it has hitherto suffered from, especially the tendency to self-define in terms of binary division and exclusion ('Being Who we Are', in Rose, *Bisexual Horizons*, pp. 16–20, esp. p. 18).

8 'Love, the loosener of limbs shakes me again, an inescapable bittersweet creature' (*The Penguin Book of Greek Verse*, ed. C. A. Trypanis, p. 150). This metaphor of love as loosener of limbs was common in Greek writing about desire and signalled the unwelcome yet irresistible unbinding of the defended self which desire entailed. A fascination with the way desire undermines rather than confirms identity goes back at least this far.

9 Most recently, Judith Butler, in *The Psychic Life of Power* (chapter 5), elaborately theorized loss in relation to Freud's concept of melancholy, identification and introjection.

Chapter 3   Wishful Theory

1 See *Radical Tragedy*, and *Sexual Dissidence*.

2 Judith Butler, 'Imitation and Gender Insubordination', in *Inside/Out: Lesbian Theories, Gay Theories*, ed. Diana Fuss (Routledge, London, 1991), p. 21.

3 *Straight Sex: the Politics of Pleasure*, p. 234. Segal's book is, more generally, thoughtful defence of female heterosexuality against the reductive accounts of it to be found in the sexual politics of recent decades – feminist, lesbian-feminist, gay and otherwise.

4 Cora Kaplan, ' "A Cavern Opened in my Mind": the poetics of homosexuality and the politics of masculinity in James Baldwin', p. 32.

5 This interview, given in 1993 and published the following year in *Radical Philosophy*, serves as an excellent introduction to Butler's work up to that point. She remarks that 'the popularising of *Gender Trouble* – even though it was interesting culturally to see what it tapped into, to see what was out there, longing to be tapped into – ended up being a terrible misrepresentation of what I wanted to say!' (p. 33).

6 'It is becoming clear that there is no straightforward relationship between self-proclaimed sexual identity and sexual behaviour' ('Heterosexual behaviour in a large cohort of homosexually active men in England and Wales', P. Weatherburn et al., *AIDS Care*, vol. 2, no. 4, 1990; cited from Field, p. 140).

7 This sentence is repeated in Butler's later book, *The Psychic Life of Power* (pp. 146–7), where the argument is pursued in greater detail (chapter 5).

8   See too John M. Ellis, *Literature Lost*. My shift here to Shakespeare may seem abrupt. The connection lies in the fact that in both these books and most others like them, it is canonical figures like Shakespeare, and the high culture to which they belong, which are said to be most under threat from theory. I return to this in Part II and Part III.

9   '[I]t seems important to point out that the whole Freudian edifice has been drastically undermined, with severe consequences for any literary criticism based on it' (Vickers, p. 273).

Chapter 4   Sexual Disgust

1   This suggests another aspect of the complexity of disgust as both experience and social interaction; that is to say, it is a response complicated by the fact that it's not always possible to distinguish between a real as distinct from an imagined threat. Of course there *is* a distinction: we can fear something as a threat when it clearly is not; but the fearing of something can already be part way towards making it a 'real' threat. Disgust enables that 'real-ization'.

2   *Si le grain ne meurt* was published in 1920; the following diary entry is dated February 1918, but there is some uncertainty about the exact dating of these entries.

3   On sexual attraction and repulsion in racial narratives see Robert Young in *Colonial Desire*, esp. chapters 4 and 6.

4   Camille Paglia seems to suggest that for men to experience women as disgusting is not only inevitable but reasonable. This derives from her belief that civilization is necessarily a reaction formation against nature, and female sexuality and reproduction is the embodiment of nature and, as such, essentially chthonian: it is a 'miasmic swamp whose prototype is the still pond of the womb'. This means that feminism has been simplistic in arguing that certain pejorative female archetypes were politically motivated falsehoods by men. On the contrary, the historical repugnance to woman has a rational basis: 'disgust is reason's proper response to the grossness of procreative nature.' She also identifies disgust as integral to the aesthetic response; it is a rational fear of, or at, 'a melting borderline' (*Sexual Personae*, pp. 12, 93).

5   Foucault has something to answer for here:

> The body is the inscribed surface of events (traced by language and dissolved by ideas), the locus of a dissociated Self (adopting the illusion of a substantial unity), and a volume in perpetual disintegration. Genealogy, as an analysis of descent, is thus situated within the articulation of the body and history. Its task is to expose a body totally imprinted by history and the process of history's destruction of the body. ('Nietzsche, Genealogy, History', p. 148)

6   'Dirt is matter out of place': Mary Douglas recirculated this seductive aphorism in recent times, and it is often attributed to her. But it has a longer history. How old exactly? Freud uses the phrase in 1908. He is

trying to explain why people who repress their anal eroticism become boring – mean, obstinate, and obsessed with orderliness. Now Freud is convinced this involves sublimation, but is unsure as to how, or why, exactly: 'The intrinsic necessity for this connection is not clear, of course, even to myself.' But he suggests that these character traits 'are reaction formations against an interest in what is unclean and disturbing and should not be part of the body'. It's then that he adds: 'dirt is matter in the wrong place' ('Character and Anal Eroticism', p. 173). In Freud's original German text this phrase appears in English, in brackets, in quotation marks, and without any annotation or source. In other words, in 1908 Freud apparently regards this proposition as something like an English proverb or aphorism. It's not surprising then to find that Cobham Brewer records it in the 1894 edition of his *Dictionary of Phrase and Fable*. Brewer is irritated by the aphorism. He comments, dismissively and tersely, 'this is not true. A diamond . . . lost on the road is matter in the wrong place, but certainly [it] is not dirt.' That's all he says. Even more interesting is the person to whom he attributes this aphorism – none other than Lord Palmerston, a British Prime Minister. I've been unable to track down when and where Palmerston supposedly coined the phrase, but this was what he declared in 1829:

> I confess I should not be sorry . . . to see the Turk kicked out of Europe . . . We want civilisation, activity, trade and business in Europe, and your Mustaphas have no idea of any traffic beyond rhubarbs, figs and red slippers; what energy can be expected from a nation who have no heels to their shoes and pass their whole lives slip shod?

Do we here have an entire dirty race out of place?

7   Lynne Segal shows the smug and self-deluding complacency of this attitude in her intelligent defence of women's heterosexual pleasure, *Straight Sex*; see esp. pp. xi and 215–16.

8   This is from Peter Stallybrass and Allon White's influential *The Politics and Poetics of Transgression*, p. 191. They arrive at this formulation through analysis of identity formation in dominant groups, especially the bourgeoisie. The 'high' bourgeois subject came to define himself through the repression and exclusion of the 'low' other, typically characterized in social, sexual and racial terms. But what was excluded socially remained psychically central: bourgeois fantasy life came to be constituted by the return of what it excluded or repressed. Stallybrass and White recognized that in psychic and social life repression and exclusion are often inseparable, and this was one reason why they deployed both psychoanalytic and materialist or anthropological accounts of identity, and in fact kept the psychoanalytic subordinate to the anthropological. But out of context that phrase which has become so influential – 'disgust always bears the imprint of desire' – has come to be used in a primarily psychoanalytic sense even by those who would not count themselves as exclusively psychoanalytic, or who are suspicious of, or even hostile to it. Such is the enduring influence of Freud

9   See Miller, *Anatomy of Disgust*, especially chapter 6.

10 Plutarch then goes on to talk of a love affair which survives this development but it is clear that this is the exception which testifies to the reverse being more typical – see Flacelière, *Love in Ancient Greece*, p. 56.

11 Cf. pp. 12–13: 'My mother had been carried to the graveyard when I was five. I scarcely remember her at all, yet she figured in my nightmares, blind with worms, her hair as dry as metal and brittle as a twig, straining to press me against her body; that body so putrescent, so sickening soft, that it opened, as I clawed and cried, into a breach so enormous as to swallow me alive.' On the representation of the feminine in this novel see Cora Kaplan, '"A Cavern Opened in my Mind": the poetics of homosexuality and the politics of masculinity in James Baldwin', in *Representing Black Men*, eds Marcellus Blount and George P. Cunningham.

12 Rupert Haselden, interviewed by Simon Garfield in *The End of Innocence: Britain in the time of AIDS*.

13 Haselden later denounced such places and in terms which led others to denounce him – see the same interview with Garfield.

14 In the *Three Essays* Freud says that the mental forces like disgust which resist the libido like dams are not only the product of education but, more fundamentally, 'are organically determined and fixed by heredity' (p. 93). This is his theory of so-called organic repression, a consequence of evolution, and it drives this struggle even deeper into life; that's to say it isn't only a struggle between civilization and instinct, culture and nature, but is now somehow 'inside' nature itself.

15 Remembering that for Freud these instincts are typically sublimated into highly respectable social identities and activities, consider the following not untypical case. A man sublimates his homosexuality into the role of a scoutmaster. When, in relation to one particular youth, the sublimation begins to break down, his re-awakened homosexuality continues to be deeply influenced by the residual sublimation. The result is that intense shame about homosexual desire coexisted with intense idealization of it.

16 The problems begin when disgust is investigated by Freud as one of the key symptoms of phobia, hysteria and neurosis. Most notably, under the pressure of repression, disgust paradoxically becomes a symptom of pleasure; repression actually 'transforms a source of internal pleasure into one of internal disgust' (*The Complete Letters of Sigmund Freud to Wilhelm Fliess*, p. 281).

17 Jean Baudrillard gives one of the most extreme (and reductive) versions of this view:

> the 'Human' is from the outset the institution of its structural double, the 'Inhuman'. This is all it is: the progress of Humanity and Culture are simply the chain of discriminations with which to brand 'Others' with

inhumanity and therefore with nullity. (*Symbolic Exchange and Death*, p. 125)

18 Mary Douglas writes similarly but with greater anthropological awareness (and caution) about dirt: 'Reflection on dirt involves reflection on the relation of order to disorder, being to non-being, form to formlessness, life to death' (*Purity and Danger*, p. 5).

19 'The meaning of eroticism escapes anyone who cannot see its *religious* meaning!' (*Tears of Eros*, p. 70).

20 See Michael Richardson, *Georges Bataille*, chapter 5.

21 The question takes different forms – see especially Elizabeth Wilson, 'Is Transgression Transgressive?', in Bristow and Wilson (eds), *Activating Theory*; Alan Sinfield, chapter 7 of *Gay and After*: 'How Transgresssive do we want to be? What *about* Genet?'; and Roger Shattuck, *Forbidden Knowledge*, chapter 7.

22 Bataille describes Mussolini and Hitler as representing a '*force* that situates them above men, parties, and even laws: a *force* that disrupts the regular course of things . . . (the fact that laws are broken is only the most obvious sign of the transcendent, *heterogeneous* nature of fascist action' (*Visions of Excess*, p. 143). On this essay see Anthony Stephens, 'Georges Bataille's Diagnosis of Fascism and some Second Opinions', and Martin Jay, *Force Fields*, pp. 56ff.

23 By taking up Bataille's partial but crucial sense of nature I do not mean to ignore the enormously complex history of the term itself. See especially Kate Soper, *What is Nature?*; and Peter Coates, *Nature*.

Chapter 5   Daemonic Desires

1 I follow Camille Paglia in using *daemonic* to distinguish the concept from the Christian *demonic*; in other respects, as will become apparent, my usage differs from Paglia's (see *Sexual Personae*, pp. 3–4).

2 Male sexuality is especially insecure, says Paglia. Always haunted by the prospect of failure and humiliation ('a flop is a flop'), even when successful it is inherently mutable, going from erection through orgasm to detumescence: 'Men enter in triumph but withdraw in decrepitude. The sex act cruelly mimics history's decline and fall.' Which also means that male sexuality is inherently manic-depressive (p. 20).

3 See, for example, Elizabeth Wilson, 'Is Transgression Transgressive', p. 114; and bell hooks, *Outlaw Culture*, chapter 7: 'Camille Paglia: "Black" Pagan or White Coloniser?'

4 Paglia frequently subscribes to a binary antagonism between nature and culture which is reductive of both:

> Moral codes are always obstructive, relative, and man-made. Yet they have been of enormous profit to civilization. They *are* civilization. Without them, we are invaded by the chaotic barbarism of sex, nature's tyranny, turning day into night and love into obsession and lust. (*Sexual Personae*, p. 150)

5   See my 'Transgression and Surveillance in *Measure for Measure*', in *Political Shakespeare* (eds Dollimore and Sinfield).

Chapter 6   Dangers Within

1   On the thaw metaphor as indicative of death not life, compare John Donne: 'Mankind feeling now a general thaw, / . . . / The cement which did faithfully compact / And glue all virtues, now resolved, and slacked' (*An Anatomie of the World*, l. 47); and George Herbert: 'When age grows low and weak, / Marking his grave, and thawing ev'ry yeare / Till all do melt' ('Mortification').

2   Recall Schopenhauer: 'Awakened to life out of the night of unconsciousness, the will finds itself as an individual in an endless and boundless world, among innumerable individuals, all striving, suffering, and erring; and, as if through a troubled dream, it hurries back to the old unconsciousness' (*The World as Will and Representation*, vol. 2, p. 573).

3   *Sexual Dissidence*, esp. chapter 15, and pp. 33–5, 249–75.

4   On 'ocular prohibition' in myth see especially Shattuck, *Forbidden Knowledge*, pp. 18–21.

5   Compare Ted Hughes's poem 'A Childish Prank' which describes how Crow, on the eve of creation, when man and woman were sleeping, bit a worm 'Into two writhing halves', stuffing the tail-half into man, the head-half into woman. The latter calls 'its tail-half to join up quickly / Because O it was painful'. Man awoke 'being dragged across the grass. / Woman awoke to see him coming. / Neither knew what had happened.'

6   For fuller exploration of these encounters see Dollimore, *Sexual Dissidence*, especially parts 3 and 8, and also, *Death, Desire and Loss in Western Culture*, especially chapters 7, 10, 18 and 19.

Chapter 7   Those who Love Art the Most also Censor it the Most

1   Conor Cruise O'Brien: 'A few lines of poetry, the selected aphorisms of a retired man of letters, may liberate the daemon of a charismatic political leader' (*The Suspecting Glance*, p. 52).

2   I explore this more fully in *Sexual Dissidence*, especially Part 3, 'Subjectivity, Transgression and Deviant Desire'.

3   Even some of the novel's strongest defenders, including Ezra Pound, also wanted to curtail some of what was most challenging about it. Hovering around this censorship are some of the most intransigent psychic realities: sexual disgust is a motivation, and its targets include the novel's refusal to separate clearly the erotic from the excremental, and sex from death (Vanderham, pp. 1, 19–28). See also Valente (ed.), *Quare Joyce* (especially the afterword by

Christopher Lane, pp. 273–88); Richard Brown, *James Joyce and Sexuality*.

4   *The New York Review of Books*, 14 May 1992, p. 42; cited from Vanderham, p. 162.

5   See especially Souhami, *The Trials of Radclyffe Hall*, chapters 19–25, to which the following account is indebted; and Alan Travis, *Bound and Gagged: A Secret History of Obscenity in Britain*.

6   Many of those who defended the novel also found it disturbing if not sexually disgusting but didn't say, at least not in public. In private it was a different matter. E. M. Forster, himself homosexual, allegedly told Leonard Woolf that 'he thought Saphism disgusting; partly from convention, partly because he disliked that women should be independent of men' (Virginia Woolf, *Diary*, 31 August 1928, p. 193).

7   Unsurprisingly, this view was shared by Joynson-Hicks – see Thomas, *A Long Time Burning*, pp. 304–5.

8   Draper (ed.), *D. H. Lawrence*, pp. 93–5. For an account of the suppression of the novel and its possible political motives, see Kinkead-Weekes in the Cambridge Edition of *The Rainbow*, pp. xlv–li.

9   Cited from Alan Travis, *Bound and Gagged: A Secret History of Obscenity in Britain*, pp. 67–8.

10 For an account of the trial proceedings see Rolph (ed.), *The Trial of Lady Chatterley*, and for the events which led up to it, see Travis, *Bound and Gagged*, chapter 6: 'The hounding of D. H. Lawrence and the hunt for missing witnesses.'

11 The core of legal censorship for obscenity lies in the so-called 'Hicklin judgement' of 1868:

> The test of obscenity is whether the tendency . . . is to deprave and corrupt those whose minds are open to such immoral influences and into whose hands a publication of this sort might fall.

The new 1959 Act legislated that the effects of the book had to be taken 'as a whole' and that there could be no conviction if publication were proved to be 'in the interests of science, literature, art, or learning' (Rolph, *The Trial of Lady Chatterley*, pp. 4, 10–11).

12 See especially his *D. H. Lawrence: Novelist*.

13 Mellors, according to his wife, has a propensity for anal sex with women – or at least so she gives out publicly in order to turn the community against him (pp. 275, 277, 279–80).

14 *Sexual Dissidence*, pp. 268–75; *Death, Desire and Loss*, chapter 18.

Chapter 8   Critical Wars and Academic Censors

1   Originally in *Shakespeare: Select Bibliographical Guides*, second revised edition, ed. Stanley Wells (Oxford University Press, Oxford, 1990), and then in *Radical Tragedy*, p. xxxiii.

2   *The Culture of Redemption*, esp. pp. 1–4, 22; *Homos*, esp. chapter 4.

3   He was the most influential and controversial of a group of critics

associated with the journal *Scrutiny*. As Francis Mulhern cautions, 'the power of disturbance so often ascribed to his person was in reality that of a whole cultural current' (*The Moment of Scrutiny*, p. viii). On Leavis and Leavisism generally see also Chris Baldick, *The Social Mission of English Criticism*; and Ian MacKillop, *F. R. Leavis: a Life in Criticism.*

4   On Nordau see especially Danial Pick, *Faces of Degeneration*; William Greenslade, *Degeneration, Culture and the Novel*; Kelly Hurley, *The Gothic Body*; and my own *Death, Desire and Loss*. Leavis's writing has been contextualized by both Francis Mulhern and Chris Baldick (among others) though with no substantial reference to Nordau that I'm aware of. It may be that Nordau was not a direct influence on any of the *Scrutiny* critics; indeed, for my purposes, the resemblance becomes the more significant if he was not.

5   For example, the world-view of science which Nordau believed would help guarantee the survival of culture, Leavis thought would destroy it.

6   Leavis's description of Lawrence as being 'normal, central and sane to the point of genius' (*For Continuity*, p. 152) is even closer to Nordau.

7   Nordau cites approvingly a melancholy perception of mutability from Heine in which mood finds embodiment in external perception: 'the driving gust of wind, the hurrying gulls, now seen, now lost to sight, the rolling in and trackless ebbing of the surf' (p. 98). Nordau appreciates here the same kind of 'objective correlative' (T. S. Eliot's phrase) of feeling which Leavis will approve in Hardy and which becomes a major strand of the modernism which in other respects Nordau abhors. Nordau contrasts Heine with poets like Swinburne, who allow mood to override and supplant the real.

8   Both essays originally appeared in *Scrutiny* and are reprinted by Leavis in the first of his two-volume *A Selection from Scrutiny* (1968), and again in *The Living Principle* (1975).

9   Elsewhere, and famously, Shelley's 'passivity' endears him to us as a drama queen (s/he who is always in control, especially at the height of dramatic excess): 'I fall upon the thorns of life, I bleed!'

10 Cf. Leavis on Shelley's *The Cenci*: 'Shelley, as usual, is the hero – here the heroine' (*Revaluation*, p. 223).

11 Compare Nordau on Rossetti: 'Rossetti is not in a condition to understand, or even to see the real, because he is incapable of the necessary attention' (p. 91).

12 Others who have read the poem more attentively and sympathetically than Leavis still find the death in life theme difficult. One representative way of handling it is to regard the pathological tendencies it suggests as somehow transmuted by art into something more familiar and acceptable. Thus Cleanth Brooks finds the sombre irrationality of the poem redeemed by its clarity of design (*The Well Wrought Urn*), and Leo Spitzer agrees (Killham (ed.), *Critical Essays*, p. 199). Similarly

Graham Hough finds evidence of the 'psychopathic' in Tennyson but concludes that here, the artist in him 'so orders these morbid emotions that they come to correspond with the general experience of the human species' – whatever that might be (Killham (ed.), *Critical Essays*, p. 191).

13 This is the argument of my *Death, Desire and Loss in Western Culture*.

14 This is Leavis, not Nordau. And to be fair, it's offered by Leavis as a maxim for the study of English, not the elimination of degenerates. It occurs in a review of *A Critical History of English Poetry* by J. C. Grierson and J. C. Smith, which is Leavis at his best, ruthlessly exposing the banalities of what then passed as establishment literary history ('Catholicity or Narrowness?', p. 292).

15 Robert Potts, 'Erotic Balance', *The Guardian, Saturday Review*, 25 March 2000.

16 It appears in G. Singh, *F. R. Leavis: a Literary Biography* (opposite p. 121) and is reprinted in (and misdated by) *The Times Literary Supplement* for 8 September 2000, front cover.

Chapter 9   Shakespeare at the Limits of Political Criticism

1 I'm using 'political' eclectically. My own past writing engages with these debates, but they are not my concern here. See also Alan Sinfield, *Faultlines*; and John Brannigan, *New Historicism and Cultural Materialism*.

2 For example, Annabel Patterson writes persuasively on how 'the most striking fact about the Elizabethan chronicles is that the moral they claim to draw is emphatically contradicted by the story they tell' ('Censorship and the 1587 "Holinshed's" Chronicles', in P. Hyland and N. Sammells (eds), *Writing and Censorship*, p. 27). See also Patterson's *Censorship and Interpretation*.

Chapter 10   The Aesthetic Attraction of Fascism

1 The influence of Futurism on fascism was significant but limited and short-lived; see James Joll, 'F. T. Marinetti: Futurism and Fascism', in *Three Intellectuals in Politics*.

2 See Martin Jay, *Force Fields*, chapter 6: 'The Aesthetic Ideology'; Andrew Hewitt, *Fascist Modernism*; David Carroll, *French Literary Fascism*; and Lutz P. Koepnick, 'Fascist Aesthetics Revisited'. Earlier studies include John R. Harrison's *The Reactionaries*; and Saul Friedlander, *Reflections on Nazism*.

3 Benjamin observed that mankind's 'self-alienation has reached such a degree that it can experience its own destruction as an aesthetic pleasure of the first order. This is the situation of politics which Fascism is rendering aesthetic. Communism responds by politicizing art' (*Illuminations*, pp. 241–2).

4 See my *Death, Desire and Loss*, Part VI, for an exploration of this aesthetic in relation to Nietzsche, Georges Bataille and D. H. Lawrence.

5 'Passion and Cunning', p. 273. This important essay gave impetus to a continuing argument about Yeats's politics, and its influence on his verse. Significant earlier commentators on Yeats's fascist tendencies included Orwell in the essay mentioned, and Louis MacNiece, in *The Poetry of W. B. Yeats* (1941). More recently Grattan Freyer, in his judicious *W. B. Yeats and the Anti-Democratic Tradition*, qualifies some of O'Brien's claims while confirming their substance; see especially chapter 8: 'At Posterity's Bar'. Elizabeth Cullingford in *Yeats, Ireland and Fascism* shows the full extent of the divergence between continental fascism and Yeats's later views. Most recently Marjorie Howes argues that Yeats's politics in the crucial period of the 1930s were based on a philosophy of race 'which accorded with European fascism in some respects and differed from it in others'. But, she adds, even where they differ, his politics were hardly more compatible with liberal democracy than fascism, being authoritarian and eugenicist, based on race and the inevitability of violence, and committed to fighting degeneration (*Yeats's Nations*, esp. pp. 160, 185). My concern here is not to brand Yeats a fascist but to show how his verse is rooted in an aesthetic shared by fascists and others.

6 On Nietzsche's influence on Yeats, see Bohlmann, *Yeats and Nietzsche*.

7 'Violence, Recognition, and Some Versions of Modernism', p. 23; see also Nicholls' full-length study, *Modernisms: a Literary Guide*.

8 Yeats, writing in 1937: 'A poet writes always of his personal life, in his finest work out of its tragedy, whatever it be, remorse, lost love, or mere loneliness' (*Essays and Introductions*, p. 509).

9 On the bow metaphor of line 8, cf. Nietzsche: 'it is precisely through the presence of opposites and the feelings they occasion that the great man, *the bow with the great tension*, develops' (*Will to Power*, p. 507).

10 Cf. 'The Secret Rose': 'heavy with the sleep / Men have named beauty'.

Chapter 11   Desire: Art against Philosophy?

1 *Poetical Works* (London, 1836), p. 276; here cited from Donald Thomas, *A Long Time Burning*, p. 4. As Thomas points out (chapter 1), the cost of the offending literature has always been crucial in deciding whether or not it should be censored: the cheaper it is, the more likely it is to be accessed by the 'vulnerable'.

2 See, most recently, Pearson's *Women's Reading in Britain 1750–1835*.

3 Montesquieu discerns something important about our fascination with the representation of suicide in art, and also anticipates Freud's views on narcissism, when he describes suicide as the supreme act of self-love, a sacrifice of our being for the love of our being; the suicide is driven by a 'natural and obscure instinct that makes us love ourselves more than our very life'. Similarly, in 1796 Madame de Staël remarks: 'there

is something sensitive or philosophical in the act of killing oneself that is completely foreign to a depraved being' (Minois, pp. 229, 275).

4 Thus Keats: 'What shocks the virtuous philosop[h]er, delights the camelion Poet' (*Letters*, p. 157).

5 Although it has been criticized for showing the influence of reductive Marxism, Karl Popper's claim that Plato's philosophy was formed as a reaction to the experience of social change (experienced as social decline), seems plausible to me. Perhaps it would be better to describe Plato's philosophy as a 'reaction formation' to change, thereby invoking Freud not as a substitute for Marx, but as a way of sidestepping the charge of reductive Marxism (a charge which has itself become a reductive kind of thinking). Popper also argues that philosophy more generally arises from the breakdown of the 'closed' society; see his *The Open Society and its Enemies*, especially chapters 3 and 4, and pp. 18, 188–201).

6 One also wonders, in relation to Karl Popper's claim that Plato betrayed and misrepresented Socrates in the dialogues (*Open Society and its Enemies*, pp. 169–226), whether this is a glimpse of the real Socrates. Unable to judge the truth of Popper's claim, I have found it plausible enough to attribute the text to Plato, even though it is Socrates speaking. In the *Phaedrus* and the *Laws*, both later works, Plato/Socrates modifies his criticism of art, and in the *Phaedrus* even allows for a kind of divinely inspired madness as the inspiration for great poetry and preferable to mundane human sanity. But it remains a highly controlled and directed kind of madness.

7 See Annabel Patterson, *Censorship and Interpretation: the Conditions of Writing and Reading in Early Modern England*.

Conclusion

1 *The Consolations of Philosophy* (Hamish Hamilton, London, 2000). Reviewing this book Mary Margaret McCabe declares: 'this is not the dumbing down of philosophy, it is a dumbing out' (*TLS*, 23 June 2000, p. 14).

2 *The Sunday Times* (*Culture* section), 6 June 1997.

3 He is not alone; Stuart Morgan declares that the 1995 Tate exhibition called *Rites of Passage*, 'proposes that artists have an important role in society: that they be considered as *passeurs*, priests (perhaps) of that secular religion that art has become' (*Rites of Passage*, p. 12).

4 Cited by Martin Jay in ' "The Aesthetic Ideology" ', p. 73.

5 The book in question is Kenneth R. Johnston's *The Hidden Wordsworth*, and the remark is quoted in a news article on the book in the *Guardian* for 23 May 1999 (p. 3).

6 Postface to Artaud's *The Theatre and its Double*, p. 108.

7 'There's not much to say about my few poems', Larkin once wrote, 'without venturing into the region of psychiatric analysis, and I don't

want to do that!' Cited from Andrew Motion, *Philip Larkin: A Writer's Life*, pp. 271–2.

8 Larkin again: 'what one writes depends so much on one's character and environment – either one writes about them or to escape from them' (Motion, *Philip Larkin*, p. 271).

9 By, for example, Terry Eagleton in *Literary Theory*, pp. 142–3.

10 If only because he has fallen into disrepute, I want to acknowledge being influenced here by Louis Althusser's thoughts on art as a form of internal distancing.

Bibliography

Ariès, Philippe, *The Hour of Our Death* (1977), trans. Helen Weaver, Oxford: Oxford University Press, 1991.

Artaud, Antonin, *Selected Writings*, ed. with introd. Susan Sontag, Berkeley: University of California Press, 1975.

Augustine, *Enchiridion*, trans. Bernard M. Peebles, in *Writings of St Augustine*, vol. IV, Washington DC: Catholic University of America, 1947.

Bagehot, Walter, *The Literary Essays*, 2 vols, in Norman St. John-Stevas (ed.) *The Collected Works of Walter Bagehot*, London: The Economist, 1965.

Baldick, Chris, *The Social Mission of English Criticism 1848–1932*, Oxford: Clarendon Press, 1983.

Baldwin, James, *Giovanni's Room* (1956), London: Corgi, 1977.

—— *Another Country*, London: Michael Joseph, 1963.

Barthes, Roland, *Sade, Fourier, Loyola*, New York: Hill and Wang, 1976.

—— *Camera Lucida: Reflections on Photography* (1980), trans. Richard Howard, New York: Hill and Wang, 1981.

Bataille, Georges, *The Accursed Share*, trans. Robert Hurley, 3 vols, New York: Zone Books, 1988 (vol. 1), 1991 (vols 2–3).

—— *Erotism: Death and Sensuality* (1957), trans. Mary Dalwood, San Francisco: City Light Books, 1986.

—— *Guilty*, trans. Bruce Boone, introd. D. Hollier, Venice, California: Lapsis Press, 1988.

—— *Literature and Evil* (1957), trans. Alastair Hamilton, London: Marion Boyars, 1985.

—— *The Tears of Eros* (1961), trans. Peter Connor, foreword by J. M. LoDuca, San Francisco: City Light Books, 1989.

——*The Trials of Gilles de Rais: Documents presented by Georges Bataille* (1965), trans. Richard Robinson, Los Angeles: Amok, 1991.

——*Visions of Excess: Selected Writings 1927–1939*, ed. and introd. Allan Stoekl, trans. Allan Stoekl with C. R. Lovitt and D. M. Leslie, Manchester: Manchester University Press, 1985.

Baudrillard, Jean, *Symbolic Exchange and Death* (1976), trans. Iain Hamilton Grant, introd. Mike Gain, London: Sage Publications, 1993.

Bawer, Bruce, *A Place at the Table: the Gay Individual in American Society*, New York: Touchstone, 1993.

Benjamin, Walter, *Illuminations*, ed. Hannah Arendt, trans. Harry Zohn, New York: Schocken, 1969.

Bermel, Albert, *Artaud's Theatre of Cruelty*, New York: Taplinger, 1977.

Bersani, Leo, 'A Conversation with Leo Bersani', *October* 82 (1997), 3–16.

——*The Culture of Redemption*, Cambridge, Mass. and London: Harvard University Press, 1990.

——*Homos*, Cambridge, Mass.: Harvard University Press, 1995.

Bohlmann, Otto, *Yeats and Nietzsche: an Exploration of Major Nietzschean Echoes in the Writings of William Butler Yeats*, London: Macmillan, 1982.

Botting, Fred, *Gothic*, London: Routledge, 1996.

Bowen, Elizabeth, *Eva Trout* (1969), London: Vintage, 1999.

Bowlby, Rachel, *Shopping With Freud*, London: Routledge, 1993.

Brannigan, John, *New Historicism and Cultural Materialism*, London: Macmillan, 1998.

Bristow, Joseph, and Wilson, Angelia R. (eds), *Activating Theory: Lesbian, Gay and Bisexual Politics*, London: Lawrence and Wishart, 1993.

Broadbent, John (ed.), *Poets of the Seventeenth Century*, vol. 2, New York: Signet, 1974.

Brontë, Emily, *Wuthering Heights and Poems*, introd. Margaret Drabble, ed. Hugh Osborne, London: Everyman, 1993.

Brooks, Cleanth, *The Well Wrought Urn: Studies in the Structure of Poetry* (1949), Harvard: Harvard University Press, 1956.

Brown, Norman O., *Life Against Death: The Psychoanalytic Meaning of History*, London: Routledge, 1959.

Brown, Richard, *James Joyce and Sexuality*, Cambridge: Cambridge University Press, 1985.

Burchill, Julie, *Absolute Filth: an A to Z of Sex*, pamphlet, no place of publication, publisher or date given.

Burke, Kenneth, 'Epilogue: Prologue in Heaven', in *The Rhetoric of Religion: Studies in Logology* (1961), Berkeley: University of California Press, 1970.

Butler, Judith, *Bodies that Matter: On the Discursive Limits of 'Sex'*, New York and London: Routledge, 1993.

——'Gender as Performance: an interview with Judith Butler', *Radical Philosophy* 67 (Summer 1994), 32–9.

——*Gender Trouble: Feminism and the Subversion of Identity*, London: Routledge, 1990.

——'Imitation and Gender Insubordination', in Diana Fuss (ed.), *Inside/Out: Lesbian Theories, Gay Theories*, 21.

——*The Psychic Life of Power*, Stanford: Stanford University Press, 1997.

Califia, Pat, 'Unraveling the Sexual Fringe: A Secret Side of Lesbian Sexuality', *Advocate* (27 December 1979), 19–23.

Carroll, David, *French Literary Fascism: Nationalism, Anti-Semitism, and the Ideology of Culture*, Princeton: Princeton University Press, 1995.

Cesarani, David, *Arthur Koestler: The Homeless Mind*, London: Heinemann, 1998.

Coates, Peter, *Nature: Western Attitudes since Ancient Times*, Cambridge: Polity, 1998.

Conrad, Joseph, *Heart of Darkness* (1899), Harmondsworth: Penguin, 1973.

Corrigan, Paul, *Shakespeare on Management: Leadership Lessons for Today's Managers*, London: Kogan Page, 1999.

Cullingford, Elizabeth, *Yeats, Ireland and Fascism*, London: Macmillan, 1981.

Däumer, Elisabeth, 'Queer Ethics; or, the Challenge of Bisexuality to Lesbian Ethics', in *Hypatia* 7, 4 (Fall 1992), 91–105.

Dean, Tim, 'How Can Psychoanalysis Help Safe-sex Education?', *Journal for the Psychoanalysis of Culture and Society* 2, 2 (Fall 1997), 1–19.

Dollimore, Jonathan, *Death, Desire and Loss in Western Culture*, Harmondsworth: Penguin, 1998.

——*Political Shakespeare: Essays in Cultural Materialism* ed. with Alan Sinfield, Manchester: Manchester University Press, second edition, 1994.

——*Radical Tragedy: Religion, Ideology and Power in the Drama of Shakespeare and His Contemporaries*, second edition, Hemel Hempstead: Harvester Wheatsheaf, 1989.

——*Sexual Dissidence: Augustine to Wilde, Freud to Foucault*, Oxford: Clarendon Press, 1991.

Donne, John, *The Complete English Poems*, ed. A. J. Smith, Harmondsworth: Penguin, 1971.

——*Selected Prose*, ed. with introd. Neil Rhodes, Harmondsworth: Penguin, 1987.

Donoghue, Denis, *Yeats*, London: Collins/Fontana, 1971.

Douglas, Mary, *Purity and Danger: An Analysis of the Concepts of Pollution and Taboo*, London: Routledge and Kegan Paul, 1966.

Draper, R. P. (ed.), *D. H. Lawrence: the Critical Heritage*, London: Routledge, 1970.

Drummond, William, of Hawthornden, *Poems and Prose*, ed. R. H. MacDonald, Edinburgh: Scottish Academic Press, 1976.

Eadie, Jo, 'Activating Bisexuality: Towards a Bi/Sexual Politics', in Bristow and Wilson (eds), pp. 139–70.

——'We should be there bi now', in *Rouge* 12 (1993), 26–7.

Eagleton, Terry, 'F. R. Leavis', in The European English Messenger 7, 2 (1998), 49–51.

——*Literary Theory: An Introduction*, Oxford: Blackwell, 1983.

Eliot, T. S., *Four Quartets* (1944), London: Faber, 1954.

——'The Waste Land' (1922), in *Selected Poems*, London: Faber, 1954.

Ellis, John M., *Literature Lost: Social Agendas and the Corruption of the Humanities*, New Haven and London: Yale University Press, 1997.

Euripides, *The Bacchae and other Plays*, trans. by Philip Vellacott, Harmondsworth: Penguin, 1977.

——*Medea and other Plays*, trans. Philip Vellacott, Harmondsworth: Penguin, 1963.

Farber, Celia, 'Unprotected', *Continuum* 5, 5 (Mid-winter 1999), 62–3.

Faulkner, William, *The Unvanquished* (1934), Harmondsworth: Penguin, 1955.

Field, Nicola, *Over the Rainbow: Money, Class and Homophobia*, London: Pluto Press, 1995.

Flacelière, Robert, *Love in Ancient Greece* (1960), trans. James Cleugh, London: Frederick Muller, 1962.

Flint, Kate, *The Woman Reader: 1837–1914*, Oxford: Clarendon Press, 1993.

Foucault, Michel, 'Nietzsche, Genealogy, History', in *Language, Counter-Memory, Practice: Selected Essays and Interviews*, ed. with introd. D. F. Bouchard, trans. D. F. Bouchard and Sherry Simon, Oxford: Blackwell, 1977.

Freud, Sigmund, *Beyond the Pleasure Principle* (1920), in *On Meta-psychology: the Theory of Psychoanalysis* (The Pelican Freud Library, vol. 11), Harmondsworth: Penguin, 1984.

—'Character and Anal Eroticism', (1908) in *The Standard Edition of the Complete Psychological Works of Sigmund Freud*, London: Hogarth, 1959, vol. 9, pp. 167–78.

—*Civilization and its Discontents* (1929–30), in *Civilization, Society and Religion* (The Pelican Freud Library, vol. 12), Harmondsworth: Penguin, 1985.

—' "Civilized" Sexual Morality and Modern Nervous Illness' (1908), in *Civilization, Society and Religion* (The Pelican Freud Library, vol. 12), Harmondsworth: Penguin, 1985.

—*The Complete Letters of Sigmund Freud to Wilhelm Fliess 1887–1904*, trans. and ed. Jeffrey Moussaieff Masson, Cambridge, Mass.: Harvard University Press, 1985.

—'Dora – Fragment of an Analysis of a Case of Hysteria' (1901), in *Case Histories I* (The Pelican Freud Library, vol. 8), Harmondsworth: Penguin, 1977.

—*The Ego and the Id* (1923), in *On Metapsychology: the Theory of Psychoanalysis* (The Pelican Freud Library, vol. 11), Harmondsworth: Penguin, 1984.

—'Psychopathic Stage Characters' (1905–6), in *Art and Literature* (The Pelican Freud Library, vol. 14), Harmondsworth: Penguin, 1985.

—*The Question of Lay Analysis* (1926), in *Historical and Expository Works on Psychoanalysis* (The Pelican Freud Library, vol. 15), Harmondsworth: Penguin, 1986.

—'Repression' (1915), in *On Metapsychology*, (The Pelican Freud Library, vol. 11), Harmondsworth: Penguin, 1984.

—*Three Essays*, in *Sexuality* (The Pelican Freud Library, vol. 7), Harmondsworth: Penguin, 1977.

—(with Josef Breuer) *Studies on Hysteria (1893–95)*, (The Pelican Freud Library, vol. 3), Harmondsworth: Penguin, 1974.

—'Why War?' (1932/33) in *Civilization, Society and Religion* (The Pelican Freud Library, vol. 12), Harmondsworth: Penguin, 1985.

Freyer, Grattan, *W. B. Yeats and the Anti-Democratic Tradition*, Dublin: Gill and Macmillan, 1981.

Friedlander, Saul, *Reflections on Nazism: An Essay on Kitsch and Death* (1982), trans. Thomas Weyr, Bloomington and Indianapolis: Indiana University Press, 1993.

Garber, Marjorie, *Vice Versa: Bisexuality and the Eroticism of Everyday Life*, New York: Simon and Schuster, 1995.

Garfield, Simon, *The End of Innocence: Britain in the time of AIDS*, London: Faber, 1994.

George, Sue, *Women and Bisexuality*, London: Scarlet Press, 1993.

Gibson, Andrew, *Postmodernity, Ethics and the Novel: From Leavis to Levinas*, London and New York: Routledge, 1999.

Gide, André, *If it Die* (1920), trans. Dorothy Bussy, Harmondsworth: Penguin, 1977.

——*The Journals of André Gide*, trans. Justin O'Brien (vol 2: 1914–27), London: Secker and Warburg, 1948.

Goldstein, Richard, 'Gay Studies Spawns a Radical Theory of Desire', *Village Voice* (29 July 1997), 38–41.

Greenblatt, Stephen, 'Invisible Bullets: Renaissance Authority and its Subversion', in Dollimore and Sinfield (eds), *Political Shakespeare: Essays in Cultural Materialism* pp. 18–47.

Greenslade, William, *Degeneration, Culture and the Novel 1880–1940*, Cambridge: Cambridge University Press, 1994.

Greville, Fulke, *Selected Poems*, ed. and introd. Neil Powell, Manchester: Carcanet, 1990.

Griffin, Roger (ed.), *Fascism*, Oxford: Oxford University Press, 1995.

Hall, Marguerite Radclyffe, *The Well of Loneliness* (1928), London: Falcon Press, 1949.

Hamilton, Alan, *The pay's the thing for business Bard*, in *The Times*, 7 April 1999, p. 9.

Hangstrum, Jean H., *The Romantic Body: Love and Sexuality in Keats, Wordsworth, and Blake*, Knoxville: University of Tennessee Press, 1985.

Harding, D. W., 'A Note on Nostalgia', in *Determinations: Critical Essays*, introd. F. R. Leavis, London: Chatto and Windus, 1934.

Harrison, John R., *The Reactionaries*, pref. William Empson, London: Victor Gollancz, 1966.

Hart, Lynda, *Between the Body and the Flesh: Performing Sadomasochism*, New York: Columbia University Press, 1998.

Haraway, Donna, 'A Manifesto for Cyborgs: Science, Technology and Socialist Feminism in the 1980s', in Linda J. Nicholson (ed.), *Feminism/Postmodernism*, London: Routledge, 1990.

Hemmings, Clare, 'Resituating the Bisexual Body', in Bristow and Wilson (eds), p. 11, n. 138.

Herbert, George, *The English Poems*, ed. by C. A. Patrides, London: Dent, 1974.

Hewitt, Andrew, *Fascist Modernism: Aesthetics, Politics and the Avant-Garde*, Stanford: Stanford University Press, 1993.

Holmes, Richard, *Shelley: the Pursuit*, London: Weidenfeld and Nicolson, 1974.

Hooker, Richard, *Of the Laws of Ecclesiastical Polity* (1593–7), 2 vols, London: Dent, 1968.

hooks, bell, *Outlaw Culture: Resisting Representations*, London: Routledge, 1994.

Howes, Marjorie, *Yeats's Nations: Gender, Class and Irishness*, Cambridge: Cambridge University Press, 1996.

Hughes, Ted, *New Selected Poems 1957–1994*, London: Faber, 1995.

Hurley, Kelly, *The Gothic Body: Sexuality, Materialism, and Degeneration at the Fin de Siècle*, Cambridge: Cambridge University Press, 1996.

Hyland, Paul and Neil Sammells (eds), *Writing and Censorship in Britain*, London: Routledge, 1992.

Jarvis, Simon, 'Reflections in the Golden Bowl', *Times Literary Supplement*, 8 May 1998, p. 25.

Jay, Martin, ' "The Aesthetic Ideology" as Ideology: Or What Does it Mean to Aestheticize Politics?', in *Force Fields: Between Intellectual History and Cultural Critique*, London: Routledge, 1993.

Jeffares, A. Norman, *A Commentary on the Collected Poems of W. B. Yeats*, London: Macmillan, 1968.

Johnston, Kenneth R., *The Hidden Wordsworth: Poet, Rebel, Spy*, New York: Norton, 1998.

Joll, James, 'F. T. Marinetti: Futurism and Fascism', in *Three Intellectuals in Politics*, New York: Pantheon Books, 1960.

Joyce, James, *A Portrait of the Artist as a Young Man* (1916), Harmondsworth: Penguin, 1969.

—— *Ulysses* (1922), Harmondsworth: Penguin, 1969.

Kaplan, Cora, ' "A Cavern Opened in my Mind": the poetics of homosexuality and the politics of masculinity in James Baldwin', in Marcellus Blount and George P. Cunningham (eds), *Representing Black Men*, London: Routledge, 1996, pp. 27–54.

Keats, John, *Letters*, selected and ed. Robert Gittings, Oxford: Oxford University Press, 1970.

Kermode, Frank, 'The Men on the Dump: a Response' in Margaret Tudeau-Clayton and Martin Warner (eds), *Addressing Frank Kermode*, Basingstoke: Macmillan, 1991.

Killham, John (ed.), *Critical Essays on the Poetry of Tennyson*, London: Routledge, 1960.

Kipnis, Laura, *Bound and Gagged: Pornography and the Politics of Fantasy in America* (1996), Durham State: Duke University Press, 1999.

Koepnick, Lutz P., 'Fascist Aesthetics Revisited', *Modernism/Modernity* 6, 1 (January 1999), 51–73.

Kristeva, Julia, *Powers of Horror: An Essay on Abjection* (1980), trans. Leon S. Roudiez, New York: Columbia University Press, 1982.

Kurtz, Benjamin J., *The Pursuit of Death: A Study of Shelley's Poetry* (1933), New York: Octagon, 1970.

Larkin, Philip, *Required Writing: Miscellaneous Pieces 1955–1982*, London: Faber, 1983.

Lawrence, D. H., *Aaron's Rod* (1922), Harmondsworth: Penguin, 1968.

——*Lady Chatterley's Lover* (1928), Harmondsworth: Penguin, 1960.

——*The Plumed Serpent*, Ware: Wordsworth, 1995.

——*The Rainbow*, ed. Mark Kinkead-Weekes, (The Cambridge Edition of the Letters and Works of D. H. Lawrence), Cambridge: Cambridge University Press, 1989.

——*Women in Love* (1921), Harmondsworth: Penguin, 1977.

Leavis, F. R., 'Catholicity or Narrowness?', *Scrutiny* XII (1944–5), 292–5.

——*D. H. Lawrence: Novelist* (1955), Harmondsworth: Penguin, 1964.

——*For Continuity*, Cambridge: Minority Press, 1933.

——'The Greatness of *Measure for Measure*', *Scrutiny* X (1941–2), 234–47.

——*The Living Principle: 'English' as a Discipline of Thought*, London: Chatto and Windus, 1975.

——*Revaluation: Tradition and Development in English Poetry* (1936), London: Chatto and Windus, 1962.

——*A Selection from Scrutiny* (2 vols), Cambridge: Cambridge University Press, 1968.

Lister, David, 'Can Immoral Artists Produce Great Works? Discuss (With Examples)', *Independent, The Wednesday Review*, 30 December 1998, p. 4.

Loomba, Ania, *Gender, Race, Renaissance Drama*, Manchester: Manchester University Press, 1989.

MacKillop, Ian, *F. R. Leavis: a Life in Criticism*, London: Allen Lane, 1995.

Mailer, Norman, *The Prisoner of Sex*, London: Weidenfeld and Nicolson, 1971.

Mann, Thomas, *Death in Venice* (1912), in *Selected Stories*, trans. with introd. David Luke, Harmondsworth: Penguin, 1988.

——*Dr Faustus: the Life of the German Composer Adrian Leverkühn as told by a Friend* (1947), trans. H. T. Lowe-Porter, Harmondsworth: Penguin, 1968.

——'Nietzsche's Philosophy in the Light of Recent History', in *Last Essays*, trans. Richard and Clara Winston and Tania and James Stern, London: Secker and Warburg, 1959.

Marcuse, Herbert, *Eros and Civilisation: A Philosophical Inquiry into Freud* (1955), with new preface by author, Boston: Beacon Press, 1966.

Marinetti, Filippo, *Marinetti: Selected Writings*, ed. with intro. R. W. Flint, trans. R. W. Flint and A. A. Coppotelli, London: Secker and Warburg, 1972.

Marriot, David, *On Black Men*, Edinburgh: Edinburgh University Press, 2000.

Marx, Karl, and Friedrich Engels, *The Communist Manifesto* (1848), introd. A. J. P. Taylor, Harmondsworth: Penguin, 1967.

Medhurst, A. and S. Munt (eds), *Lesbian and Gay Studies: a Critical Introduction*, London: Cassell, 1997.

Merck, Mandy, *Perversions: Deviant Readings*, London: Virago, 1993.

Miller, William Ian, *The Anatomy of Disgust*, Cambridge, Mass.: Harvard University Press, 1997.

Millett, Kate, *Sexual Politics* (1969), London: Virago, 1977.

Milton, John, *Paradise Lost*, ed. Alastair Fowler, London: Longman, 1968.

Minois, Georges, *History of Suicide: Voluntary Death in Western Culture* (1995), trans. Lydia G. Cochrane, Baltimore and London: Johns Hopkins University Press, 1999.

Morton, Donald, 'Queerity and Ludic Sado-Masochism: Compulsory Consumption and the Emerging Post-al Queer', in Donald Morton et al. (eds), *Post-ality: Marxism and Postmodernism, Transformation* 1, Washington DC: Maisonneuve Press, 1995, pp. 189–215.

Motion, Andrew, *Philip Larkin: A Writer's Life*, London: Faber, 1993.

Mulhern, Francis, *The Moment of Scrutiny*, London: Verso, 1979.

Nicholls, Peter, 'Violence, Recognition, and Some Versions of Modernism', *Parataxis* 4 (1993), 19–35.

——*Modernisms: a Literary Guide*, London: Macmillan, 1995.

Nietzsche, Friedrich, *The Birth of Tragedy* (1872) and *The Genealogy of Morals* (1887), trans. Francis Golffing, New York: Doubleday, 1956.

——*Ecce Homo: How One Becomes What One Is* (1888), trans. with introd. R. J. Hollingdale, Harmondsworth: Penguin, 1979.

——*Human, All Too Human* (1878), trans. R. J. Hollingdale, introd. Erich Heller, Cambridge: Cambridge University Press, 1986.

——*Twilight of the Idols* (1889), and *The Anti-Christ* (1895), trans. with introd. R. J. Hollingdale, Harmondsworth: Penguin, 1968.

——*Untimely Meditations*, trans. R. J. Hollingdale, introd. J. P. Stern, Cambridge: Cambridge University Press, 1983.

——*The Will to Power*, trans. Walter Kaufmann and R. J. Hollingdale, ed. with commentary by Kaufmann, New York: Vintage Books, 1968.

Nordau, Max, *Degeneration* (1892), trans. from second edition, New York: Appleton and Co., 1895. Reprinted with introd. George Mosse and index from 1900 reprint, Lincoln, Nebraska and London: University of Nebraska Press, 1993.

O'Brien, Conor Cruise, 'Passion and Cunning: An Essay on the politics of W. B. Yeats', in A. Norman Jeffares and K. G. W. Cross (eds), *In Excited Reveries: A Centenary Tribute to William Butler Yeats 1865–1939*, London: Macmillan, 1965.

——*The Suspecting Glance*, London: Faber, 1972.

Orwell, George, 'W. B. Yeats', in *Collected Essays*, London: Secker and Warburg, 1961.

Pagels, Elaine, *Adam, Eve and the Serpent*, London: Weidenfeld and Nicolson, 1988.

Paglia, Camille, *Sexual Personae: Art and Decadence from Nefertiti to Emily Dickinson* (1990), Harmondsworth: Penguin, 1992.

Pascal, Blaise, *Pensées*, trans. with introd. A. J. Krailsheimer, Harmondsworth: Penguin, 1966.

Patterson, Annabel, *Censorship and Interpretation: the Conditions of Writing and Reading in Early Modern England*, Madison: University of Wisconsin Press, 1984.

Pearson, Jacqueline, *Women's Reading in Britain 1750–1835: A Dangerous Recreation*, Cambridge: Cambridge University Press, 1999.

Penwarden, Charles, 'Of Word and Flesh: an interview with Julia Kristeva', in Stuart Morgan and Frances Morris (eds), *Rites of Passage: Art for the End of the Century*, London: Tate Gallery Publications, 1995.

Pick, Daniel, *Faces of Degeneration: A European Disorder, c.1848–c.1918*, Cambridge: Cambridge University Press, 1989.

Plato, *Apology*, and *Phaedo*, in *The Last Days of Socrates*, trans. with introd. Hugh Tredennick, Harmondsworth: Penguin, 1969.

——*The Republic of Plato*, trans. with introd. F. M. Cornford, Oxford: Oxford University Press, 1945.

——*The Symposium*, trans. Robin Waterfield, Oxford: Oxford University Press, 1994.

Popper, Karl, *The Open Society and its Enemies* (1945), London: Routledge, 1995 (single volume edition).

Punter, David, *The Literature of Terror: a History of Gothic Fictions from 1765 to the Present Day*, vol. 2: *The Modern Gothic*, London: Longman, 1996.

Raleigh, Sir Walter, *The History of the World*, ed. C. A. Patrides, London: Macmillan, 1971.

——*Poems*, ed. Agnes M. C. Latham, London: Constable, 1929.

Richards, I. A., *Poetries and Sciences* (1926), London: Routledge and Kegan Paul, 1970.

Richardson, Michael, *Georges Bataille*, London: Routledge, 1994.

Rolph, C. H. (ed.), *The Trial of Lady Chatterley*, Harmondsworth: Penguin, 1961.

Rose, Sharon et al. (eds), *Bisexual Horizons: Politics, Histories, Lives*, London: Lawrence and Wishart, 1996.

Safranski, Rudiger, *Schopenhauer and the Wild Years of Philosophy*, Cambridge, Mass.: Harvard University Press, 1990.

Said, Edward, *Culture and Imperialism*, London: Chatto and Windus, 1993.

Sanders, Wilbur, *The Dramatist and the Received Idea: Studies in the Plays of Marlowe and Shakespeare*, Cambridge: Cambridge University Press, 1968.

Scholder, A., and I. Silverberg (eds), *High Risk 2: Writings on Sex, Death and Subversion*, London: Serpent's Tail, 1994.

Schopenhauer, Arthur, *The World as Will and Representation* (1819/1844), trans. E. F. J. Payne, 2 vols, New York: Dover, 1966.

Sedgwick, Eve Kosofsky (ed.), *Novel Gazing: Queer Readings in Fiction*, Durham and London: Duke University Press, 1997.

Segal, Lynne, *Straight Sex: the Politics of Pleasure*, London: Virago, 1994.

Shakespeare, William, *The Complete Works*, ed. Stanley Wells and Gary Taylor, Oxford: Clarendon, 1988.

——*The Sonnets and A Lover's Complaint*, ed. with introd. John Kerrigan, Harmondsworth: Penguin, 1986.

Shattuck, Roger, *Forbidden Knowledge: from Prometheus to Pornography*, New York: St Martin's Press, 1996.

Shelley, Percy Bysshe, *Shelley*, selected by Kathleen Raine, Harmondsworth: Penguin, 1974.

Sherman, S. P., 'Forde's Contribution to the Decadence of the Drama', in W. Bang (ed), *Materialien zur Kunde des älteren englischen Drama*, 23 1908.

Sidney, Sir Philip, *An Apology for Poetry*, in *Sir Philip Sidney:*

Selected Poetry and Prose, ed. David Kalstone, New York and Toronto: New American Library, 1970.

Signorile, Michelangelo, 'Bareback and Reckless', *Out* (July 1997), 36–8.

Simpson, Mark (ed.), *Anti-Gay*, London: Cassell, 1996.

Sinfield, Alan, *Faultlines: Cultural Materialism and the Politics of Dissident Reading*, Oxford: Oxford University Press 1992.

——*Gay and After*, London: Serpent's Tail, 1998.

Singh, G., *F. R. Leavis: a Literary Biography*, London: Duckworth, 1995.

Soper, Kate, *What is Nature?: Culture, Politics and the Non-Human*, Oxford: Blackwell, 1995.

Souhami, Diana, *The Trials of Radclyffe Hall* (1998), London: Virago, 1999.

Spenser, Edmund, *The Faerie Queene*, ed. Thomas P. Roche Jr, Harmondsworth: Penguin, 1978.

Stallybrass, Peter and Allon White, *The Politics and Poetics of Transgression*, London: Methuen, 1986.

Steiner, George, *Heidegger*, second edition, London: Fontana, 1992.

Stephens, Anthony, 'Georges Bataille's Diagnosis of Fascism and some Second Opinions', *Thesis Eleven* 24 (1989), 71–89.

Sullivan, Andrew, *Virtually Normal: An Argument About Homosexuality*, London: Picador, 1995.

Tennyson, Lord Alfred, *Poems of Tennyson* (Oxford Edition), introd. T. Herbert Warren, London: Humphrey Milford, 1917.

Thomas, Donald, *A Long Time Burning: the History of Literary Censorship in England*, London: Routledge and Kegan Paul, 1969.

Travis, Alan, *Bound and Gagged: A Secret History of Obscenity in Britain*, London: Profile Books, 2000.

Tribe, David, *Questions of Censorship*, London: Allen and Unwin, 1973.

Trypanis, C. A. (ed.), *The Penguin Book of Greek Verse*, Harmondsworth: Penguin, 1971.

Valente, Joseph (ed.), *Quare Joyce*, Ann Arbor: University of Michigan Press, 1998.

Vanderham, Paul, *James Joyce and Censorship: The Trials of Ulysses*, London: Macmillan, 1998.

Vickers, Brian, *Appropriating Shakespeare: Contemporary Critical Quarrels*, New Haven and London: Yale University Press, 1993.

Walder, Dennis, *Ted Hughes* (Open Guides to Literature), Milton Keynes: Open University Press, 1987.

Walton, Izaak, *Lives*, introd. George Saintsbury, London: Oxford University Press, 1927.

Warner, Michael, 'Why gay men are having risky sex', *Voice* 15, 5 (31 January 1995), 33–6.

Wawrzycka, J. W., and M. G. Corcoran (eds), *Gender in Joyce*, Gainesville: University Press of Florida, 1997.

Webster, John, *Selected Plays*, ed. Jonathan Dollimore and Alan Sinfield, Cambridge: Cambridge University Press, 1983.

Wells, Matt, 'Sex on the Edge', *Guardian* (*G2*), 14 March 2000, pp. 2–3.

Wilde, Oscar, *The Importance of Being Earnest* (1895), ed. Russell Jackson, London: Ernest Benn, 1980.

——*The Picture of Dorian Gray* (1890–91), Harmondsworth: Penguin, 1949.

Wilson, Elizabeth, 'Is Transgression Transgressive?', in Bristow and Wilson (eds), *Activating Theory*.

Woolf, Virginia, *The Diary of Virginia Woolf*, vol. 3, 1925–30, ed. Anne Oliver Bell, Harmondsworth: Penguin, 1982.

Yeats, W. B., *Collected Poems*, London: Macmillan, 1971.

——*Essays and Introductions*, London: Macmillan, 1961.

——*Letters*, ed. Allan Wade, London: Hart-Davis, 1954.

Young, Robert, *Colonial Desire: Hybridity in Theory, Culture and Race*, London and New York: Routledge, 1995.

Name Index

Subject Index

Other Books by the Same Author

Radical Tragedy:
Religion, Ideology and Power in the Drama of
Shakespeare and His Contemporaries

Political Shakespeare
(editor, with Alan Sinfield)

Sexual Dissidence:
Augustine to Wilde, Freud to Foucault

Death, Desire and Loss in Western Culture